Charles L. Cherry
George D. Murphy

Villanova University

WRITE UP THE LADDER

A Common Sense Guide to Better Business Communication

Goodyear Publishing Co. Inc.
Pacific Palisades, California

Library of Congress Cataloging in Publication Data

Cherry, Charles L
   Write up the ladder.

   Includes index.
   1. Commercial correspondence–Handbook, manual, etc.
I. Murphy, George D., joint author.   II. Title.
HF5726.C5   651.7'5   75-11184
ISBN 0-87620-990-8

Copyright © 1976 by
Goodyear Publishing Company, Inc.
Pacific Palisades, California

Current printing (last digit):

10 9 8 7 6 5 4 3 2 1

ISBN: 0-87620-990-8
Y: 9908-8

Cover and interior design: Jackie Thibodeau

Printed in the United States of America

CONTENTS

PREFACE

If you examine business writing texts that are currently on the market, you will see that many are very imposing volumes. They offer a variety of situations and structures to teach students to cope with both the practical necessities and the fine points of business communications. This is good. To our minds, however, other texts are often unnecessarily intimidating and overly complicated. The art of business communications is not particularly mysterious—all it really takes to develop skill at communication is a command of some basic theory, and practice. We wrote WRITE UP THE LADDER to provide these and to help you develop your skill.

Parts I and II examine the essential theory and psychology of written communications. We suggest a basic approach to use in writing, and discuss ways to handle common writing experiences. Part III presents, in a simple and direct manner, rules of language you need in order to avoid embarrassing yourself or your employer. In each chapter we have provided a number of practical exercises and sample letters that allow you to test your developing skill. Finally, the Appendices offer additional sample communications as well as general exercises that reinforce the lessons of the text as a whole.

ACKNOWL-EDGMENTS

We are eager to express our gratitude to several people—to our wives, Caroline Cherry and Mary Lou Murphy, for their editorial insights, and sundry comforts and encouragements; to Miss Barbara Brown for her *pizzicato* touch at the typewriter and for logistical support beyond all telling; to Villanova University for its support; and to Jan Deming of Goodyear Publishing Co. for her handling of our manuscript.

We are also happy to acknowledge debts to Mr. Tom Walsh, Mr. Frank Sherry, Mr. Robert Ritchie, Mr. Joseph P. Corcoran, and Mrs. Joyce Munro. We are deeply grateful to Mr. Jack Craig.

Finally, one of us has for years been indebted to both the late John Hugh Esslemont Slater and to Jerome Fischer, the "onlie begetters" of what skill at grammar he has.

Thanks to all.

Part I
THE BASIC APPROACH

Chapter 1

WRITING AS A SKILL

Every book promises its prospective readers that they'll get something in return for the time they spend reading it. That something can be entertainment or expertise, information or escape, but something is always promised, and sometimes the promise is kept.

This book is no exception, for it too makes a promise, one we are reasonably sure can be kept. The something the reader can get from this book in return for his time is the improvement of his skill at written business and technical communication. We do not say that this book will enable anyone to master the art of communication, for that promise it cannot keep. No one can really master communication, if for no other reason than that language is an artificial convention; by its nature it is inadequate to convey all the shades of feeling and intricacies of thought that exist. But we do say that everyone can improve, if not master, communication skill.

There are, however, skills and skills. There are millions of people who are expert at transplanting kidneys, playing chess, making lamps out of beer bottles, and hot-wiring cars. Some of these skills are more useful—not to mention legal—than others, but they all take a good deal of time and effort to acquire. It is not easy to write well and it is legitimate to wonder whether it is worth the trouble. Every time someone approaches us with a proposition, we ask—or should ask—"What's in it for me?" Right now you should be asking that question about our promise to improve your skill at written communication.

There are at least two answers to your question. One is that there is a reward of self-satisfaction that comes from acquiring any skill. People climb Mount Everest because "it's there," and elderly men jog two miles a day simply because they like to know they can do it. Many people write simply for the personal reward derived from expressing themselves clearly and cogently. Another answer to the question, however, is that writing well can make you money. That's more than can be said for jogging.

Everyone knows that writing a hit play or a Pulitzer Prize-winning novel can earn impressive money indeed, but it is admittedly more difficult to see the connection between writing ordinary business memos, letters, and reports, and affluence. Nevertheless, the connection does exist.

Some years back, the *Harvard Business Review* took a poll of its readers, among whom are many of the world's most influential executives. Readers were asked what qualities they looked for in considering subordinates for promotion. Interestingly enough, the quality most valued by readers of the *Harvard Business Review* was skill at communication, and the importance of written communication was especially stressed.[1]

These executives regarded communications ability as the most important among *many* vital executive qualities. But, don't forget that the very term *communication* presupposes that you have a message to transmit; you know something that will be of value to others if it can be transmitted clearly. Auditors or marketing people, engineers or personnel experts, those who know their jobs *and* are able to communicate to others how well they know their jobs—these are the people who succeed. The formula for their success consists of a mixture of equal parts of job expertise and communication ability.

There is an old philosophical riddle which asks, "If a tree falls in the forest, and there is no one to hear it, does the tree make any sound when it falls?" We can re-phrase that riddle for our own purposes and ask whether it is possible for a person to be a good accountant or a good engineer if he can not helpfully transmit information and recommendations to other members of his organization? What if, for example, Dr. Jones, a scientist in charge of research and development, cannot clearly report his estimated production schedule for a new product to a marketing director? Can Dr. Jones be said to be good at research and development? The answer is clearly, "No." Conversely, if Mr. Smith, the marketing director, could not communicate to the people in research and development the importance of having a certain item in production by a given date, then he too will have failed at an important part of his job.

These are theoretical examples as anything involving Smiths and Joneses must surely be. In reality, no one could become either a marketing director or head of research and development unless, in addition to being a master of statistical sampling or stress analysis, he could successfully communicate these and other mysteries to intelligent laymen.

It may have occurred to you that you know of many white collar jobs in business and government that require little, if any, written communication. So do we. There are millions of people comfortably situated in offices all over the country who are never called upon to write a memo, much less a letter or report, from one year to the next. We met one the other day, in fact. We can't give you his real name, but his nickname, as he proudly announced, was "Bolts." For the past fifteen years he had sat at a desk (the same desk) buying bolts for the Department of Defense. He would make a few telephone calls every day to suppliers, but for the most part he simply sent out order forms in quadruplicate and filled in the blanks on pre-printed contracts. He planned to retire in ten years. He also planned to spend that ten years buying more bolts. He said he liked his job.

Managerial success, however, as opposed to simple security, requires that we see how the parts of an organization relate to one another and how the whole organization relates to the world beyond it. Communication is the most basic form of relation; it is the relation of one mind to others. As we rise up the ladder of managerial success, our perspective improves and our ability to communicate, particularly in writing, provides tangible evidence of how well we comprehend the complex relationships of today's organizational world. Communication, then, is at once a function and a cause of managerial promotion, and it is for this reason that we say that it is possible to *write up the ladder of success.*

1. John Fielden, "What Do You Mean I Can't Write?" *Harvard Business Review* (May/June, 1964), pp. 144-156.

Chapter 2

COMMUNI=CATIONS STRATEGY

So much for why you should be concerned with writing well. Now we must get down to the more complicated matter of how it is done.

Actually, it is not so complicated as you may think, and one of the greatest barriers to successful business correspondence is an exaggerated notion of its difficulty. Look at it realistically; you will not, after all, be called upon to write a novel or sonnet sequence, but letters and memos. Your purpose will not be to inflame the imagination of millions, but simply to make, in as personable and direct a way possible, a few things perfectly clear to a few people.

It may be of some encouragement to know that the quality of much public writing is so low that, with a little practice and thought about tactics, you may become, if only by default, a better than average writer. In fact, by reading only as far as you have in this book, you already enjoy an advantage over the average writer. You have already displayed a willingness to do something that most people in business never do, and that is to concern yourself with a study of the fundamental techniques of successful writing. Usually when an average person is promoted into a job which requires him to write, he uses the files of correspondence his predecessors generated as models. His predecessors probably had done the same thing. It is not an exaggeration to say that most business writing consists of imitating an imitation of an imitation ("Little fleas have littler fleas upon their backs to bite 'em").

But we hope you aspire to become a good writer and not merely a better than average one. To do this it is first important to have confidence in your ability to write and not be overly worried about grammar and punctuation. Anxiety about writing can be a great barrier to skillful communication. In Chapter 10 we will discuss the writer's psychology, or *your* state of mind as you confront the experience of learning to produce effective letters, memos, and reports. We will try to motivate you and to dispel any excessive concern you may have about writing. But for now, let's direct our focus from the psychology of the writer to the other participant in the communication process—the *reader*.

3

Your success as a writer will depend heavily on your capacity to be a common sense, grassroots psychologist. Like most people, writers are primarily concerned with their own needs and feelings. But the successful writer is not only concerned with what he wants and needs to communicate, but with the emotional and intellectual *effect* of his communication upon his reader.

Speaking of psychology, psychologists have discovered that people conceptualize in two different ways. The classification is made on the basis of how people respond to a spoken word. If, for example, when a person hears the word **triangle**, he actually visualizes a shape, a three-sided polygon, on his mental screen, he's said to be a visual thinker. But if, instead of a shape, he sees a word, **t-r-i-a-n-g-l-e**, then he is an abstract thinker. Which is the best way to think? Neither way is better. The differences just exist, like brown eyes or blue eyes.

Likewise there are two ways of thinking about writing, and here one way is distinctly better than the other. When you think about writing a letter do you

> *Think of the letter?* That is, the letter you must write, the written task that has to be fulfilled?

> or do you

> *Think of the reader?* Do you realize that you haven't completed your task when you have signed and mailed the letter, but only when the letter has reached the reader and motivated him in the way you desire.

The first approach can be called BUSINESS WRITING. The second approach is BUSINESS COMMUNICATION.

If we want to communicate instead of simply churning out paper, we have to be at least as much concerned with our reader's psychology as our own, and, in order to touch his mind and positively motivate him we must be simultaneously concerned with three aspects of good communication strategy:

> *Tone:* The climate of feeling our message generates.

> *Information:* The presentation of *correct* information, and *sufficient* information to motivate our reader to the action or conclusion we desire.

> *Organization:* The presentation of information *clearly* and *strategically*.

Tone, Information, and *Organization* are the basic ingredients of effective communication. The trick now is to remember the formula. Let's see what the first letters of the three concepts spell when put together. T + I + O make TIO . . . which spells nothing in English. This is unfortunate because there's nothing like a snappy acronym like P.A.N.I.C. or S.E.X. to keep formulas spotlighted in our memory.

However, waste not, want not. Let's revive that triangle we just finished discussing and use it for our memory gimmick.

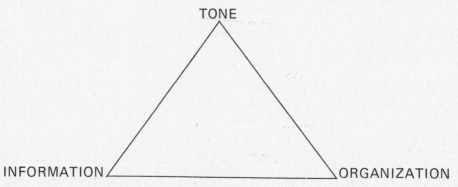

When you think of writing, THINK OF THE TRIANGLE.

SAMPLE LETTERS

Keeping the triangle in mind, let's examine a couple of actual letters. We've changed the wording a little, but only to conceal the identity of their authors. Read through them carefully and, as you do so, put yourself in the position of the people who received them. From that point of view, are they good, bad, or indifferent letters? Briefly, what would their psychological effect on their recipient be?

The first letter (Figure 2.1) is from a defense contractor who has had difficulty in completing the manufacture of an order of turnbuckles by the contractually stipulated date. He wants an extension of his delivery schedule.

The next letter (Figure 2.2) is from a claims agent for an insurance company to a lawyer. The lawyer has written on behalf of a client, for whom he has power-of-attorney, to collect under a supplemental hospitalization policy the client carries.

Which is the better letter—the defense contractor's or the claims examiner's? We feel that the contractor's letter is so dramatically bad that we hesitated to use it in this book for fear that our readers would believe that we had made it up. The sad fact is, however, that Mr. Royer's letter (Figure 2.1) is real, or rather it is very much like a real letter which was abbreviated, to save our readers fatigue, and altered a little, to save its real author some well-deserved embarrassment. The really sad fact about Mr. Royer's letter is not simply that it is bad, but that so many other business letters which are written also share its badness, though in less exaggerated ways.

What is wrong with it? For openers, it failed its most important and practical test—it didn't work. The real "Mr. Royer" was denied his extension.

If we consider Mr. Royer's letter with respect to the triangle of *Tone*, *Information*, and *Organization*, we must agree that *Tone* is its most deficient area. You have undoubtedly thought of a phrase or two of your own that might describe its style, but we'll say that it can be fairly described as pompous and overinflated. Mr. Royer has filled it with some stuffy clichés of business writing that were the rage of the 1880s and are now about as trendy as a stiff wing collar on a bank teller. Note, in this connection, Mr. Royer's use of such terms as "twenty-eighth instant," "subject noted," and "herewith respectfully petition," and see Chapter 15 for more examples of dated, threadbare phrases and some suggested substitutes.

Mr. Royer seems to be a past master of redundancy, seizing every opportunity to use two, or three, or four words where one would do nicely. Note his phrase "one last, final (and of short duration) extension of time." What would be wrong with saying "one last, short extension"? Even where he does use one word rather than several, Mr. Royer prefers the exotic to the garden variety. Does not "dearth," for example, mean the same thing as "shortage," and could not he have said "many" rather than "manifold"? Faults such as these are merely annoying, but there are times when Mr. Royer's fancy taste in vocabulary absolutely obscures his message. In his second paragraph, you find the word "allo-centric." What does it mean? We looked it up when we first read his letter, but we've forgotten its meaning already. It is not a very useful word.

There are one or two spots in his letter where Mr. Royer's fancy phrasing conveys a meaning that he almost certainly did not intend. For example, look at his second paragraph where he writes about the "prima facie" reasons for his delinquency. The correct application of the term *prima facie* is to facts or evidence that appear obvious "at first sight." If the reader of Mr. Royer's letter is aware of this meaning he may wonder whether there are other reasons that do not appear at first sight and which Mr. Royer is concealing.

Mr. Royer, who probably prides himself on his vocabulary, undoubtedly considers himself to be an impressive writer. He's right about this, for he is an impressive, even an unforgettable writer. But good business writing is not concerned with impressiveness for its own sake, but with function— with persuasion, explanation, motivation, and information. The Commander of the Defense Supply Depot simply wanted to know where his turnbuckles were. He was not disposed to be impressed by

ELKINS ROYER, INCORPORATED
6613 Winston Boulevard
San Diego, California 92014
(714) 732-4399

April 16, 197__

Commander
Defense Supply Depot
618 Alleghany Avenue
Philadelphia, Pennsylvania 19146

Attention: DSEF-PBAI

Subject: Request your permission to grant one last, final (and short duration) extension of time for us to effectuate total quantity delivery of your FSL 5380-334-9819, Turnbuckle Assembly.

Gentlemen:

In response to your letter of the twenty-eighth instant, and in connection with subject noted, we herewith respectfully petition your concurrence to allow one last set-back of the present delivery schedule due date, i.e., FROM: 3 June, 197__ TO: 31 July, 197__ (final and firm commitment).

The prima facie reason(s) for our apparent delinquency is (are) manifold and, in our way of thinking, should be explained in a causatively sequential manner so as to best serve the allo-centric interests, empathy, and understanding of your activity to our rather unenviable performance record in execution of this contract.

(1) As you are undoubtedly well aware, for the past several months there has been a dearth of qualified help available in this area—lay-offs in the Aerospace Industry notwithstanding—which, of course, results in a rather restricted productive capability. We have in force training programs for unskilled, underprivileged, and disadvantaged persons in compliance with your ARPS criteria (Section IX, Part 4) but, as you know, time is needed (more time than is necessary in many instances) to do the job.

(2) This same condition applies to our subcontractors who, repeatedly, have disappointed us by not being able to meet their performance commitments and this, thus in turn, has adversely contributed to compounding our position of delinquency with your agency.

(3) Moreover, about halfway downstream toward completion of this order, we did have some labor problems whereas despite federal regulation governing wage adjustments, we encountered some difficulty in the relative interpretation thereof (to our employees); the result of which precluded our being able to exact any overtime from our factory personnel for a period of nearly two months, i.e., until a satisfactory negotiated wage accommodation could be resolved.

Consequently, in view of the foregoing, we ask that you accept our proposal for shipment of the totality of your hardware by the date (31 July, 197__) specified herein. Please oblige.

Thank you. We shall esteem your usual prompt attention and courtesy regarding our request for extension of the delivery schedule and stay of default proceedings.

Very truly yours,
ELKINS-ROYER, INCORPORATED

Sunderland E. Royer
Vice President, Sales

SER:la   *Bad*

Figure 2.1.

**DROVERS AND PECULATORS
ASSURANCE CORPORATION**
9931 Reedon Plaza, Baltimore, Md. 21229
(301) 644-9600

October 7, 197__

Reginald Ponder, Esquire
Ponder, Ponder and Surmise
207 East Atkins Boulevard
Largesse, Nevada 89109

Dear Mr. Ponder:

Enclosed is our claim check in the amount of $600 to the order of Miss Mabel Z. Donner.

This check represents the hospitalization benefits due her for her confinement from July 27 through September 25, 197__, a total of 60 days.

When we checked on September 25, we were informed by the hospital that Miss Donner was still confined. Therefore, I am enclosing an additional claim form so that you can have it completed upon her discharge from the hospital and submit it to us along with the appropriate information. We will be glad to issue an additional benefit check at that time.

In your letter, you mention that you expect Miss Donner to be transferred to Winsocket Lodge, a nursing home. It should be noted that the benefits for hospitalization under the terms of Miss Donner's policy do not include confinements in nursing homes. Therefore, her benefits will terminate upon admission to the nursing home.

It has been a pleasure to be of service to you, and we look forward to completing our responsibility in this claim.

Sincerely,

Felton Mather
Claims Examiner

FM:gd

Good

Figure 2.2.

Mr. Royer's linguistic trapeze act. He might, on the other hand, have been a little amused, but not amused enough to keep him from cancelling the contract and leaving Mr. Royer's company with a lifetime's supply of undelivered turnbuckles.

The second letter, the one from the claims examiner to the lawyer (Figure 2.2), is a much better example of business communication. It is, of course, an easier letter to write, for it is less difficult to give someone six hundred dollars than to explain why you can't make delivery on an important contract.

The *Tone* of Mr. Mather's letter is not very dramatic, but it is quietly courteous. Note the last paragraph in which he writes that "it has been a pleasure to be of service" and goes on to remark that his company "looks forward" to completing "our responsibility." This conclusion is undoubtedly a formula which Mr. Mather has used many times in his career as a claims examiner. We will discuss the use of readymade formulas more fully later, but we should mention now that *originality* is more often a deterrent than an aid to effective business communication. Most messages are concerned with formulated situations, and communications efficiency requires the use of a number of stock responses to stock situations. Mr. Mather's formulas, however, are simple, direct, and relatively human, as opposed to Mr. Royer's, which seem offensively pompous and impersonal.

The *Informational* and *Organizational* elements of Mr. Mather's brief letter are also satisfactory. He gets immediately to his point and sticks to it. He also uses the simple but effective strategy of beginning on the most positive note available to him: "Enclosed is our claim check in the amount of $600." Notice here that Mr. Mather has organized his letter in a way that anticipates further, time-consuming writing; he encloses a supplemental claims form, and he warns Miss Donner's lawyer of the termination of her benefits, should she be transferred to a nursing home.

To sum up these two samples of written communication, we can say that Mr. Royer's letter is pompously inept, while Mr. Mather's is courteously efficient. Mr. Mather has evolved a clear strategy for communication. Mr. Royer has not.

EXERCISES

Think about the three questions below without looking back over the material you have just read. Jot brief answers down on a sheet of paper and *then* check back in the text to see how well you remembered the material covered.

1. Can you briefly describe the basic difference between Business Writing and Business Communication? *Business Writing — Your thinking oof the letter.*

2. What are the three basic aspects of communication? *Business Communication = your thinking of the reader* *Tone, Information & Organization*

3. How do most people learn to write business letters?

Chapter 3

THE UNITY OF EFFECT

In this chapter we will discuss in more detail the three points of our communication strategy triangle: *Tone, Information,* and *Organization*. We want to give you a fuller sense of what each of these aspects of communication implies, and, more practically, we'd also like to suggest a few specific tactics to help you gain greater proficiency within thses areas. We'll start with *Tone*. In later chapters these three elements will be restated regarding different types of communications. Here, however, we will discuss them in terms of general theory.

TONE

We've often heard people criticize a speaker: "It isn't *what* he said, it's the *way* he said it!" What they are complaining about is tone. We all know how much gestures, facial expressions and variations in volume can affect response in conversation, but too often, in writing, we forget about the importance of tone. Tone is extremely important, particularly in letters, which are the most personal form of written message.

The disturbing thing about tone is that you have it whether you want it or not. That is to say, even if you are not consciously aware of controlling the tone of your written message, your writing nevertheless will have a certain tone, one that very likely may seem indifferent to the human feelings of its recipient. So, if you want your messages to create and sustain goodwill and to elicit cooperation, you must be in conscious control of your tone.

The right tone requires the right *balance* of personalities—yours and the reader's—and it generally pays to put the emphasis on the reader's personality. We are all a little paranoid these days about our individuality, and we tend to mutter darkly about computers and automation, so it is now more important than ever to make your reader believe that he is receiving your personal attention. He should feel that he is corresponding with a human being who regards him as another human being and not as a category or punch card.

If you want to give your letters this personalized tone, it is important to *stress what we call the* **you approach** *as opposed to the* **I** *or* **we approach**.

The simplest and most direct way of cultivating the **you approach** is to make sure that your opening lines contain some direct reference to the reader. Consider such opening techniques as these:

> Thank *you* for *your* memo. . . .
>
> *Your* request has been approved. . . .
>
> Thank *you* for the interest *you* showed. . . .

Another technique you may use to personalize your correspondence is to refer to your reader by name once or twice in the course of your letter. Don't overdo this, however, as it is a gambit much employed by direct-mail promoters of retirement condominiums in Death Valley and off-shore burial plots. You have probably received several of these obvious form letters in which your name appears in every other sentence with the ink just a little lighter or darker than the rest of the type. However, just because snake-oil salesmen overuse this technique doesn't mean that its moderate use is a bad idea.

Be aware at all times of the **connotative** *and* **denotative** *meanings of words* that you use. Almost any word you use has both. The *denotation* of a word is its logical, dictionary meaning while its *connotation* is the emotional meaning or implication it carries. The connotation of words is obviously important in poetry and advertising, but it is too often overlooked in routine business correspondence. Be careful in selecting denotatively synonymous terms; their connotations may not be as interchangeable as you think. Remember the old saying: "I am firm-minded. My friends are often stubborn. My enemies are pig-headed."

Consider the connotative differences between the following pairs of words which have essentially the same denotation:

state/claim	disturbed/irate
dislike/resent	weak/feeble
inexpensive/cheap	

In establishing a favorable tone, *try to* **empathize** *with your reader.* Empathize means more than sympathize; it means trying to put yourself in your reader's place. Here is where it is important to carefully *preview* an incoming letter from a psychological as well as informational standpoint before replying to it. What do you know or can you deduce about your reader? Is he young or old, angry or worried? Is he confused? Is he a businessman or a little old lady? Adjust your tone to match what you know about your reader.

Be particularly on guard when corresponding with the public that you do not let a bored, routine tone creep into your letters. Remember that, although you may have answered a particular question a thousand times, this may be the first time your reader has asked it.

In creating tone, watch out for the following pitfalls:

Excessive humility	Preachiness
Obvious flattery	Pomposity (remember Mr. Royer!)
Condescension	

Above all, *cultivate plain, old fashioned* **courtesy**. Courtesy is not something that comes naturally to us. We learn to practice it in our social life through trial and painful error because it makes social relations pleasanter and easier for us. We also practice courtesy because we have learned

her threat to "cancel all!" SurFuture Investment Company could easily have responded in a briefer, clearer, more appropriate, and more pointedly helpful manner, as in Figure 3.3.

Dear Mrs. Dalton:

I have received your recent correspondence regarding the above policies.

Policy 00821 has a due date of December 22, 197__. The rates for this policy are: $10.93 monthly, $31.70 quarterly, $61.21 semiannually, and $120.23 annually.

Policy S 21006 has a due date of May 10, 197__. The rates for this policy are: $7.50 monthly, $20.38 quarterly, $40.50 semiannually, and $75.00 annually.

Because of your existing policy with our company we were pleased to be able to provide you with coverage for six months under a Special Supplemental Accident Policy. The accident protection was issued and became effective May 15, 197__. There was no requirement for the first six months.

Policy N286520 and policy N286521 have due dates of May 15, 197__.

I trust this information has been helpful. If you have any further questions, please do not hesitate to contact me.

Sincerely,

Harriett W. Armstrong
Policy Owner's Service

Figure 3.2.

Dear Mrs. Dalton:

Thank you for your recent inquiry.

In checking our records, I see that you have four policies with SurFuture. Policy 00821, with a due date of December 22, 197__, costs $120.23 annually, while Policy S 21006, due May 10, 197__, costs $75 annually.

In addition to these base policies, you have two supplemental policies (N286520, N286521), due May 15, 197__, and costing $8.25 each.

The total annual cost of all four policies accounts for the $211.73 expended since January. I might add that this is money well spent, for taken together these policies provide total health and accident protection for your entire family. The attached booklet describes your coverage in detail.

Should you have additional questions, please do not hesitate to write.

Sincerely,

Harriett W. Armstrong
Policy Owner's Service

Figure 3.3

In addition to providing essential information, this version of the letter takes the *extra step* by trying to persuade Mrs. Dalton to keep her policies. By taking the time to translate and interpret the data, Ms. Armstrong helps both Mrs. Dalton and SurFuture.

ORGANIZATION

The notion of *interpreting* rather than simply *presenting* information leads naturally into a consideration of the last side of our communication triangle, **Organization**. *Organization* is nothing more than the technique of displaying information to the best advantage.

Here again, a *preview* is necessary, for, before writing, we should consider our intended message from an organizational angle, essentially asking ourselves the following three questions:

1. What is the conclusion I want my reader to reach?
2. What is the best plan to follow in arranging my information to lead my reader to the desired conclusion?
3. What techniques can I use to make sure that my reader is able to follow my informational plan to its conclusion quickly and easily?

Answer the first question first. If you want to lead your reader to reach certain conclusions, you want him to do more than simply finish your message, staying with it all the way to "Sincerely yours." You want him to think or act in specific ways in response to it. When you preview your message, *be specific about your purpose in writing* it. You may think it impossible that anyone in his right mind would bother writing anything without a definite purpose, but the sad truth is that, when it comes to writing, many people are not altogether in their right minds. The very thought of writing so disconcerts them that they can't achieve a state of creative relaxation, and they become so preoccupied with the *task* of communicating that they fail to keep firmly in mind their *reason* for communicating.

So your first concern must be to establish precisely what it is that you want your message to do, and this requires more than simply determining the general subject of the message. A typical interoffice memo form, such as the one shown in Figure 3.4, has four headings printed at the top: "Date," "To," "From," and "Subject." In the "Subject" blank we might find "Accounts receivable," or "Monthly sales meeting," or "Atkinson case." But such statements of the *subject* of a memo do not define the *purpose* of the memo or establish the conclusion you may want your reader to reach after he has read it. The *purpose,* as opposed to the *subject,* of such a memo might be "determining

CAUSTIC UNGUENTS, LTD.

Date: _____

To: _____   From: _____

Subject: _____

Figure 3.4. *A typical interoffice memo form.*

why accounts receivable are lower in July than in June," or "seeking reasons for changing the monthly sales meeting from Fridays to Mondays," or "setting forth reasons for not renewing the Atkinson lease."

The next step after having formulated the specific purpose of your message is to ask yourself the second question, that is, how should you arrange your information in a way that will elicit the desired conclusion from your reader? It is at this point that you should decide on your basic communication strategy, which will be determined as much by the nature of the data you must organize as by your preconceived purpose.

Do you want, for example, to describe a process? Then you might well use a *chronological* or *sequential* arrangement, proceeding logically from step one to step two and so on. Have you reached a decision with which you want others to agree? Then you might consider a *deductive* strategy in which you begin by stating your conclusion and then citing the particular reasons which led you to it. The same problem could be tackled *inductively* by beginning with the particulars that support your conclusion. Again, it might well be that you are simply concerned with marshalling all the relevant considerations that will enable someone else to make an informed decision. In this situation you could proceed by listing all the "pros" followed by all the "cons," or you might elect to balance each "pro" with a "con" as you go. The point is that there are obviously many ways to skin each problematic cat. You should decide beforehand on a strategy and follow it consistently, not simply leap in and unsystematically tear the poor creature apart.

You might find an *outline* helpful. It is the rare person who has emerged from the American school system without having had to (1) memorize a poem by Longfellow and (2) prepare at least one outline. A kind of mystique has grown up around the outline with its meticulous protocol governing the relative hierarchy of Roman numerals, capital letters, Arabic numerals, and so on. But what some instructors often overlook is that an outline in itself is of no great importance; it is only useful as a tool for the construction of something more--the larger, written message. The outline is to the writer what the blueprint is to the contractor. It keeps the creative process from going astray.

The great virtue of the outline for the writer is that the very act of putting it together forces him to think clearly and decide firmly on what his purpose is and on how he is going to achieve it. The longer and more complicated a job of writing, the more necessary a blueprint for its construction will be. But an outline can be helpful in the construction of very short messages as well.

Forget about the beautiful, descending array of numerals and letters in the formal, textbook outline! Just a few basic points jotted down in their most effective order can be invaluable in helping you to focus your purpose and determine your strategy. This kind of casual blueprint is especially important if you are going to dictate your communication.

Now for the third and last question you should ask yourself before beginning the actual process of writing: What techniques can you use to make it as easy as possible for your reader to follow your informational plan to its conclusion? The first and most basic technique available to you is to *use intelligent* **paragraphing**.

Remember that paragraphs are not simply decorative. The indentation that signals the beginning of a new paragraph is not designed just to please the eye but also to rest the mind. A paragraph primarily indicates to your reader that you are moving on to another important subdivision of your overall logical plan. Nothing disconcerts a reader more than to encounter a number of lengthy paragraphs in a message, for this subconsciously alerts him to the fact that his head is about to hurt. Looking at that vast, unbroken expanse of print or typescript, the reader suspects one of two things: either the writer is so indifferent to his mental comfort that he hasn't bothered to break his message down into the easily assimilated units of thought called paragraphs, or the writer is so confused himself that he is unable to organize his material coherently. Either way, the reader knows that there is heavy going ahead.

As a general rule, the more complicated the material, the more paragraphs you should have, but take care that these paragraphs are *legitimate* paragraphs. Some writers seem to paragraph as the

whim takes them. This sort of thing is the written equivalent of "urr's" and "ahh's" in oral communication. A paragraph break of this sort does not alert the reader that he has arrived at another important element of the message, but only that the writer needed a little time to get his thoughts
together.

Another technique for leading your reader through the complexities of your message is to
enumerate the major divisions of your thought. If, for example, you believe that there are three
basic reasons for moving that sales meeting from Friday to Monday, there's nothing wrong with num-
bering the paragraphs in which you consecutively take them up, or introducing them like this: "The
first reason is . . . ." "The second reason is . . . ." and so on. This may not be the most sophisticated
kind of organization, but it does the job.

Another way to guide your reader through difficult passages is to *use repetition and parallelism*.
If you repeat key terms you keep your reader on the track of the subject at hand, and if you take
care to use similar grammatical structures (parallelism) throughout a complicated element of your
message, you keep the pattern of that message clearly before the reader. Notice how John Henry
Newman—one of the great prose stylists of the last century—uses these devices to enable his reader
to follow him through a complex inventory of the attributes of the well-trained mind:

> It [the well-trained mind] is almost prophetic from its knowledge of history; it is almost
> heart-searching from its knowledge of human nature; it has almost supernatural charity from
> its freedom from littleness and prejudice; it has almost the repose of faith, because nothing
> can startle it; it has almost the beauty and harmony of heavenly contemplation, so intimate
> is it with the eternal order of things and the music of the spheres.[1]

This passage is not the easiest thing in the world to comprehend even as it stands, but imagine its
difficulty if it lacked the repetitions and parallelism which knit it together!

Use transitional words and phrases as another way to conduct your reader smoothly from one
point to another along the pathway of your prose. Such terms as "moreover," "in spite of this,"
"in addition to," "because of that," and "meanwhile, back at the ranch," not only alert your reader
to the fact that you are making a transition from one point to another, but also indicate the logical
relationship of what is to come to what has gone before. Such words are like road signs; they not
only tell the reader where he is going, they remind him of where he has been. We'll discuss transitions and parallel structure in greater detail in Chapter 14.

Most business writing is *expository* in nature, which is to say that it is chiefly concerned with
explaining or defining things and concepts. Despite everything you may have heard to the contrary,
man is not naturally a logical animal. He may be naturally intelligent, but that is not the same as
being logical. Logic is the method used to convey the results of our thinking to others: it is not
necessarily the way we think. As a matter of fact, psychologists still are not very clear about how
we do think, but they do know that it is rarely in the manner we call logical.

You may find it interesting, as well as disconcerting, to eavesdrop on your own thought processes.
If, for example, you are trying to come to a decision about something, you will find that your mind
holds in suspension enormous amounts of data and emotions, much of which is apparently irrelevant,
until at some point in your turbulent stream of consciousness you almost inexplicably make the
decision. It is only when we want to convey the reasons behind that decision to another person that
we must use logic, that is, translate the subjective shorthand of our thinking into linear longhand
that can be understood by someone else.

Logic is essentially the process of making clear to anyone else the connections which exist between one thought and another. Unfortunately, a connection that may be very obvious to us, may
be unclear to anyone who could not look inside our head while we were thinking. The most im-

---

1. John Henry Newman, "Discourse VI," from *The Idea of a University* as reprinted in Charles F. Harrold
   and William D. Templeman, eds., *English Prose of the Victorian Era* (New York: Oxford University
   Press, 1938), p. 594.

portant quality a good ~~expository~~ writer can cultivate is skill at establishing clear connections between ideas, the ability to translate his own intellectual shorthand into the conventional, artificial, but vital longhand called logic.

Many times we have had the experience of pointing out to a student that we fail to see the connection between one of his sentences or paragraphs and the next, only to have him counter with, "Well, if you'd just stop and think for a second, you'd see the connection!" Our usual response is, "Why the devil should you expect us to stop, even for a second?"

Ideally only the innate difficulty of the material with which a message deals should require the reader to "stop and think." If an intelligent reader must stop to devise his own connections, translate the writer's shorthand, then he is being forced to do the writer's job for him. The writer has disregarded a fundamental element of *Organization*.

Up to now we've been treating organization from the point of view of structure and coherence—the clear development of a central purpose in a logically ordered sequence of sentences and paragraphs. Yet, there is also a psychological dimension to organization, for it is just as important to organize your messages in a *psychologically strategic* manner.

Let's examine this point by reviewing a particular case. Mr. Alvin R. Summers, Assistant to the Dean of Hargrove College, writes to a number of foundations requesting their support in establishing and endowing two kinds of scholarships: 1) a post-graduate scholarship of $1,000.00 for a graduating senior who best exemplifies the ideals of Hargrove College and whose service to the community has been most impressive; 2) a number of $1,000 scholarships (renewable on merit for a four year period) for academically superior students of limited means who are applying to Hargrove. These endowed scholarships would be named as indicated by the donor. Within a few weeks, Mr. Summers begins to receive answers to his request. These are shown in Figures 3.5, 3.6, 3.7, and 3.8.

Carson Metals Foundation
Radon Boulevard
Middleton, Connecticut 06457
March 26, 197__

Mr. Alvin R. Summers
Hargrove College
Wilmington, Delaware 19898

Dear Mr. Summers:

I am pleased to inform you that your institution has been selected as the recipient of a Carson Scholarship Endowment.

Under the terms of this grant, your school will receive $10,000 each year for four years for the support of academically gifted students unable to meet the costs of their education; such students will be designated as "Carson Scholars." You are free to select the students and to distribute the funds as you deem necessary. A check for $10,000 will be sent to Hargrove each July for the next four years.

I offer you my congratulations and wish your institution every success.

Sincerely,

Terrence M. Bellinger
Executive Secretary

Figure 3.5.

In the four responses Mr. Summers receives, one is positive, three are negative. In our single "Yes" letter—Figure 3.5—we see a good example of positive organization. The writer immediately communicates the big idea with the word "pleased." Thus the reader has a positive frame of mind in which to consider the necessary administrative details of the next paragraph. The writer then only needs to add a brief farewell, for he has been the bearer of glad tidings.

But consider the problems of the other foundation representatives. Every day requests for money come in, and every day they must reject many of them. There is nothing more difficult than to compose a good "No" letter. Consider the problems involved. First, you are the bearer of ill tidings and are sure to make your reader unhappy, if not downright miserable. Second, you must be diplomatic enough to soften the blow, so that you retain the good will of your reader. In other words, you must use sound psychology or tact in structuring your response. This applies whether you are rejecting a request for money, firing an employee, or refusing an offer of marriage.

In Figure 3.6 Mr. Watson displays no such tact. Rather, he implies that he speaks from a position of power and wealth, and has little time for requests that he cannot honor. Thus his early use of "regret," appearing at the beginning of the letter, immediately strikes a negative note, a discordant tone not compensated for but compounded by the hurried, almost brusque closing that follows. Mr. Watson's response may well leave Mr. Summers either feeling guilty for having bothered Diamond Trust in the first place, or grumbling vindictively about tax dodges.

Diamond Trust
201 Quince Street
Washington, D.C. 20006
April 12, 197__

Mr. Alvin R. Summers
Hargrove College
Wilmington, Delaware   19898

Dear Mr. Summers:

   Regarding your request for scholarship assistance, I regret that the Diamond Trust will not be able to undertake any such commitment. We have not provided for such support in the past and have no present intention of moving in this direction.

Sincerely,

Marvin K. Watson
Director

Figure 3.6.

Notice the difference, however, in Figures 3.7 and 3.8. Mr. Summers does no better with these foundations than he did with Diamond Trust. He comes away penniless, but with a better taste in his mouth. The letters by Moran and Carmichael are much more diplomatic in part because of their organization. In each case they begin not with "I regret" or "Unfortunately" or "Sorry"—negative elements—but with points on which they and the reader can agree. Then gradually, in the second paragraph, both writers inform Mr. Summers that they are unable to help. Yet they do so without costing themselves the good will of Hargrove College. Their letters are concerned, pleasant, and sincere.

MainLine Foundation
102 West 49th Street
New York, New York 10017
March 25, 197__

Professor Alvin R. Summers
Assistant to the Dean
Hargrove College
Wilmington, Delaware 19898

Dear Professor Summers:

Thank you for your letter of March 15, in which you request scholarship assistance from our foundation.

What you are proposing to do is the right thing, I believe, in the context of current educational needs, and you are to be congratulated for your initiatives on behalf of the students. Regrettably, however, other budget commitments preclude our assistance—and I do not expect that funds will become available for this sort of undertaking for at least the foreseeable future.

Thus, all I can do is wish you well and hope that you are successful in securing an alternate source of funds.

Thank you for writing and good luck.

Sincerely,

Alice K. Moran
Program Officer

Figure 3.7.

Keep in mind, then, the following simple rules for proper psychological organization of "Yes" and "No" letters. *For the "Yes" letter, always begin immediately with the positive statement:*

I am happy to inform you that you have won the competition.

Congratulations on your recent promotion.

Your request is approved.

Yes, you are eligible for our bank loan.

This places your reader in the proper frame of mind to receive any supporting details. *For the "No" letter, always start with something you and your reader can agree on:*

The cost of living is certainly rising.

Belk, Inc. appreciates the skill with which you have handled your position in recent years.

You are to be congratulated on your desire to help the sick.

Then proceed in a courteous, tactful manner to inform the person that mortgage money is not presently available, or that his desired raise will not be forthcoming, or that the Red Cross cannot accept donors with a history of venereal disease. Finally, in both the "Yes" and "No" letters, conclude in a pleasant, sincere manner to retain goodwill. In every case, always ask yourself how you would feel if *you* were the recipient of the letter you write.

Belco Chemicals Foundation
103 Fidelity Building
East Lansing, Michigan 48823
March 22, 197__

Mr. Alvin R. Summers
Assistant to the Dean
Hargrove College
Wilmington, Delaware 19898

Dear Mr. Summers:

Thank you for your letter of March 15. For many years our company has recognized the importance of supporting higher education, and we do so, very liberally, through a program of matching the gifts of our employees, on a dollar for dollar basis, to the colleges and schools of their choice. Limits are high—namely, $800 per year for sustaining funds and $8,000 from any individual for capital funds.

We can fully appreciate your need for funds as outlined in your letter, but we have not been in the practice of making outright grants for fellowships or special projects such as you described.

Even though unable to be of assistance at this time, we wish you every success in finding the funds to carry on your very worthwhile endeavor.

Sincerely,

G. S. Carmichael
Executive Secretary

Figure 3.8.

EXERCISES

Once again, think about the questions below without looking over the material you have just read. Jot your answers down on a sheet of paper and *then* look back in the text to check your recall of the material covered.

1. What is the difference between *connotation* and *denotation?*

2. Briefly define the concept of *Tone* in writing.

3. Can you recall the difference between *sympathize* and *empathize?*

4. How many pitfalls can you think of which endanger effective *Tone?*

5. Explain what the terms *upward* and *downward* communication mean.

6. What is *expertitis?*

7. What is meant by *previewing* an incoming message?

8. What is meant by taking the *extra step?*

9. What, briefly, is the difference between the *purpose* and the *subject* of a message?

10. What is the basic purpose of paragraphing?

11. Jot down three transitional words or phrases.

12. What do *repetition* and *parallelism* have to do with *Organization?*

Part II
COMMUNICATIONS SITUATIONS

Chapter 4

LETTER FORMS

As the leading dandy of Regency England, "Beau" Brummell dictated the proper dress for the well-dressed man. Favoring a simple but elegant look, he disliked perfumes, garish materials in men's clothing, and fantastic tailoring. Thus when he was once told about a man who was so well-dressed that people turned to stare at him whenever he entered a room, Brummell observed, "Then he was not well-dressed."

We can learn something about business communication from Brummell's quip, namely that our letters should not be so highly style conscious nor so outlandish that they call attention to themselves. This means that they should not distinguish themselves by color or complexity of letterhead (current taste dictates simple lines and plain colors). Neither should they be radically innovative in form or embarrassingly deficient in grammar and spelling. The latter problems, along with writing style, are dealt with in other sections of the text. Our present concern in this chapter is with the form of business communications.

There are six basic parts of the business letter: the heading, including the return address or letterhead and date, the inside address, the salutation, the body of the letter, the complimentary close, and, of course, the signature. We'll go over each of these six parts briefly; for models you can refer to the commonly used block and semiblock letter forms shown in Figures 4.2, 4.3, and 4.4.

A. THE HEADING

The heading gives the full address (with zip code) of the writer and the date of the letter. End punctuation is not used and the heading is blocked either to the right or left margin of the paper, and lines up with the complimentary close and the signature. If a letterhead containing the address is used, the date may be written immediately under it or flush with the right or left margin.

villanova
university

VILLANOVA, PENNSYLVANIA 19085

Date

February 8, 197__

Inside
Address

Mr. Robert T. Pope
Director of Admissions
Brewster School of Law
201 E. 34th Street
New York, New York 10011

Salutation

Dear Mr. Pope:

Body

Mr. Thomas K. Johnson has asked me to support his application to your institution. I am happy to do so.

I have known Mr. Johnson since he was a student in my Business Communication class in spring 197__. He displayed in that course the kind of skills that should help him in the legal profession: a clear ability to articulate his ideas in both verbal and written form; a knowledge and application of sound scholarly procedure; an admirable desire for learning.

In my contacts with him outside the classroom, I have always found him to be a friendly, capable person. Also, his varied background and experiences qualify him as the kind of well-rounded student most schools desire. He has worked as a life-guard during the summers at a New Jersey resort. He is an accomplished worker in woods, able to construct both wood sculptures and traditional cabinets. Finally, his full-time job with a local insurance company has afforded him valuable practical experience in the business community.

I am confident that Mr. Johnson will bring credit to your school.

Compli-
mentary
Close

Sincerely yours,

Malcolm L. Bass

Signature

Malcolm L. Bass, Ph.D.
Associate Professor

mb:bb

Figure 4.1. *Letter typed in block style with date, complimentary close, and signature at left-hand margin.*

B.　THE INSIDE ADDRESS

The inside address should be identical to the address on the envelope itself. It gives the full name and address (and the title, if known) of the person you are writing. The inside address is typed flush with the left margin from two to six lines below the dateline. Be *sure* to spell the name correctly and always use some title before the name.

C.　THE SALUTATION OR GREETING

The salutation begins at the left margin two spaces below the inside address. Before writing or dictating the greeting, consider how well you know the person. Your greeting will generally match your complimentary close in tone. Thus if you begin with "Dear Bill," you will close with "cordially yours" or "best regards" rather than the more formal "yours truly" or "respectfully yours."

When you are writing to a company rather than to an individual, use the term "Gentlemen" (rather than Messrs. Smith, Kline and French). When you are writing an individual, such as the president of a company, and do not know that person's name, begin with "Dear Sir." Always try to determine the proper name and title of the person to whom you are writing; this little effort shows care and helps avoid possible embarrassment.

Here are some common salutations:

Dear Sir

Dear Dr. Jones (*Mr., Mrs.* and *Dr.* may be abbreviated; other titles, such as *General,* should be spelled out in the salutation, even though they may be abbreviated in the heading)

Dear Miss Jones

Dear Mrs. Jones

Dear Ms. Jones (Female executives will frequently indicate the proper form in the signature of their letter. If not known, use *Miss* or *Ms.,* depending on your own sense of which they might prefer. *Ms.* is becoming more common and acceptable, but is still resented by some.)

Dear Madam

Mesdames (plural of *madam*)

Ladies (better substitute for *mesdames* when writing a group of women or a company composed of women)

My dear Madam

My dear Sir　　　(Try to avoid these formal salutations: they imply strained relations.)

Sir

In case you are writing to a diplomat, an archbishop, or the Pope, consult any good dictionary for a listing of proper salutations. Always follow the salutation with a colon.

D.　THE BODY

The body of the letter begins two lines below the salutation. Depending on the form chosen, the first sentence begins flush with the left hand margin (block style) or is indented five typewriter spaces from the margin (semiblock style). In either case, the sentences should follow the principles of good writing (with particular attention to tone, information, and organization). Double space between paragraphs. If the body goes into a second page, type the name of the recipient, the page number, and date across the top of the page or at the margin. This helps prevent problems should the two pages become separated.

villanova
university

Department of English

February 8, 197__

Mr. Robert T. Pope
Director of Admissions
Brewster School of Law
201 E. 34th Street
New York, New York 10011

Dear Mr. Pope:

Mr. Thomas K. Johnson has asked me to support his application to your institution. I am happy to do so.

I have known Mr. Johnson since he was a student in my Business Communication class in spring 197__. He displayed in that course the kind of skills that should help him in the legal profession: a clear ability to articulate his ideas in both verbal and written form; a knowledge and application of sound scholarly procedure; an admirable desire for learning.

In my contacts with him outside the classroom, I have always found him to be a friendly, capable person. Also, his varied background and experiences qualify him as the kind of well-rounded student most schools desire. He has worked as a lifeguard during the summers at a New Jersey resort. He is an accomplished worker in woods, able to construct both wood sculptures and traditional cabinets. Finally, his full-time job with a local insurance company has afforded him valuable practical experience in the business community.

I am confident that Mr. Johnson will bring credit to your school.

Sincerely yours,

Malcolm L. Bass

Malcolm L. Bass, Ph.D.
Associate Professor

mb:bb

Figure 4.2. *Letter typed in semiblock style with date, complimentary close and signature centered.*

Department of English
Villanova University
Villanova, Pennsylvania 19085
February 8, 197__

Mr. Robert T. Pope
Director of Admissions
Brewster School of Law
201 East 34th Street
New York, New York 10011

Dear Mr. Pope:

Mr. Thomas K. Johnson has asked me to support his application to your institution. I am happy to do so.

I have known Mr. Johnson since he was a student in my Business Communication class in spring 197__. He displayed in that course the kind of skills that should help him in the legal profession: a clear ability to articular his ideas in both verbal and written form; a knowledge and application of sound scholarly procedure; and admirable desire for learning.

In my contacts with him outside the classroom, I have always found him to be a friendly, capable person. Also, his varied background and experiences qualify him as the kind of well-rounded student most schools desire. He has worked as a lifeguard during the summers at a New Jersey resort. He is an accomplished worker in woods, able to construct both wood sculptures and traditional cabinets. Finally, his full-time job with a local insurance company has afforded him valuable practical experience in the business community.

I am confident that Mr. Johnson will bring credit to your school.

Sincerely yours,

Malcolm L. Bass

Malcolm L. Bass, Ph.D.
Associate Professor

mb:bb

Figure 4.3. *Letter in semiblock style without letterhead; heading, complimentary close and signature at right-hand margin.*

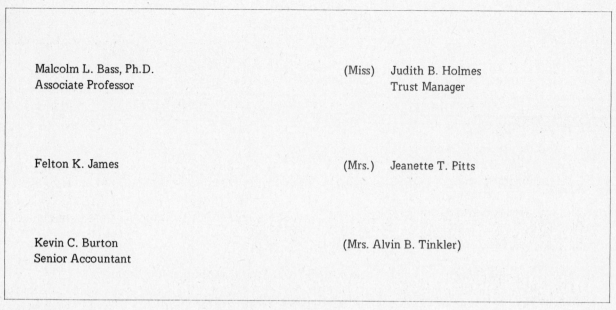

Malcolm L. Bass, Ph.D. Associate Professor	(Miss)	Judith B. Holmes Trust Manager
Felton K. James	(Mrs.)	Jeanette T. Pitts
Kevin C. Burton Senior Accountant		(Mrs. Alvin B. Tinkler)

Figure 4.4. *Some examples of several types of signature.*

E. THE COMPLIMENTARY CLOSE

The complimentary close, typed two spaces below the last line of the body, generally appears in line with the date. When a letterhead is used, the date is centered or flush with either margin. When a letterhead is absent, the date is usually placed at the right margin, along with the return address.

As we indicated earlier, the complimentary close used depends on the salutation. The most common forms, however, are: "Sincerely yours," "Cordially yours," "Yours truly," and "Respectfully yours." Many correspondents simply drop the "yours" and close with "Sincerely," "Regards," or "Cordially." These are more informal yet nonetheless acceptable endings.

F. THE SIGNATURE

The signature appears four lines below the complimentary close and is typed neatly for your reader. Your handwritten name, either matching the full name in the signature or abbreviated in accordance with your relationship to the correspondent, appears directly above the typed signature.

Titles or positions should be indicated in the signature as an aid to someone writing you in the future. Also, women should indicate how they wish to be addressed. Figure 4.4 indicates some different ways of styling a signature.

Business correspondence should generally be typed or printed on standard business stationery—usually 20-pound white bond in 8½ by 11 inch sheets—unless you have a good reason for choosing other colors or quality paper. You should always follow standard forms, except perhaps in sales letters. For sales you may wish to use cartoons or striking designs or green parchment in order to capture someone's attention. Marketing research will indicate the advisability of such approaches. Sales figures will indicate their effectiveness.

Chapter 5

LETTERS OF APPLICATION AND RESUMÉS

It is now time to deal with the communications strategies involved in getting a job or what is more politely called "a position." Since most Americans consider that what they are hunting for really is a "job," despite what they call it in letters and interviews, that's what we'll call it too. But before we settle down to the nuts and bolts business of constructing effective letters of application and resumés, let's consider the extensive preparation that precedes that stage of the successful job hunt.

ORGANIZING YOUR STRATEGY

A. MENTAL PREPARATION

The first stage of preparation is to make a personal inventory of your assets. This is not an easy task, and part of the difficulty is in accepting the fact that anxiety, if not downright fear, is a normal psychological state while job hunting. But though it is normal, it is not pleasant, particularly since it is necessary to project an image of cool confidence in letters of application and in employment interviews.

Much anxiety stems from the fact that everyone has a fear of the unknown. And, despite everything we hear about the grand old American spirit of individualism, we all tend to derive a great deal of self-definition from institutions with which we identify. For many millions of us, changes in our psychological states are consistent with our continually evolving identification with a series of institutions.

The first institution with which we are affiliated is the family, and our earliest self-image is defined in its terms. The next major institution which absorbs and shapes us is school, or rather the series of schools through which we progress. Think back to the time when you graduated from, say, grammar school to junior high school, and remember how disturbing that transition was. If you hadn't felt a little anxious at the prospect of all those strange kids from strange parts of town, those strange teachers teaching strange subjects like algebra, and those grimly anonymous rows of lockers in the unfamiliar halls, you would have been distinctly abnormal. But think too of how quickly you adjusted to the new institution, how your anxiety gradually faded and the school became, if not a festival of delight, at least tolerable.

When you can persuade yourself that a certain amount of anxiety is normal when you are facing the big transition from the familiar institution of school to the institution of the job, then the next step in self-inventory should be to examine your skills and aptitudes. It helps to use paper and pencil and to jot down, in no particular order, but simply as they occur to you, your various interests, hobbies, proficiencies, your educational training, and whatever full- or part-time jobs you may have previously held.

Then, put that list aside for awhile. Come back to it from time to time, study it, and add things to it as they suggest themselves. Remember too, that your school's placement center or guidance office can very often make available to you, either free or at bargain rates, a battery of aptitude tests which can be helpful to your self-inventory. They may reveal that you have abilities for jobs you might never have considered, or, even more important, they may prevent you from making a false start in a job for which you are psychologically unsuited.

Your personal inventory will provide the raw material out of which you will later construct your letter of application and your resumé. But at this stage of the campaign, it should be open-ended and you must feel free to add to it and subtract from it at will. Also, while you are compiling your personal inventory, you should be thinking of the types of jobs available to you.

B. THE JOB MARKET

Ours is an extraordinarily complex economy, and legions of people make money in ways that wouldn't occur to someone with a rigid or limited notion of suitable employment. For example, you have certainly noticed the large ash trays which stand in the lobbies of theaters and the corridors of office buildings. Have you noticed that they are often filled with a very fine-grained sand which extinguishes the cigarette butts dropped into them? Have you ever asked yourself how that sand got there? Do you imagine that the management of each theater and office building sends someone to the seashore every month or so with a shovel and half a dozen burlap bags? Consider the fact that somewhere in every city at least one person sells sand to fill ashtrays.

Well, the sand business may not be the commercial opportunity of your dreams, but it's just one example of the thousands of occupations which exist somewhere between ditch digging and neurosurgery. The more occupational slots you are aware of, the more intelligently you can take your personal inventory.

A very common complaint of liberal arts majors and general business majors is that their education has not qualified them to fit immediately into a precise job slot. It is true that "generalists" do experience more difficulty in finding their first job than do "specialists," but consider this:

> The generalist who's been out of college for 5, 10, 15 years invariably reports that he is 'happy'
> or 'very happy' with his career (90 percent), that he would 'repeat his major' (80 percent plus)
> and that he's making as much money as his specialized classmate.[1]

Conversely, the vocationally specialized student often gets psychologically locked in to his speciality. If he is an engineer, he may be blind to challenging and lucrative opportunities in sales,

1. Statistics drawn from Robert Calvert, Jr., *Career Patterns of Liberal Arts Graduates* (Cranston, R.I.: Carroll Press, 1969). Reprinted from *Careers and Jobs,* a monograph prepared by the Career Development Center, Villanova University, 1973, p. 3.

administration, or marketing, for example. In our highly fluid economy, it is distinctly p sible to become over-specialized. How many buggy whip makers have you met lately?

C. WHERE TO FIND JOB OPENINGS

How can you discover the various types of jobs for which you may be fitted by training, apt de, or inclination? The best source of information is your school's placement office—keep in mi that you can usually still use their services after leaving school. There are, however, other sources job leads. Here are a few:

1. Classified Ads. Look not only in newspapers but in specialized trade and professional journ (like *Sunnyside and Casket* if you are interested in the undertaking profession or selling embalm fluid).

2. Federal, State, County, and Municipal Civil Service. Civil Service openings at all levels of gover ment are legally required to be posted (look in your nearest Federal Building) and qualifying exam inations for the various jobs are advertised. Take as many examinations as you can.

3. Private Employment Agencies. These vary widely as to quality and the types of employment in which they specialize. Check out any agency with people who have used it before, read any agreement very carefully before signing it, and avoid any situation in which the employer does not pay the agency fee. That is, accept only "fee-paid" jobs.

4. State Employment Agencies. Quality varies widely from state to state and none are particularly strong in managerial or professional opportunities. But they are free, and many offer a computerized print-out of available jobs.

5. Word-of-Mouth Advertisement. Advertise your availability to friends, neighbors, and friends of friends, and don't overlook present and former teachers. Although it is not necessarily true that "it's not what you know but who you know" that counts, it certainly doesn't hurt to know someone who can put you on the inside track for a job opening.

D. HOW TO APPROACH PROSPECTIVE EMPLOYERS

All right, let's assume that you've made your personal inventory, given some careful, creative thought to working out a list of jobs that your inventory suggests you could fill, and discovered a number of actual or potential job openings through one or more of the sources we've just discussed. You are now set for the communications stage of your employment campaign; that is, you must now put your ego on the line and advertise your availability to prospective employers. Unless your personal inventory reveals that you are qualified for just one, unique type of job—designer of tools for left-handed diamond cutters, perhaps—and unless you have found after a diligent search that there is only one job opening in that line of work in the whole world, you must advertise your availability to a number of prospective employers simultaneously. Remember that you are conducting a full-scale campaign, not engaging in a series of isolated skirmishes.

There are four basic ways of advertising your availability, but only one of them is really much good.

1. Placing Your Own Advertisement. A classified ad in the "Positions Wanted" section of a newspaper is frankly not a very productive source of acceptable job opportunities. A slightly better bet would be a carefully-written advertisement in a specialized trade journal read by people in the field you want to enter. There have been instances of successful use of the personal advertisement approach to job hunting, but the odds are heavily against the success of this technique.

2. The Drop-in Approach. You may appear unannounced at an employer's office just seconds after

after he discovers that he has an urgent need for a designer of left-handed diamond cutter's tools. In this case you'll be welcomed like a combination of the Prodigal Son and the payroll clerk. But the odds are greater that you will be politely intercepted by a receptionist or other lower-echelon employee of the organization, and shunted over to the personnel office. There you will be given many forms to fill out and sent on your way with some variation of the "don't call us, we'll call you" routine. Incidentally, avoid filling out application forms whenever possible. They are usually a waste of time unless you are reasonably certain that there is a genuine opportunity for a job with an organization.

3. The Telephone Approach. This has all the disadvantages of the "drop-in" strategy and more. A telephone call is very easily intercepted by a secretary who will either switch you over to personnel or ask you to send in a letter and resumé (which is what you should have done in the first place).

4. The Letter and Resumé Approach. This is the most common technique, and it is common because it is the most effective. The reason for its effectiveness is that it permits you to conduct a positive, broadly based job hunting campaign with a minimum of effort. It does not require you to wait for a few replies in response to a series of expensive ads. Neither will you have to trudge around from employer to employer, or make a series of trying phone calls to anonymous secretaries. The letter of application and resumé tactic enables you to simultaneously reach scores, even hundreds of potential employers. What is more, as matchbook ads for mink farming promise, you can do this in the privacy of your own home! This technique also brings you and your skills directly to the attention of the particular person in the organization who can authorize hiring you—the marketing director, the controller, or the head of design, for example.

The letter of application (sometimes called the "cover letter") and the resumé (also known as the "vita" or "data sheet") should be submitted together, but now we'll take them up separately, beginning with the letter of application.

EXERCISES

1. Run a personal inventory on yourself, jotting down your estimate of your skills, personality strengths, and training. Set up a "debit column" as well, with a frank estimate of your weaknesses.

2. Compile a list of jobs which you think are consistent with your personal inventory. Don't be rigid—remember the sand salesman! Don't get hung up on starting salary or security, but think of potential income and satisfaction as well.

3. Submit your personal inventory and your job list to members of the class. Let them see what additions to your job list they can come up with.

10 unusual jobs - and a brief description of what the person does

LETTERS OF APPLICATION

Make them brief! Your letter of application should rarely be more than one page. It is designed to be read by a busy executive, and you must use it to present your most attractive qualities and your fitness for a job as concisely as possible. Long, rambling cover letters are irritating to the recipient and, as often as not, go unread. Therefore, since brevity is the soul of the letter of application, the *Information* and *Organization* aspects of written communications are important considerations in their composition.

The purpose of the letter of application is not to give the employer all the relevant facts about you. That is the purpose of the resumé. The letter is designed to give him just enough carefully selected information to motivate him to go on to read your resumé and, perhaps, call you in for an interview. In fact, the purpose of both the letter and the resumé is not to get you a job, but rather to get you an interview which will, in turn, result in a job offer.

Both the letter of application and the resumé must be composed with all the care that an advertising copy writer devotes to an advertisement, because that's really what they are—advertisements for yourself.

Your letter of application must be typed and must be original. It should be obvious that it was specially prepared for a particular application. Your resumé, on the other hand, can be photocopied or offset printed, because you will almost certainly be sending the identical information to many employers who will not expect you to present them with an original resumé. They will expect an original cover letter, though, one that indicates that you have taken the time to consider how your special aptitudes mesh with their special needs.

In addition to being typed and original, *your letter should be as personalized as possible.* Try to send your letter to a person rather than to a title. Don't, for example, write to

> Personnel Director
> Caustic Unguents, Inc.

when you can address it to

> Mr. Richard Prater
> Personnel Director
> Caustic Unguents, Inc.

"Dear Mr. Prater" is a much more effective salutation than "Dear Sir." If you have ever resented the impersonal tone of junk mail addressed to "Resident" or "Occupant," you will understand what we mean about the psychological advantage of personalizing any letter, not to mention crucial ones like letters of application. Personalizing your letter may require some research on your part, but the advantage in *Tone* will be worth it. Your school library or placement service can provide you with current directories of businesses and corporations that, in many cases, will supply you with a name to go with a title. If you are applying to a local organization, a call to its switchboard can provide you with the name of its Personnel Director, Plant Supervisor, Sales Manager, or whomever you want to write. (Important: make sure you get the full name from the operator, and be sure to check the spelling with her!)

Remember too that the most effective, personalized letter of application is usually not directed to the personnel executive of a company, but to the head of the specific department in which you want to work. He is the one who will ultimately activate the personnel machinery.

Your next concern is to *catch your reader's interest as soon as possible.* This is the most ticklish aspect of the letter. It involves the most careful consideration of *Tone.* Your strategy, of course, is to draw attention to yourself, but in such a way as to get yourself hired, not laughed at. If you walked down a busy street firing a starter's pistol and wearing a sombrero, pink velvet overalls, and a sequined cape you would draw attention to yourself, but, even if you escaped the attention of the police, you would never get hired for any job other than advance man for a freak show.

Your problem is essentially this: you must immediately provoke your reader's interest in your talents and personality while, at the same time, avoiding any suggestion that you are egocentric, peculiar, or in any way unable to fit smoothly into the corporate groove. Though businessmen loudly, and doubtless sincerely, proclaim their interest in individuality, they are also very much concerned about not rocking the boat, even to bail it out.

Maybe you really don't want to get a job and are perfectly happy drawing unemployment checks. Then an opening like the following is guaranteed *not* to result in an interview:

> If your organization needs a dynamite financial analyst with one thousand and one mind-blowing ideas on how to make the next fiscal year fat city, I am your man!

On the other hand, an excessively modest, humble opening is just as bad:

> If your company should happen to have an opening for a financial analyst, I believe that I may be qualified to fill the position.

But, bad as both these openings are, they do have one virtue: the egomaniacal one and the humble-pie one are both specific, that is, they focus on one particular job. Never, never write asking simply for *a* job; ask to be considered for a *specific* job or jobs. Even if you are a generalist, fresh out of school and with no vocational training, it is still possible to be reasonably specific. Consider this approach:

> My education and interests lead me to believe that I can best serve Caustic Unguents, Inc. in any one of a number of "people-oriented" positions such as public relations, sales, or personnel administration.

This might not be the best possible, attention-grabbing opening for a letter of application, but it is better than the two previous examples. It is courteous, direct and as specific about job desires as the writer's qualifications allow. But let's examine some other possible openings.

> I believe that my master's degree in business administration, along with my five years experience in both radio and television broadcasting make me a prime candidate for the position of station manager of KOOT AM and FM.

> or

> I have a master's degree in Library Science. I have published two children's books. I have worked in the public relations field for three years, and I love to travel. These are just a few of the things that make me think I can successfully fill the position of field representative for the children's and young adults division of the Faber and Constable Publishing Company that was recently advertised in *Publisher's Weekly*.

> or

> Could your export firm use a secretary who is fluent in English, German, and French and who can type fifty words a minute as well as receive dictation at one hundred words a minute?

> or

> This June I'll graduate with a degree in Business Administration from Coventry College. A lot of other job hunters will be able to say as much, however, and the important question is, what else do I have going for me? For the past six years I have worked part-time in every phase of my family's very successful restaurant, so I know the food service business in every phase from dishwasher up as well as being well-grounded in general business theory. Could Amalgamated Restaurant Supply use a management trainee like me?

It should be obvious that, in addition to being arresting, succinct, personalized, and specific, you should *organize your letter of application in such a way as to put your best foot forward.* Look over your personal inventory while at the same time putting yourself in your prospective employer's shoes. Pick out the one or two items in that inventory you think would most interest this particular employer. Emphasize them early in your letter as the writers of the sample openings above have done. While you're at it, take a look at the "debit column" of that inventory. What are your major drawbacks for this job? Organize your letter in such a way as to play these down.

Both your letter of application and your resumé must be factual, of course, but it is possible to organize the facts in the most effective, or least damaging, manner. Let us say, for example, that you have been a brilliant student, graduating second in your class with a 3.9 out of a possible 4.0 cumulative average. On the other hand, your academic record has been achieved at the cost of your social and extracurricular life. You have never, for example, held a part-time job; you have never joined, much less been an officer of, a social organization; you have never been the manager of the campus frisbee team. Your tactics in the letter of application are obvious: you must place dramatic emphasis on your academic success and conveniently ignore the other areas.

Now let's suppose that you were a less than brilliant student who stumbled across the finish line with a 2.1 cumulative average after repeating Advanced Basket Weaving twice. However, you held a full-time job all through school. Here the tactic is equally obvious. Simply assert that fact that you are a graduate. There is no need to mention your cumulative average or enlarge upon the challenge that basket weaving posed for you. Move on to emphasize the stamina you displayed by completing your education while working full time.

Closing the letter of application is a relatively cut and dried operation. The thing to remember here is that you don't want your reader simply to file and forget your application. You should leave him with the impression that you expect him to reply to your letter, if only to say that he has no opening for you. Your accompanying resumé will contain your address and phone number, and your letter of application will of course show your address in its heading. Nevertheless it is an effective practice to remind your reader in your closing paragraph that you can be reached "at the above address" and to provide him with a phone number.

Use the closing paragraph to reinforce the fact that you want an interview, and that you certainly expect at least a response. Any variation of the following formulas will serve:

> I await your reply with eagerness.
>
> I look forward to hearing from you about an interview at your convenience.
>
> I look forward to your response.

THE RESUMÉ

The resumé which accompanies your cover letter should be a clear, concise, chronological summary of your life, that is, those aspects of your life that are relevant to employment. Neither the resumé nor the cover letter is, you will recall, designed to get you a job; they are designed to procure you an interview. Save your more dramatic self-selling techniques for the interview and keep your resumé relatively conventional. Employers react just as negatively to eccentrically catchy resumés as they do to gimmicky letters of application. However, although the format of the successful resumé is relatively confining, there is no reason why you can't organize your strategies so as to put yourself in the best light possible.

A. THE PHYSICAL LAYOUT

The resumé should be neatly and accurately typed. Although electric typewriters provide the most impressive typescript, stick to the standard elite or pica typeface and pass up the more exotic typefaces available. The resumé should be short, no more than two pages, if possible. If it doesn't *seem* possible, *make* it possible! Use standard, white, high quality paper. Avoid high gloss, colored, or oversized paper.

Ideally, you should prepare a freshly-typed resumé for each application since this will enable you to tailor the resumé to the special situation each application represents. You could, for example, head your resumé with a custom-made title like the following one:

The Qualifications of
ELTON R. HAGGERTY
for
Traffic Manager at
Southeast Air Freight

But since it is more likely that you will engage in a widespread job hunt, it will be more realistic and efficient to prepare a standard ready-made resumé which you can have photo duplicated or offset printed. Do not, by the way, have your resumé mimeographed because a significant number of employers are put off by a mimeographed resumé.

B. ORGANIZATION OF THE RESUMÉ

The invariable, standard opening should present your name, your address, and your telephone number. If you are already employed, you may want to include your business address and phone number. But if you don't want your boss to know that you are shopping around for a new job you'll want to avoid being phoned at work, so omit the business address and phone number from your opening. If you do include them, label them:

Elton R. Haggerty

Home Address: 6106 Passyunk Drive
                      Sarasota, Florida 32801

Home Telephone: (305) 734-4399

Business Address: Caustic Unguents, Inc.
                      403 Culpepper Road
                      Sarasota, Florida 32803

Business Phone: (305) 658-9900
                      Ext. 264

The next item on the resumé should be a clear description of the job or jobs you're looking for. Many applicants omit this, and it understandably exasperates employers who can't tell from the résumé whether the writer wants to be an <u>apprentice j</u>anitor or executive vice president. Your letter of application will be specific about this matter, of course, but resumés and cover letters are often detached from each other while the organization that receives them shunts them around from office to office. This section can be headed "Position Sought," "Career Goals," or "Professional Objective." For example:

> Position Sought: Entry level position as sales or marketing trainee.

or

> Position Objective: Growth-oriented, beginning level opening in financial management.

You have a choice in the next section. You can list your educational training first, or you can elect to give your job experience first. Decision, decisions! Actually, your personal inventory should solve this knotty problem for you. If you have had little or no job experience, your training or education must receive top billing.

In presenting your educational experience, begin with the highest degree you hold. If you do not yet have a degree, an associate degree, or a technical certificate, give the expected date of its acquisition. You will naturally give the name of the degree-awarding institution as well as your major. If you have an exceptionally high average, mention it. If not, don't mention it. It is also an excellent idea—particularly when applying for technical jobs—to list courses you have taken that are relevant to the job. For example:

> <u>Education</u>:   Bachelor of Science in Mechanical Engineering.
> Coventry College—degree anticipated May, 1976.
> Relevant Courses:

Mechanics of Materials	Dynamics of Systems
Electrical Engineering Principles	Machine Designs
Advanced Calculus	Thermodynamic Analysis I & II
Engineering Thermodynamics I & II	Measurement Techniques
Fluid Mechanics	Experimental Mechanical Engineering I
Electrical Engineering Lab I	Metal Processing
Design of Machine Elements	Heat Transfer
Engineering Electronics	

> Maintained a 3.2 (out of 4.0) cumulative average.

or

> <u>Education</u>:   Bachelor of Science in Business Administration (Finance Major), Coventry
> College, 1975
> Related Courses:

Accounting Principles I & II	Business Law
Economics Principles I & II	Statistics I & II
Elements of Administration	American Economic Problems
Introduction to Computers	Marketing Principles
Managerial Economics	Intermediate Statistics
Finance I & II	Operations Research
Investment I & II	Financial Institutions & Markets

If you have made the Dean's List, won any scholarships, or qualified for membership in any honor societies, these achievements should be advertised in this section as well.

The job experience section should begin with the job you now hold, or the job you most recently held. Give the dates of employment, the name and location of the firms, and the titles of your positions as well as a brief description of your duties. Always clearly distinguish between full-time and part-time or summer jobs. For example:

Experience: Summer, 1975–Staff announcer, Radio Station KNCA, Resume Speed, Nevada. Delivered live commercial announcements, produced and was the host of the "Music for Dining" show one hour daily, wrote and delivered four five minute local news shows daily.

Summer, 1974–Summer Intern, Johnson City *Daily Intelligencer,* Johnson City, Idaho. General reportorial and rewrite work for the 31,000 circulation daily newspaper.

After listing your job and educational experience, you may, if you think it strategic, list your special interests and hobbies. If these hobbies can be seen as somehow job-related, or if they reveal you as an attractive All American boy or girl, it will be to your advantage to present them. If you don't have any impressive outside interests, it is best to ignore this section rather than noting casually that you like to read or take long walks. If you are applying to the United States Forest Service and you are an enthusiastic bird watcher and rock climber, by all means advertise these hobbies. If, however, you are into Satanism or belong to one of the more flamboyantly psychotic motorcycle clubs, these activities should be tactfully passed over.

Whether you choose to list your outside interests or not, your resumé should include a section on personal data. Some resumé writers prefer to put this section just before the education and job experience section, others later. No matter where you position it on your resumé, the personal data section should state at least your age, marital status, height and weight, and general health. If you are a little young for a job or a little old, you need not give your age straight out; simply give your birth date and let your prospective employer perform the arithmetic if he cares to.

Be optimistic about your health. Discount any tendencies toward hypochondria you may have –if you honestly feel that you can perform the duties of the job and can walk up the stairs for the interview, describe your health as "fine" or "good." Also, if you have any physical handicaps, but feel they will not impair your job efficiency, don't volunteer that information on your resumé. If your handicap is obvious, the face-to-face job interview is the best place to deal with the problem; if it is not obvious, why worry?

Do not give your race, religion, or political affiliation. Ideally, these matters will have no bearing on your fitness for a job. This is not an ideal world, of course, so there is no need to invite an employer's prejudices to operate either for or against you.

The final section of your resumé should be devoted to the matter of personal and professional references. You have three options. You may ignore the whole matter of references entirely on the legitimate assumption that they are not really important unless the employer is interested enough in your general qualifications to ask you in for an interview. If he continues to be interested in you, he will ask you for a set of references during the interview; it goes without saying that you should enter each interview equipped with a set of references. This approach has the advantage of slimming the bulk of your resumé down to attractive and efficient proportions.

On the other hand, if your resumé does seem a little thin, you may want to flesh it out by including a list of references at the end. And, if you have some especially impressive references like the president of a large steel company or the second cousin of the Shah of Iran, you will want to spotlight this fact on your resumé.

Perhaps the best approach in resumé writing as in other areas of life is a compromise. Omit the references from your resumé but close with a statement to the effect that personal and professional references will be supplied upon request.

One final word about references and, for that matter, about resumés–it is common courtesy, as well as intelligent strategy, to ask potential references if they object to your submitting their names.

Figures 5.3 and 5.4 show some examples of typical resumés.

LOUIS R. CADENZA
1482 Mt. Holly Avenue
Coventry, Penna. 19014
(215) 833-3367

(Home address—after 5/10/76)
6 Whitfield Drive
Rochester, New York 14029
(212) 329-5841

Professional Objective	Growth oriented entry level opportunity in the financial and business functions. Interests include business planning, budgets and measurements, management information systems, as well as related areas.
Education	B.S. in Business Administration (Finance major), Coventry College, expected May, 1976

Cumulative average: 3.3/4.0; Deans List — 5 semesters
Elected to Who's Who in American Colleges, 1975

Related Courses:

Accounting Principles I & II	Business Law
Economic Principles I & II	Introductory Statistics I & II
Elements of Administration	American Economic Problems
Introduction to Computers	Marketing Principles
Managerial Economics	Intermediate Statistics
Finance I & II	Operations Research
Investments I & II	Financial Institutions & Markets

Experience Summer 1975	Arthur L. White & Co., Webster, New York SUMMER INTERN with this medium-sized CPA and financial counseling firm. Assisted in two client audits; performed semi-independent asset valuation analysis for small public transportation company. Position provided excellent orientation to "middle market" businesses.
Summers 1974, 1973, 1972	PARADISE REGAINED, Mt. Pocono, Pa. Beginning as combination busboy/laborer at this summer resort, progressed to waiter and substitute maitre d'. During third summer, concurrently organized arts and crafts program for up to 45 teenagers.
Part-time	During semester vacations and after school in high school, worked at variety of odd jobs (e.g., mailman, caddy, store clerk).
Interests	International relations; dramatics; golf.
Extra curricular Activities	President, Delta Pi Epsilon (Commerce & Finance fraternity); Belle Masque Dramatic Society; Coventry Cry (Newspaper) and BELLE AIR (Yearbook); Junior Week Committee.
Personal	Age 21 Married 5'9", 165 lb Health fine
References	References supplied upon request.

Figure 5.3.

RICHARD F. GRIGGS
2703 E. 183rd Street
Bronx, New York 10041
(212) 329-5648

(college address to 5/15/76)
P. O. Box 2018
Coventry College, Coventry, Pa. 19014
(215) 527-3584

POSITION OBJECTIVE: BSME entry position emphasizing new design responsibilities. The specific
products or processes are not as important as the opportunity for applying creativity
and analytical ability and the chance for growth eventually into management.

PERSONAL DATA: Age 23   Single   Health excellent
6'2", 200 lb.

EDUCATION: BSME, Coventry College (anticipated 5/76)
Maintained 2.7/4.0 cumulative average (2.85 in major) while holding a
20-30 hr/week part-time job

Technical Courses:

Mechanics of Materials	Dynamics of Systems
Electrical Engineering Principles	Machine Design
Advanced Calculus	Thermodynamic Analysis I & II
Engineering Thermodynamics	Measurement Techniques
I & II	Experimental Mechanical Engineering
Physical Metallurgy Lab	I & II
Fluid Mechanics	Metal Processing
Electrical Engineering Lab I	Heat Transfer
Design of Machine Elements	Engineering Electronics

EXPERIENCE:

Summers
1974 & 73

Laboratory Technician, E. A. Swift Mfg. Co., N.Y., N.Y.
(425-employee manufacturer of materials handling equipment)

Activities ranged from construction of prototype and pilot systems to assisting
the Plant Engineer in designing expanded manufacturing and test facilities.

Summers
1972-73

Successively: lifeguard at family pool; highway construction crew helper;
counselor at boys' camp.

Part-time
1972 Present

Various positions—handyman, laborer, shipping clerk, grocery clerk, etc—to help
finance education.

COLLEGE
ACTIVITIES:

Coventry BSME Student Chapter (Secretary, 2 years); Glee Club; intramurals.

HOBBIES: Auto repair and remodeling; hi-fi equipment construction.

REFERENCES: Personal and professional references supplied upon request.

Figure 5.4.

EXERCISES

THE RESUMÉ

1. Make up your own personal resumé. Have a specific job field in mind as you compose it. Have your instructor evaluate the finished product.

2. Write a hypothetical resumé and letter of application in response to one of the following advertisements.

a.
Management Trainee

Young furniture company seeking individual to become integral part of production team. Will be learning skills in inventory control, purchasing, expediting, etc. Prefer College Grad with some business bkgd. Exc. growth position, salary negotiable. Send application and supporting documents to Mr. Blimm, P. O. Box 83, Levittown, Pa. 19057.

b.
Management Trainee
HEALTH CLUB

needs sharp & enthusiastic people for ladies division willing to work and learn. Begin as instructor and advance at your own rate. No exp. necessary. Must be physically fit and alert. Write J. DaCrema, Hadrian's Health Spa, 606 Appian Road, Rome, Georgia 60791.

c.
SALES

Immediate opening w/a leading Specialty Chemical Manufacturer. This is an opportunity for an aggressive individual. Responsibilities for developing present & future sales in the N.J. area. Exp. in field not a necessity, for we will train you for the opening. Offer above average income (sal plus comm), benefits, vehicle furnished w/ expenses. Seek ambitious, personable individual w/ two years of college. Write Bader & Bass Employment Agency, 387 Woolworth Way, South Orange, New Jersey 07079

Chapter 6

ABSTRACTS AND SUMMARIES

Once you have a job, it is unlikely that you will be called upon to do much writing during the early phase of your employment. And when you are called upon to do some writing, you won't start out by producing full-scale reports or by taking sole charge of the correspondence with important clients. What is more likely is that you will be asked to perform in a support capacity for those who do have the responsibility for writing important communications.

One way of looking at the structure of a typical business or government organization is as an extended "information chain." The higher a person climbs up the organizational ladder, the more frequently he is called upon to make decisions, and the higher he climbs on the ladder, the more significant and critical those decisions become. The best decisions are based on the best available information.

Over the past century a sort of Information Explosion has taken place, so that no matter where you go you find intelligent, concerned people, in every phase of human activity, complaining that it is humanly impossible to keep on top of the important information in their field. Computers have been a help, of course, but they have been a hindrance as well. They make it possible to store enormous quantities of information, but in turn they must receive quantities of data from people who can program them concisely. Human beings all along the chain of information govern what information is relevant to any given decision and pass only selected data along to the next echelon of decision-makers. Computers, libraries, and data banks store and classify the avalanches of information that are at once the blessing and the curse of modern man, but people generate all the information. Hence the importance, particularly in the early years of your career, of writing clear abstracts or summaries of available information.

So what are abstracts and summaries? These are really two names for the same thing. Another synonym, *précis,* a word derived from the French, is defined by one dictionary as "a concise summary of essential points, statements, or facts." One root meaning for the word *abstract* is "to take out," and this meaning gives a very accurate description of what the act of producing a summary involves—the taking out from the general stream of facts and opinions only those which are relevant to your specific needs. Such summaries are, in business, the basis for all decisions, whether to negotiate a merger with another firm, open a new branch office, or raise a secretary's pay.

All this is to say that it is inevitable that some time early in your employment one of your superiors is going to ask you to supply him with information he needs either to make a decision or to recommend a decision to someone else further up the ladder. If you are asked to present that information in written form, a short report or a memo, you will be writing a summary. But this should not disconcert you too much, because you have been summarizing and abstracting things all your life. As a matter of fact, you are almost certainly doing it now.

Out of all the time we spend studying in school, a great deal is spent in summarizing material in textbooks. We may not consciously think of it as summarizing, but when we are assigned to read a chapter or two in a history, or economics, or English textbook, we do not—unless we are either very naive or very inefficient—sit dutifully down and carefully read every word. Even back in grade school no one needed to tell us that life was too short for such a painstaking process, and we soon learned to skim through assignments. And, as we skim through material, we engage in a primitive form of summarizing or abstracting. When faced with fifty pages of history to read before a test the next day, we automatically ask ourselves: "How much of this stuff is important? How much do I really need to know?"

Actually, all the information is important, but some parts of it are more important than others. Much written material is illustrative or explanatory, designed to expand on or reinforce the major points. In skimming, we want to find out what the major points are and concentrate on them.

Some of us are better at the process than others, as the results of examinations show. Very probably, those of us who get the poorer grades have not mastered the art of skimming carefully. That sounds like a flagrant contradiction in terms, but it's not, because to skim something successfully does not mean that we can rush through printed material carelessly. Successful summarizing requires considerable concentration.

So, what is a successful summary? It's one that works, that proves-out in reality. Let's put it this way: If, after skimming through fifty pages of history, you get a 98 percent on an exam, your skimming worked. You correctly decided which were the major points in the text and concentrated your attention on them. Or, let's assume that you're working for an organization and your superior asks you to read a 150-page government manual on plant safety and give him a fifteen-page summary of its contents. Your summary will be successful if it accurately represents all the essential information contained in the original in a concise form. If your superior can use your summary of the government manual as a guide to preparing your plant to pass a federal safety inspection, and the plant passes that inspection, then you have written a successful summary—one that works.

Now to some basic questions. One question is, how long should a good summary be? Someone once said about a girl's dress that it should be "short enough to be interesting, but long enough to cover the subject." A variation on that line can be adapted to the summary; it should be short enough to be useful, but long enough to be correct.

In other words, a summary has two functions, (1) to save a reader time, and (2) to convey accurate information. It stands to reason that if your summary is long and rambling your reader might just as well turn to the original text. On the other hand, if it is so abbreviated that it leaves out important elements of information or fails to establish adequate connections between data and conclusions, then the summary is simply not reliable. It gives a distorted, fun house mirror view of the original.

However, when you are asked to write a summary, you will usually be given some indication of how long your superior would like it to be. Most likely, he'll ask you to "boil this down to a couple of pages," or to "give me the gist of this in about a thousand words." On the average, the length of a useful summary should be less than 20 percent of the original text.

A second fundamental question is, how do you write a good summary? The usual textbook method at this point would be to set down a series of techniques and then ask you to apply them to a concrete example. But since there's a good chance that you already have an instinctive grasp of the techniques, you don't need our recipe. However, let's find out.

We'll start small, with the paragraph. We'll start with the paragraph for three reasons. First, the paragraph is the next-to-smallest unit of logic in writing (the smallest is the sentence). Second, if you can adequately summarize a paragraph, the difference between this and summarizing whole articles, reports, and books is only a matter of degree. And third, if you can't summarize a paragraph easily and accurately, learning to do so will give you the basic tools needed to condense longer units of writing. Below you'll find a paragraph which has about 185 words (not counting the articles). As you read through it, concentrate on the major points and think about how to summarize the paragraph in about fifty words. You may want to jot down some notes.

> Expending time and energy on attempts to reduce tax liabilities naturally uses up some of the scarce resources of individuals and firms. Nevertheless, such activities represent a rational response to potential government appropriation of income as long as the gain from successful tax avoidance more than offsets these resource costs. If the revenues generated by tax-reduction activities were less than these costs, profits would be reduced and the actions should not be undertaken. For example, tax-free municipal securities sell at lower interest rates than taxable corporate bonds, and this yield differential represents part of the "cost" of buying municipal bonds. If corporate bonds are yielding 8 percent and municipals 5 percent, the cost is $30 per $1,000 of tax-exempts purchased. If the tax rate is 50 percent, however, an investor saves $40 in taxes by purchasing the municipal security. Since the tax saving exceeds the cost, the tax exempt bond is the superior investment. If the rate on municipal bonds is 3 percent, however, the cost exceeds the benefit, and the taxable security should be purchased. Similar sorts of calculations must be made for other activities which reduce taxes, and the costs may well include hiring the services of specialized tax lawyers and accountants. An activity should be undertaken *only* if it contributes positively to profits after taxes.[1]

Now let's see how you did. If your summary is basically (not exactly) like the one below, you already have a good grasp of the technique of summarizing.

> Undertake tax saving activities only if their profit exceeds their cost (which can include the cost of tax experts). If tax free municipals yield 5 percent and corporate bonds 8 percent and the tax rate is 50 percent, you save $40 per $1,000 with the municipal. But if the municipal yields 3 percent, its cost exceeds tax savings.

When you were mentally summarizing that paragraph above, you may have begun by trying to isolate the sentence which seemed to contain the *core idea* of the passage, for that is how many people begin. This sentence is very often called the topic sentence, a term you have very probably heard before since it is a favorite with English teachers who delight in explaining to a class that a good paragraph of expository prose must contain a sentence which states the main or "germ" idea of the paragraph. Every other sentence in the paragraph must in some way relate to the main idea, either by explaining, enlarging, or giving examples of it.

These same English teachers go on to explain that a good paragraph must have *unity*, which is achieved by structuring the paragraph around the topic sentence. Any sentence that does not relate to the topic sentence is a digression which detracts from the satisfying unity of the paragraph. Moreover, they also insist that a good paragraph should have *coherence*. By that they mean that not only should every sentence in the paragraph logically relate to the topic sentence, but also that the relation should be clearly evident to the reader.

1. Donald J. Mullineaux, "The Taxman Rebuffed: Income Taxes at Commercial Banks," reprinted from the *Business Review* of the Federal Reserve Bank of Philadelphia (May, 1974), p. 12.

Now all this is good <u>doctrine</u>, but it does not always work out in practice. It is true that a good paragraph should be coherently unified around a core idea, but that core idea cannot always be found neatly encapsulated in one sentence. For example, look back again at that paragraph we summarized. The second sentence, the one beginning "Nevertheless, such activities. . ." is the most likely candidate for the role of topic sentence, and it is the sentence most helpful to isolate at the start of any summary of the paragraph. However, the reader would not know what "such activities" were unless he had read the first sentence. And a <u>persuasive</u> case can also be made for the important role of the last sentence in the paragraph in stating—or restating—the central idea.

Now what all this really shows is that although many paragraphs do present the <u>gist</u> of their message in one independent topic sentence, many other paragraphs present the leading idea in several sentences. The <u>adept</u> summarizer should be prepared to deal with either situation.

Generally, most paragraphs present the core idea early in their development. If you are ever pressed for time and have to get through a good deal of reading quickly, one way to do it is to read only the opening sentences of paragraphs. But some paragraphs—often those most crucial to the sense of a piece of writing—do not state the core idea at the beginning. Some save this idea until the end, building toward a logical climax. Some tuck it away in the middle, while others present it in the beginning and then, for clarity or emphasis, repeat a variation of it at the end. A very few paragraphs never explicitly state their central idea, but simply imply it.

In any event, once you have settled on a paragraph's core idea, whether it's specifically set out in one topic sentence or in several sentences, you have discovered the paragraph's logical skeleton. You may then rephrase the main idea, trim away the fatty tissue, and pick and choose among the supporting ideas, and then you are well on the way toward formulating a useful summary of that paragraph.

Here are some examples of a few more paragraphs. Pick out the core idea in each of them as you read.

1.　Chief among Rockefeller's early tactics, and the one to which has been attached the most notoriety, was the railroad rebate system through which Standard Oil enjoyed a very considerable advantage over its competitors in the matter of freight rates. But John T. Flynn maintains that Rockefeller was simply availing himself of an opportunity which was open to all large-scale shippers at the time—a time when railroads were operated very much on the *laissez faire* principle and the rail barons "used the roads as if they owned them outright and without any thought of the public's right in their services." Although Rockefeller used the rebate technique against Standard Oil's competitors with ruthless efficiency, he was far from being its inventor.

2.　Now it is perfectly true that men's views of what is desirable depend upon their characters; and that the innate proclivities to which we give that name are not touched by any amount of instruction. But it does not follow that even mere intellectual education may not, to an indefinite extent, modify the practical manifestation of the characters of men in their actions, by supplying them with motives unknown to the ignorant. A pleasure-loving character will have pleasure of some sort; but, if you give him the choice, he may prefer pleasures which do not degrade him to those which do. And this choice is offered to every man, who possesses in literary or artistic culture a never-failing source of pleasures, which are neither withered by age, nor staled by custom, nor embittered in the recollection by the pangs of self-reproach.[2]

3.　Even without its tax advantages, profit-motivated banks would have no doubt embraced equipment leasing as a potentially profitable mode of operations during the expansion-minded sixties. The simple reason is that leasing represents a rational and flexible means of paying

2. Thomas Henry Huxley, "Science and Culture," *Science and Education* as reprinted in Charles F. Harrold and William D. Templeman, eds. *English Prose of the Victorian Era.* (New York: Oxford University Press, 1938), p. 1337.

for an equipment purchase. It consequently complements the various financing alternatives banks can offer their customers. The advantages typically cited for leasing include protection against risk of obsolescence, conservation of working capital, ease of negotiation, minimization of red tape, and the ready availability of ancillary services such as insurance, maintenance, and record-keeping. In addition, leasing may convey benefit to *both the lessor and the lessee*. As a purchaser of new equipment, the lessor is allowed a tax credit, presently equal to 7 percent of the value of the equipment. In addition, the lessor can take advantage of accelerated depreciation allowances, which defer tax payments to some future period. Although the liability will eventually be incurred, accelerated depreciation nonetheless yields benefits since the funds "saved" by avoiding taxes today can be invested in interest yielding assets.[3]

4.   Traditionally the construction industry has been a feast-or-famine business largely because of tight periods in the availability of credit, such as the credit crunches of 1966 and 1969-70. A crunch usually lasts for less than a year, but during the crunch banks and other institutions that normally take in customer's savings and then loan them out to investors temporarily experienced decreased deposit inflows. Deposits slow down because savers prefer to invest directly in market assets which offer higher interest rates than the legal ceilings allow savings accounts to pay. As a result, banks, S & L's, and other institutions that usually make mortgage loans have less deposit inflows available from which to make loans. So, they ration their limited supply of loanable funds to those investments which they think will earn the highest rate of return at each level of risk. Mortgage credit is usually reduced by loan officers during temporary periods of tight money because mortgage rate ceilings keep mortgage rates from rising high enough to be competitive with other investments of equal risk in which the lending institutions might invest. The resulting restriction in mortgage credit causes a big reduction in home buying. Thus, tight credit not only makes it difficult for most families to get home mortgages, but also bankrupts some construction companies that can't sell their inventory of new houses because home buyers can't get mortgages.[4]

Aside from picking out topic sentences, another practical technique for writing summaries—whether of paragraphs, articles or book length items—is to *read everything at least three times.*

By this we do not mean that each reading should be as careful and deliberate as the next. Indeed, the first time you read something you intend to summarize, you should race through it so quickly that you can hardly be said to be reading at all. The first time through, you should be primarily concerned simply with discovering what the thing is about. (We are reminded of the speed reading champion who read Tolstoy's enormous novel *War and Peace* in fifty-three minutes and forty-eight seconds flat, and when asked what it was about, replied, "Russia.")

The first reading should really be called a "skimming" because all you should be doing is flipping through the pages and discovering how long the selection is, whether it has a table of contents, whether it is broken up into divisions such as chapters or into subsections with headings, whether it's about Russia. The first quick reading is simply to acquaint you with the overall design of the piece.

Never begin actually to compose a summary just as you begin reading an article or report, for you will not be able to distinguish the informational forest from the trees. You might not be aware when you start that the first section is given over to a lot of introductory throat clearing that is not relevant to a useful summary of the entire piece. If you summarize as you read for the first time, you can waste a lot of time and ink.

Your second reading should be slower and more careful, closer to the pace of what we normally think of as studying. During this second reading you are less likely to be sidetracked from the central

3. Donald J. Mullineaux, "The Taxman Rebuffed: Income Taxes at Commercial Banks," reprinted from the *Business Review* of the Federal Reserve Bank of Philadelphia (May, 1974), p. 18.

4. Jack Clark Francis, "Helping Americans Get Mortgages," reprinted from the *Business Review* of the Federal Reserve Bank of Philadelphia (January, 1974), p. 16.

theme of the piece since your first, quick reading will have given you an idea of its grand design.

You may want to take notes after the second reading, or, if permissible, underline important passages in the text. But, once again, don't take notes as you read; do it after you finish reading. If it's a book length piece you're summarizing, read a chapter before you begin to make notes of the central points. If it's shorter than book length, read a whole section before you stop to take notes. In this way, you will not be distracted from the flow of the text, and by reading a section at a time before stopping to take notes or abstracting the main points, you will be able to isolate the important issues.

Finally, read the text through a third time, very quickly. This will serve to fix the overall development and emphasis of the original in your mind.

Now you are ready to use your notes and your underlining to compose your summary. But before turning you loose to apply these techniques in actual practice, we'd like to make two more points about the art of summary. The first is that you should use your own words. Avoid the temptation simply to string quotations from the original together and call it a summary. If you do that, you are simply creating a fragmented, incomplete version of the original. But if you take the ideas and information in the original and reformulate them in your own words, you are more likely to compose an accurate condensation. This is not to say that you should never quote the original, but that you should not let quotations substitute for your own careful, synthesizing thought processes.

The final point is that, although we have relied very heavily upon the paragraph in our discussion of the craft of summarizing, we do not want to leave you with the impression that you must summarize each paragraph in the original. Far from it! Feel free to leave out entirely paragraphs which are merely transitional, illustrative, or repetitive. Just as there are relatively unimportant sentences in a paragraph, so can there be unimportant paragraphs in a report, or, for that matter, unimportant chapters in a book.

Following are two extended selections, Figures 6.1 and 6.2. Write a useful summary of each of them, reducing each selection to about 20 percent of its original bulk.

O TANNENBAUM! O SCOTCH PINE![5]

Over 30 species of evergreens are commonly used as Christmas trees. The fir tree, the tree of song, was the Christmas favorite for a long time, but in recent years it has yielded first place to the Scotch pine. Ranking second in popularity is the Douglas fir, and third is the Balsam fir. The three together account for 61 percent of all Christmas trees produced.

A man going forth to buy a Christmas tree is told by his wife to get one that has a full, bushy, symmetrical shape, with strong enough limbs to support the ornaments and electric lights, and with branches springy enough to snap back into good shape when released from the strings that bind it for shipment. And, above all, the tree must have a fresh green color with needles that won't fall off before the New Year, be neither too tall nor too small, smell like pine, and not be too expensive. Of course, he finds that there is no such tree, but the various species displayed on the lot do approach the requested specifications with varying degrees of success.

There is good reason why the Scotch pine has become the country's leading Christmas tree. First of all, it meets a wife's demands—it shapes beautifully, its size and smell are good, and its needles hang on and on. Second, it is easy to grow. It is tolerant to a wide range of soil and moisture conditions and survives planting shock well. And of particular interest to the grower is the fact that the Scotch pine can be grown to Christmas-tree size in about eight years in contrast with the fir that requires ten to twenty years.

PLANTATION TOILS

Growing Christmas trees as a cash crop looks like easy money. The land need not be the best, the capital requirements are modest, and as Christmas approaches the buyers are in a festive mood. As a business, it is easy to enter and the size of the venture may be as small as a backyard or as large as a thousand acres. Consequently, the business has attracted all kinds of people, especially those with time on their hands and land underfoot. What beginners are likely to overlook or underestimate is the amount of tender loving care and the length of time required before the cash rolls in.

First is the planting of the seedlings which may be done by hand or by machine. The latter is up to ten times more productive, depending upon the size of the plantation and the conditions of the site. To keep the weeds from taking over, the plantation requires frequent mowing with a power mower. To keep the bugs from eating up the plantation requires periodic spraying. To help the trees attain the proper density and proper Christmas-tree shape requires yearly shearing, once the shearing has begun. As harvest time approaches, the grower must identify the trees to be cut down, line up labor to cut, tie or bale the trees, and perhaps arrange for hauling to market. Many growers sell to wholesalers, some do their own retailing, still others engage in both.

There is also the "choose and cut" plantation. Families arrive en masse, finally agree upon a tree, superintend its cutting, and take it home in triumph. The grower sells at the retail price (roughly double the wholesale price), and the customer hauls his own.

PLANTATION TROUBLES

Growing Christmas trees would not be an industry if it were without troubles. A major pitfall is planting the wrong trees. On ordering seedlings from the nursery, you may select White pine and Black spruce because you observe they are gaining in popularity. But it takes eight years for the White pine and twelve years for the Black spruce to be-

Figure 6.1.

come marketable trees, and consumers are fickle.

Moreover, part-time labor, upon which the industry must rely, is unpredictable. A crew of workers, hired to do shearing in midsummer, may decide, after the sun is directly overhead, that it is a good day to go fishing or simply knock off and do nothing.

Bugs! Over 60 different kinds of insects, from aphids to Zimmerman pine moths, feed on Christmas trees. "It is a rare tree-planting which is not subject to attack by one or more of these pests sometime during the period from planting to harvest," says Extension Bulletin 353, of Michigan State University. And the inch-long, red-headed worms of the pine sawfly come in such swarms that when they move, the whole tree appears to jump. Bugs are not the only pests, but also mice, deer, rabbits, and people.

Then, too, some trees grow crooked, one-sided, or turn yellow. Such trees are a loss—unmarketable. However, the story is told of a grower who advertised his yellowed trees as "Golden Scotch pine" and sold them at premium prices. Now some producers are dyeing Christmas trees in any color to match one's decor.

Plantation growers are also adversely affected by one aspect of what might be called the ecology crisis. Air and water pollution are real and serious, to be sure, but the subject has gotten so much publicity that some people have come to believe that it is sinful to cut down a tree. This attitude was revealed on stopping at a country store to ask directions to Mr. X's tree plantation, and the storekeeper saying, "Oh, you mean the tree butcher." Many people fail to realize that Christmas trees are crops harvested from fields which are replanted.

Arthur M. Sowder, formerly of the Forest Extension Service, in his monograph "Christmas Trees: The Tradition and the Trade," points out that shortly after Theodore Roosevelt became President, he refused the placement of a Christmas tree in the White House because he felt it a wasteful practice. However, the President changed his mind after Gifford Pinchot of Pennsylvania, who was Chief of the Division of Forestry, convinced him that natural stands of Christmas trees are frequently too thick and that removal of some of the trees affords the remaining trees more soil, sunlight, and moisture, with the result that they grow faster and healthier. Conservation is not saving for the sake of saving, but rather making the most efficient use of natural resources. In many forested areas, Christmas trees are the only practical crop, and, if left to themselves, would eventually stagnate.

One of the most serious problems the industry faces is competition from artificial trees. Made of metal, plastic, or other material, these "trees" sell at prices ranging from two to five times as much as the prices of the real Christmas trees they simulate. Of course, they are cheaper in the long run if used five to ten times, but with repeated usage they show their age. Nevertheless, artificial trees have cut deeply into the natural tree market.

ARTIFICIAL FUTURE

While the future of the Christmas tree industry appears bright, it is certain that meeting the growing demand will involve surmounting a variety of difficulties. Three of these are fickle consumer tastes, labor unpredictability, and insects. Chief among the problems producers face, however, is the burgeoning artificial "tree" business. It appears that for a growing number of consumers a tree is a tree is a tree.

5. From Evan B. Alderfer, "About Christmas Trees," *Business Review* of Federal Reserve Bank of Philadelphia (December, 1971), pp. 11-14.

Figure 6.1. *(continued)*

Chapter 7

MEMOS AND BRIEF REPORTS

In this chapter we will be concerned with some types of business communication that are difficult to define. In fact, it is easier to say what memos and short reports are *not* than to say what they are.

They are not letters. They can be longer or shorter than a letter, but they need not have the traditional form of business letters—address, salutation, complementary close, etc. They are not long formal reports, which require letters of transmittal, abstracts, tables of contents, graphics, and bibliographies. The techniques of producing formal reports comprise an art in themselves, and there are many excellent books on the subject which you may consult when your progress up the organizational ladder requires you to produce them. However, we will not discuss the formal report here.

The difference between the memo and the short report is essentially (and arbitrarily) one of length and purpose. A memo is short. It can be only one or two sentences; it rarely exceeds a page. The purpose of the memo is uncomplicated. Typically, it presents straightforward information, or requests action to be taken. The short report ordinarily runs two or more pages and its purpose is more complex. It may present and interpret information; it may present and analyze the reasons for taking or not taking an action; it may present and interpret information for the purpose of recommending whether an action should or should not be taken.

Basically, both memos and short reports are, in the jargon of modern organizations, "in-house" communications. They are typically exchanged between individuals or departments *within* an organization and are not directed to clients or the general public. Therefore, they do not represent the company to the community at large.

Before we discuss the techniques of composing effective memos and short reports (the same techniques, in general, as were established in Part I of this text), let's examine some typical examples, as shown in Figures 7.1 through 7.7. As you read through these materials keep in mind our communications triangle of *Tone*, *Information*, and *Organization*, and evaluate its use.

In these random samples of memos and short reports, you've probably noticed with regard to *Tone*, *Information*, and *Organization* that *Tone* is a less important consideration with memos and

Example A. A simple informational memo.

Caustic Unguents, Ltd.

DATE: April 9, 197__

FROM: Cecil Sump, Sales Director

TO: All Sales Personnel

SUBJECT: Sales meeting

As of today, the weekly sales meeting will be conducted on Fridays at 3:30 P.M. in the Sales Conference Room.

Cecil Sump

SALES DIRECTOR

Figure 7.1.

Example B. A somewhat more involved memorandum outlining the itinerary of a business trip.

DATE: February 14, 197__

TO: Mr. Jack Roth

FROM: Thomas J. Wells

SUBJECT: Business Trip to
Santa Barbara and Los Angeles

Dear Jack:

Below is my advance notice of absence advising you of my trip to Santa Barbara, California, and Los Angeles, California, the week of February 13, 197__. My schedule is as follows:

Sunday, February 13, 197__ – depart Philadelphia, Pennsylvania for Santa Barbara, California. I am staying at the Santa Barbara Biltmore.

Monday, February 14, 197__ – Science Spectrum in Santa Barbara. Telephone Number (802) 963-8605

Tuesday, February 15, 197__ – depart Santa Barbara, California, for Los Angeles, California. I am staying at the Marina del Rey, Los Angeles, California. I will spend the day with Mr. J. R. Mann.

Wednesday, February 16, 197__ – I will be working with Mr. B. A. Back.

Thursday, February 17, 197__ – I will be working with Mr. S. J. Spect - #11181 and possibly with Mr. J. A. Dill - #11281.

Friday, February 18, 197__ – enroute, Los Angeles, California, to Philadelphia, Pennsylvania.

Sincerely,

TJW:mpr

cc: Mr. T. G. Clark
        File

Thomas J. Wells

Figure 7.2.

Example C. A memo from the purchasing agent in a firm of ecological consultants. The memo outlines new procedures for ordering books.

Staff Memo
1 May 197__

To: All technical staff   *Answer*

Subject: Book orders

Recently I have noticed that several popular books ("kiddie books") have been purchased. These are often expensive (one illustrated book cost $35.00) and are of little or no value in the work of the firm.

Until a better screening method can be determined, all requests for the purchase of publications will be submitted to your department chairman. If the chairman approves, he will forward the request to Esther Ash. Collected requests will be reviewed by Jack McCall.

Such requests must contain the following information, at a minimum:

Author, date, title, publisher, and cost

Reason this book is necessary

Account to be charged

Person requesting and date of request

Signature of department chairman and date

Esther will date each request she receives and will provide requests weekly to me with a cover sheet showing the title of each book requested in the attachments.

This is not intended to stymie purchases of books necessary to the firm. It is intended to restrict the purchase of non-technical materials. Some non-technical publications may be useful—be sure to explain why you recommend such publications.

Jack McCall

Figure 7.3.

Example D. A memo from the public relations director of a drug manufacturer. The memo seeks to set up a regularly scheduled procedure for approving requests from physicians and other health professionals for the drug company's financial assistance in attending medical meetings and symposia.

INTERNAL CORRESPONDENCE

Date: November 14, 197__

To: Thomas J. Wells   From: John M. McCarter

Subject: Meeting Support

Dear Tom:

We have had much difficulty in gaining a quorum to judge the merits of various requests for meeting support all through 197__. Al Hymes has agreed that you, Don Carr and I may meet on a regular basis and pass judgement on requests as they come in so that an early answer can be returned to the requestors.

W__ __ begin this plan as promptly as circumstance allows. Will you please chec__ __th Don and me to determine what time of day, on what day of the week w__ __uld sit down every week and take care of whatever has come in since the __ious meeting. Let's try to make this a sacred time that will be observed ex__ __t when travel or other very important matters must take precedence.

I would suggest __ __t Friday morning, 9:00 a.m. might be a good time. If this meets with yo__ __ schedule and Don's, let's get started as soon as possible.

Sincerely,

John M. McCarter

mp

cc: A. J. Hymes
      D. O. Carr

Figure 7.4.

Example E. A memo from an executive of the same drug company to its public relations director. Memo requests him to investigate and report on the matter of an irate physician who had been conducting research on one of the company's products, drug # 1368-A.

INTERNAL CORRESPONDENCE

Date: March 11, 197__

To: T. Wells   From: Walter N. Brown

Subject: Drug #1368-A and Dr. Gante

Dear Tom:

Today, Dr. Samuel R. Gante of Coventry voiced a complaint to our salesman, Paul Ryan. Dr. Gante was bitter regarding his dealings with SURFA and his alleged work for us on 1368-A.

According to Dr. Gante he has worked many hours preparing data on 1368-A. He was advised by SURFA that this program was cancelled.

Any information that you can furnish in this regard would be greatly appreciated. Dr. Gante is a good prescriber of 1368-A and was so upset by what happened that we are concerned that this may affect his future prescription of SURFA products.

Sincerely yours,

Walter N. Brown

WB:nc

Figure 7.5.

Example F. A short report by the drug company's public relations director. The report presents the results of his investigation of the case of the understandably distressed researcher.

DATE: March 29, 197__

TO: Mr. Walter N. Brown

FROM: Thomas J. Wells

Subject: Complaint: Samuel R. Gante M.D. to SURFA Salesman over SURFA Drug #1368-A

Dear Walter:

Your March 11, 197__ memo regarding the above was as startling to me as I suspect the initial news of complaint was to you. Checking first with others in Marketing, I encountered similar reactions. Your inquiry took some digging and people to be consulted were out of the office at varying times, thus the delay in getting back to you.

Direct telephone inquiry to Doctor Gante on March 15th yielded the following information:

Doctor Gante said that he was approached by CR [Clinical Research, a division of SURFA] in early January 197__. They requested that he, as Director of Student Health Services at Coventry College, undertake a SURFA Drug #1368-A study among students at that school's Student Health Center. After negotiating with Coventry's Administration for approval of the proposed study, which was initially disapproved by them, Doctor Gante won permission to proceed. He had worked many hours on the project only to be advised by CR in early March that SURFA had changed its plans and would not be conducting a #1368-A study at Coventry College after all.

Understandably, Doctor Gante was miffed, even bitterly offended. He feels that SURFA pulled it all out from under him, leaving him to feel humiliated in the eyes of Coventry's Administration, not to mention being unrequited for his services.

CR's view expressed to SURFA is that Doctor Gante is due compensation for his efforts in this aborted project.

But, there is another side to the story: Our Medical Department reports that they asked CR to look for investigators who could provide a patient population to fulfill Drug #1368-A study protocol requirements. There was an important stipulation: CR was not to commit SURFA to a study. That's where things went amiss. CR, it would seem, may have mavericked by unilaterally giving Doctor Gante the impression that all was "go" for a study. In any event, he sprang into action, lining up the necessary clearances to proceed. The rest you know about.

SURFA Drugs is sympathetic to Doctor Gante's plight and understands his displeasure. However, Medical contends that CR is responsible and has told them so. Our Medical Department acknowledges only that SURFA has never had a commitment to Doctor Gante, either directly or indirectly, since no "go-ahead" was ever given through CR, their agent.

Paul Ryan is perfectly free to discuss the SURFA version of this impasse with Doctor Gante. If he does, and Doctor Gante would like to discuss it further, he is invited to contact Doctor Gerald A. Silver, Director of our Medical Department.

Figure 7.6.

Doctor Silver did advise me that there will be additional studies forthcoming and that Doctor Gante will be given priority consideration if he would be interested.

The foregoing represents what I understand the "cards at play" to be in this situation.

In my telephone conversation with Doctor Gante, he praised Paul Ryan, saying Paul was "on the ball" for his alert follow-through after their conversation on the subject. He also said he was pleased to have heard directly from SURFA. Though I made no commitment, I assured Doctor Gante that the information he provided to me would be conveyed appropriately.

Your concern for a favorable resolution of the present situation is shared by everyone here who is involved. Resetting the goodwill SURFA had enjoyed with Doctor Gante is a diplomatic challenge at this point.

Thank you, Walter, for bringing this problem to my attention. Please keep us advised.

Sincerely,

Thomas J. Wells

TJW:gh

cc: Mr. A. J. Hymes
     Mr. D. O. Wilson
     Mr. R. A. Pearson
     G. A. Silver, M.D.
     R. A. Lewis, M.D.

Figure 7.6. *(continued)*

Example G. A brief report distributed to instructors in the training division of a government agency.

SELECTING A VISUAL

As stated in the Report of the Commission on Instructional Technology, "Despite recent progress in educational research and development, educators still have few reliable, validated guidelines for choosing one instructional medium over another." Therefore, it should be recognized that an instructor has to work within limitations as he selects the most appropriate available resource—one that has high probability of assisting a trainee toward objective achievement.

From *Visual Materials: Guidelines for Selection and Use in Training Situations,* Training Systems and Technology Series, No. VI, U.S. Civil Service Commission, Bureau of Training, pp. 2-3.

Figure 7.7.

Selecting an appropriate and effective visual is no easy job. Many instructors have treated their visuals so casually that they have ignored the possibility that there may be better ones available. Whenever new material is taught, new visual materials must be brought into the classroom to support it. Even a slight change in the objective of an existing lesson may render an otherwise effective visual useless. To meet the requirements of changing lessons and lesson objectives, instructors must constantly reevaluate their visual materials. Certain key factors, however, should always be observed when replacing a visual or designing a new one.

Determine Need

The first, and probably the most important consideration is need. Whenever there are teaching points which are difficult to explain, a visual may be needed. If oral description fails to convey a clear and complete image to the trainee's mind, a visual may be needed. This criterion of need should be applied not only to new lessons, but to older established lessons in the program of instruction.

Visuals also may be used to motivate interest at appropriate points in the development of a lesson. However, any visual the instructor chooses to "perk up" his lesson must be related to the material he is teaching. If the visual contains an emotion laden concept, or an idea that causes the trainees to want to pursue the concept portrayed, the visual ceases to function.

Facts Required

When an instructor has decided a visual is necessary, he must next determine what the visual has to do. That is, what must the visual accomplish in terms of the lesson objective and what image should it establish in the trainees' minds.

1. Lesson objective. The lesson objective determines the level at which trainees are being taught. Given in terms of familiarization, working knowledge, or qualified knowledge, this objective helps determine the type and nature of the visuals that will be necessary for the lesson. Familiarization is the level at which "trainees learn sufficient facts and principles to be able to recognize their importance and know where to go for additional knowledge should the need arise." At this level of instruction, the clarity and simplicity of graphic visuals often provide the necessary impact and stimulate appropriate recall more conveniently and inexpensively than

other visuals. Furthermore, the instructor will find that graphic visuals satisfy trainee's curiosity as well as develop their interest in subsequent lessons.

To support the achievement of higher learning levels, more involved, detailed, and complex visual materials are often necessary. To develop a "working knowledge, trainees must possess a sufficient knowledge of related facts, principles, and techniques to enable them to perform routine practical applications under direct supervision of a qualified individual." When instruction is given at the working knowledge level, visual content should include additional facts which will build on conceptuals gained during familiarization. To develop qualified knowledge, "trainees must be capable of demonstrating sufficient knowledge to permit independent functioning in the area concerned." When instruction is given at this level, either actual equipment or suitable substitutes should be available for maximum realism. Since models etc. are often very complicated and expensive, a professional media specialist should be consulted regarding its use and handling.

2. Clear image. A distinct mental image of the visual must be established before an instructor can hope to have it reproduced. It must be the exact image he intends to transfer to his trainees. What is the right image? Simply, the one that is essential, exact, and basic. Frequently, experts in subject knowledge overlook fundamental points that are essential to trainee understanding. Consequently, they select too complicated a visual for the beginning trainee. Two simple visuals, used in sequence, are preferable to one complicated visual. . . .

3. Evaluate. Whether or not a visual will accomplish its purpose can be judged at two points: during the dry-run and in the actual classroom setting. . . . The instructor should dry-run his visual with his lesson materials to determine the appropriateness of the visual for himself. If he rehearses before other staff members, they, too, can help him with their comments and reactions. Having satisfied himself that the visual works in the dry-run, he can then use it in the lesson. Again, evaluation should be made. If the instructor senses that the trainees did not respond as anticipated, he must re-examine his visual. A few inquiries among members of the class may suggest corrections or changes that should be made.

Figure 7.7. *(continued)*

brief reports than it is with other types of communications. This is because memos and reports, as we mentioned before, are in-house communications that are mainly concerned with conveying factual information. However, don't suppose that you need not consider *Tone* when you draft a memo.

Let's consider the *Informational* aspects of memos and short reports first. Obviously, your concern should be with how much and what kind of information you need for your message. But even before you become involved with this basic consideration, you should *have the purpose of your message firmly in mind.* Do you want, as in Example A (Figure 7.1), to announce a meeting? Then, obviously, you must have at least the following information at hand—the date of the meeting, the place of the meeting, the time of the meeting. Do you want, as in Example B (Figure 7.2), to let your associates and supervisor know where you can be reached on a business trip? Then you must inform them about where you are going and when, and also where you will stay, with whom you will be working, and when you will return.

The memos and brief reports we have illustrated above make use of fairly minimal informational requirements, but even with such basic kinds of messages, unless you have your purpose clearly in mind before you begin to compose it is all too easy to omit some important piece of information. Obviously, with more complicated memos and reports like those in Examples F and G (Figures 7.6 and 7.7), it is all the more important to have your purpose clearly defined before you begin to gather and arrange your information.

Not only should you, the writer, have your purpose in mind when you compose these messages, but you should also *take care to make your purpose clearly understood to your reader.* Memos and reports, which are often concerned with either requesting or conveying information, are likely to be delivered promptly and put to immediate practical use. For this reason it is vital that your message be explicit. One criticism that can be made of Example A (Figure 7.1), for instance, is that although it clearly announces a new time and place for a meeting, it does not even hint at why the change has been made.

THE TIME FACTOR

Time is another important thing to consider in transmitting information via memoranda. This basic consideration is often overlooked. How much time should you allow between the composition of your message and the realization of its purpose? How long will it customarily take for a memo from you to reach the desk of its recipient? Will the sales personnel find out about the new meeting time three days or three hours before the meeting? When we need information, we want it, as the saying goes, yesterday, but always *consider how long it may take the recipient of your memo or report to respond.* If you've requested a simple piece of factual data that your reader may have right in front of him on his desk, that's one matter. But if the information you seek requires extensive research or a special computer run, it's another and altogether different matter. How long, for instance, do you think it took Tom Wells to gather the information for his short report, Example F (Figure 7.6), about SURFA drug # 1368-A?

A final informational factor to consider is *distribution.* You have information to convey? Who needs it? You need information? Who has it? Don't waste time and paper. Be sure that you *distribute your memos and short reports to the people and places where they will do the most good.* Obviously, if you need information about when one of your company's new products will be ready for marketing, you need not ask the company president or the guard at the plant gate. Your memo should be distributed to Research and Development, or to Production. It probably need not even be distributed throughout each of these departments, but sent only to those people in each department directly involved with the product in question.

The effective *Organization* of memos and short reports is a question which depends upon the length, nature and complexity of the message. If you simply want to announce a meeting, as in Example A (Figure 7.1), a simple "where and when" formula will suffice. But, if your message is longer and more complex, then you must consider using various organizational strategies so that the purpose of your message can be accomplished with a minimum of confusion on your reader's part.

THE OUTLINE

If your message is at all long or complicated, *jot down an outline of it before you begin to write or dictate.* An outline is the writer's equivalent of the pilot's checklist of operations before take-off. Just as the checklist forces the pilot to be absolutely certain that all the complicated mechanisms of his plane are in working condition, the outline forces the writer to be sure that he has all his information on hand and arranged in a logical, comprehensible order—before taking off on the flight of composition.

The classical outline looks something like this:

        I.
            A.
            B.
                1.
                2.
        II.
            A.
            B.
            C.
        III.
            A.
            B.
        IV.
            A.
                1.
                2.
                3.
            B.

The roman numerals (I, II, III) represent major divisions of your information or argument, the capital letters (A, B, C) indicate important subdivisions, and the arabic numerals (1, 2, 3), stand for subsidiary points within those subdivisions. You may want to incorporate this outline form into your actual message, using the various numerals and letters to clearly indicate to your reader the major thrust of your message, but if you do, keep this in mind: if you divide something, it is only logical that you divide it into at least two parts. Look at the section of an outline below:

        A.   Packaging methods
            1.   Wooden crates
            2.   Cardboard boxes

        B.   Transportation
            1.   Via rail

The last subdivision is illogical. If only one method of transportation is going to be considered, then it should not be shown as a separate subdivision. Just say "B. Transportation (via rail)." Remember, if you have A, you must have at least B; if you have 1, you must have at least 2.

Another outline technique widely used in scientific and technological memos and reports is the decimal form. This form is used in the following excerpt, Figure 7.8, from a SURFA drug company memo dealing with the proposed agenda of a conference on the marketing of drugs packed in individual "unit" doses.

STAFFING AND PERSONNEL

Pharmacist

    The discussion should include the following points.

1.0   The unit dose medication distribution system is generally mediated through the centralized or decentralized concept. The speaker should discuss the differences between these approaches and the effects of these differences on personnel requirements.

2.0   It should be helpful to discuss the roles and functions of the pharmacist in the unit dose medication distribution system versus the roles and functions of the technician in the system.

3.0   What are the criteria for staffing and personnel?

        3.1   Hours of Operation
        3.2   Completeness of the System
        3.3   Type of patient serviced (Medical, Surgical, Acute, Chronic, etc.)
        3.4   Number of pharmacy deliveries per day

Nurse

    The discussion should include the following points.

1.0   The effect of unit dose on nursing staff requirements. How is, or could, the "extra time" for the nurse be utilized?

2.0   What the nurse would be willing to transfer to pharmacy in terms of function.

Figure 7.8.

Outlines can make a report visually clear, but sometimes the use of the outline form in the body of your actual message can be inappropriate. The material you need to organize may not be complex or detailed enough to require so mechanical an approach.

Often, just using numbers to set off your major points is enough to enable your reader to follow your organizational strategy. Notice how effectively the author of Example G (Figure 7.7) uses numbers to set off the three basic considerations that determine the selection of a visual aid. Example G also incorporates another organizational device that is simple but effective: the use of subheadings to indicate important divisions of the message. The author has broken the procedure of selecting visual aids down into two steps, and has clearly marked them off by giving them the subheadings "Determine Need" and "Facts Required."

In addition to numbers and subheadings, indentation of certain portions of your message can serve as a "visual aid" to organization. Again, the author of Example G has used this method to clearly differentiate between sections of his report, as have the authors of Examples C (Figure 7.3) and F (Figure 7.4).

The most basic and indispensable organizing device is the paragraph. Paragraph intelligently, keeping in mind that the more complicated your message is, the more likely it is that you should use frequent paragraph breaks to give your reader's eyes and his mind a moment's rest before moving on to the next logical subdivision. Remember that information, like food, is easier to digest if it is consumed in small bites rather than large chunks. And, when you paragraph, don't overlook those very helpful transitional terms (*moreover, in spite of, in addition, however,* etc.) that act as logical roadsigns telling your reader where he is headed, and reminding him where he has been.

The secret of organizing any message is to break it into parts and to clearly indicate the relationship between the parts. A little time spent considering the nature and purpose of the information you wish to organize will suggest the organizational strategy which is appropriate—that is, the logical parts into which your message should be broken, and how those parts should be arranged. Material can be arranged *inductively* (beginning with facts and ending with a conclusion) or *deductively* (beginning with the conclusion followed by the facts). If you wish to describe a process, a chronological organization would be appropriate (break the process down into its phases, beginning with the earliest and concluding with the last). If you want to analyze both sides of an argument, your material could be broken down into affirmative and negative categories or, possibly, each affirmative point could be followed by a negative point. Whatever strategy of organization you use, let that strategy be clearly apparent to your reader!

TONE

Though we have said that *Tone* is not as important a consideration in creating memos and short reports as it is in other types of writing, we do not mean to give the impression that this angle of the communication triangle should be ignored. The sad fact is that many writers of memos and short reports are so preoccupied with the accuracy of their information and the clarity of its organization that they overlook *Tone* entirely—with the result of seeming unintentionally brusque and impersonal.

We suggested earlier that in Example A (Figure 7.1), the reason why the time of the sales meeting was changed should have been included. This would not only be helpful information, but it would greatly improve the tone of the memo. People like to know why things are changed and appreciate being told. As it stands, Example A seems peremptory. Look at Example F (Figure 7.6), in which Tom Wells examines the delicate question of who was responsible for Dr. Gante's embarrassing predicament. This message could not possibly have been written without a careful consideration of appropriate *Tone*.

Finally, consider the following memo, announcing a meeting and outlining its agenda (Figure 7.9).

Now this is a very ordinary memo. Its Informational and Organizational qualities are obvious: the meeting is announced and the reader is told where, when, and why. The two major subjects to be covered at the meeting are set forth and briefly described. A paragraph is devoted to each important logical subdivision of the message and certain organizational signposts are used ("The first proposal is that. . . ."; "The second proposal is that. . . .").

What may not be so obvious is the fact that the writer was at least as much concerned with the memo's *Tone* as he was with its *Information* and *Organization*.

In the first paragraph, the writer urges his reader to attend the meeting. He is aware that his colleagues frequently complain about the number and frequency of meetings they are required to attend, and does not want to give the impression that the reader *must,* or even *should* attend.

In the second paragraph, the writer mentions two "interesting" proposals. He is very much in favor of those proposals, and his first instinct was to describe them as "excellent," but he does not wish to appear biased in their favor before the staff has had a chance to discuss and approve them.

On the other hand, he does not simply call them "proposals"," because a neutral term might well offend the staff members who suggested them. Therefore, he settles on the phrase "interesting proposals."

In the fourth paragraph, the writer describes the second proposal as designed to "realign" the last two sections of the reading list for graduate students. His choice of that word "realign" is very careful. He is aware that the English department has been arguing for years about the reading list; some want it revised, some want it unchanged, and some want to abandon it. The writer does not want to reopen that particular can of worms at this particular meeting. He dare not use the word *revise* or even *change*, so he uses the term "realign" and hopes for the best.

So it is, then, that Tone has its place even in so matter-of-fact a message as the announcement of a meeting. Basic writing considerations are basic to all types of writing!

COVENTRY UNIVERSITY
Department of English

April 15, 197__

From: Lance Madrid   To: Graduate Staff

Subject: Graduate Staff Meeting

There will be a meeting of the graduate staff at 12:30 p.m. next Tuesday, April 22, in 204 Vasey. All graduate teachers are urged to attend.

Two interesting proposals regarding graduate school procedure have been made recently, and I'd like to present them to the staff for discussion.

The first proposal is that we revise the comprehensive examination procedure so that, if a candidate fails the examination, he need not be re-examined in the section (or sections) which he did manage to pass.

The second proposal is to realign the last two of the eight literary periods covered by the reading list and the comprehensive. As it stands now, they cover American literature <u>before</u> the Civil War and American literature <u>after</u> the Civil War. It has been suggested that the two classifications would reflect more realistically our actual course emphasis if the designations were changed to "American Literature until 1900" and "American Literature after 1900."

The graduate committee will be meeting later this month to select tuition scholars and teaching assistants, and we are interested in any comments the staff might make on the present candidates.

Sincerely,

Lance Madrid
Chairman, Graduate Committee

Figure 7.9.

EXERCISES

Memos and short reports are basically informational. Since you as a student may not have access to such business or government data as these messages are ordinarily concerned with, the following exercises are designed to have you organize information that is available to you in everyday life.

1. You are the secretary of a social club. The club membership voted, almost unanimously, to hold its annual dinner dance on the last Saturday in May at Schmidt's Alpine Inn. It is now April 22 and you have discovered that the Alpine Inn will not be able to accommodate your group until the first Saturday in June. Arrangements for the dinner dance must be made quickly and there is not time to have the full membership approve the changed date. You and the club's other officers have decided to contract with the Alpine Inn for the later date. Write a memo to your club membership announcing and explaining the change.

2. You belong to an investment club. Select a stock which has been recently written up in the business journals (*Forbes, Business Week, Wall Street Journal,* etc.) and write a brief report recommending whether or not your club should purchase ten shares of it. Consider the company's past performance, current sales and dividend, and the economic factors likely to affect its future prospects.

3. Write a short report in which you compare and contrast the advantages of taking your lunch to school or buying it at school. Be sure to consider the matter of relative convenience weighed against cost.

4. Write a short report presenting the economics of owning a large home freezer (150 lbs. capacity and up). Consider such matters as initial cost of the unit, daily cost of operation, the freezer life of basic foods, and the cost of bulk purchase of food as opposed to the more frequent purchase of small quantities of supermarket specials. Consult your local utility company and such publications as *Consumer Reports.*

Chapter 8

DEALING WITH THE PUBLIC

It may be that in a normal work day you will be called upon to write a variety of letters. You cannot anticipate every writing situation, but what you can do is to familiarize yourself with examples of some of the basic letters that you can expect to use in the business world. Even though we may overlook some possibilities here, if you employ the elements of sound communication discussed throughout this text you should be able to handle any problems.

SALES LETTERS

A good sales letter must capture and hold the interest of the reader. This is its first requirement. Consider all the time and money spent in direct mailing efforts to generate new business. Unless your potential customer actually reads and considers your sales letter, it is wasted effort.

Of course, many sales communications are not letters so much as leaflets, brochures, or pamphlets which contain little print, a great deal of color, and a lot of illustration. One news magazine recently attracted new business with a small, four-page mailing consisting of color photographs of former covers, a convenient business reply card (postage paid), and the text illustrated in Figure 8.1.[1]

This appeal is brief, forceful and psychologically appealing. It implies that by reading TIME regularly you can become a more knowledgeable, interesting person. This promotional piece illustrates the essential characteristics of any successful sales letter. It should be brief, clear, and interesting. Think of these characteristics when you examine full page, color advertisements in a magazine. Such advertising space is expensive, so one may be tempted to get more bang for the buck by overwhelming the reader with praise of one's product. Some ads in fact do this, but most (especially the

---

1. Reprinted by permission from *Time,* The Weekly News Magazine; Copyright Time Inc.

TO <u>KNOW</u> YOU KNOW,
READ TIME

It doesn't have to be a hassle to understand the news. With TIME, it's easy—there's never any doubt. You <u>know</u> you know what's going on. And that's vital these days.

With TIME, you get more than the headlines. You get insights, ideas, background you won't find anywhere else. In every field from Business to Books, Music to Medicine. Organized and concise. Sharply written. Every week a world of information you can think about . . . talk about . . . use.

TIME is people like Henry Kissinger and Kurt Vonnegut, Liza Minnelli and Billie Jean King, William F. Buckley, Jr. and the Rev. Sun Myung Moon. Places like the Kremlin and Capitol Hill, Wall Street and the Bourse. Events from the Super Bowl to the Stratford Shakespeare Festival.

See for yourself. Join the millions of interested, interesting people who read TIME each week. Stay well-informed the easy way—and save money too.

TIME FOR ONLY
25¢ A WEEK

That's quite a bargain, since TIME normally costs 60¢ a week on newsstands and 35¢ an issue by regular subscription.

Figure 8.1.

successful ones) are less wordy and rely on a happy amalgam of image and text, with a deemphasis of the text. Here are some examples:

Image: A snowman holding two bottles of whiskey
Text: MELT A MAN'S HEART WITH A GIFT OF OLD PEMBERTON
THE BEST OF WHISKEYS FOR THE BEST OF SEASONS

Image: A man and woman on a golf course wearing sports clothes with cashmere sweaters
Text: THE QUIET DISTINCTION OF A LORD ANGUS CASHMERE

Image: A healthy, smiling young couple sailing on a lake with cigarettes in their hands
Text: FOR A SEA-FRESH TASTE SMOKE SEA BREEZE CIGARETTES

Your sales letters, while they may not be as pictorial as these, should imitate such ads in brevity, clarity, and interest.

Don't rely on tired formulas such as the computer letter shown in Figure 8.2 with its hollow attempt to appear personalized.

While this approach relies on brief, clear paragraphs, it is neither interesting nor imaginative. It rings false because it is so obviously a form letter trying hard not to be one. Everyone knows that form letters must be used to reach large numbers of people, so why try to disguise the fact? The reader will not be fooled by such computer tricks, and to use them is to risk alienating a potential customer, for you imply that he *can* be fooled. Be more sensible, direct, and honest in your presentations.

A person will buy your product or service either because he needs it or because you make it so appealing that he wants it. But, as we stressed earlier, you must first capture his attention. This may be done by cartoons, an engaging letterhead, or a unique arrangement of your text, but it is also essential that your opening sentence be appealing. Rhetorical questions are sometimes effective:

Dear Mr. Chesno:

You are among the few persons in the Stratford area receiving the enclosed application at this time.

This piece should be of special value to you, Mr. Chesno.

It can bring you detailed information on how to begin a promising new job opportunity. And in no time at all, just by training in your own living room at 413 Bailey Road.

Simply return the postage paid envelope enclosed, Mr. Chesno, and we will send you free and without obligation an illustrated booklet describing how you may take our home correspondence course in accounting.

That's right, Mr. Chesno, for just pennies a day EDICOM can start training you for a lucrative, rewarding career. More than a hundred other individuals in the Stratford area alone have done so. So shouldn't you also try it out?

We look forward, Mr. Chesno, to hearing from you. Complete the enclosed card and mail it today.

Figure 8.2.

Do your retirement years include many warm days on sunny beaches?

Is your family tired of the same old meals?

Are your investment dollars bringing you a reasonable return?

Can you combine Danish Modern furniture with French Provincial?

In this way you gain your reader's interest, but you must answer these questions to his satisfaction as well, so that he will be motivated to buy your product or at least send for more information. Your answers should be convincing and informative, so that he feels he has something to gain. Notice how the letter in Figure 8.3[2] accomplishes this.

This BENCRAFT dealer reinforces the mention of special savings in the second sentence by stressing the other services available—delivery, installation, etc. The capitalization technique is perhaps overdone, but it varies the type and places effective stress on such key words as REBATE, SAVINGS, and BENCRAFT. This stress is essential as a follow-through on the opener. Our next example, Figure 8.4, illustrates a more straightforward letter, one that also appeals to the reader's self-interest, and makes a less obvious but still effective use of capitalization.

The profit motive is a strong one, and the letter in Figure 8.4 makes use of it—but without jeopardizing the credibility of the sender; he takes care to mention that with "unusual gains" come "obvious risks." Only swindlers and charlatans offer enormous profits without risk. It is far better to be honest, direct, and human in your salesmanship. Don't make exaggerated promises and absurd claims. Besides attracting attention and offering persuasive details, this letter provides a positive conclusion. It asks the reader to send for more information. Such information (e.g., brochures) may be included with the first letter, but this can be expensive. It is often better to send a "feeler" letter to identify more clearly those customers seriously interested in your goods or services.

By way of summary, then, let's examine the three key parts of any sales letter.

2. Courtesy Cobb & Lawless, Wayne, Pennsylvania.

DEAR CUSTOMER:

Would you agree that these are difficult times?

But in spite of RISING PRICES and INFLATION, we at COBB & LAWLESS are offering our customers quality BENCRAFT appliances at special savings of from $10 to $50 per appliance.

We have decided to take the money usually spent on newspaper advertising and REBATE it directly to our regular customers by REDUCING PRICES on merchandise in stock.

We were also fortunate in acquiring quality BENCRAFT appliances at a substantial savings from a leading BENCRAFT dealer in New Jersey who retired from business after 40 years. We are PASSING THESE SAVINGS ON TO YOU.

Included in this sale are BENCRAFT REFRIGERATORS and FREEZERS, BENCRAFT LAUNDRY EQUIPMENT, BENCRAFT RANGES AND OVENS and DISHWASHERS. We also have PRE-SEASON PRICES on high efficiency, energy saving BENCRAFT AIR CONDITIONERS.

We are a FULL SERVICE dealer: WE DELIVER—WE INSTALL—WE REMOVE THE OLD APPLIANCE, all at no extra charge. We also SERVICE what we sell.

Our KITCHEN INSTALLATION department is at your service to install whatever you buy, or for complete KITCHEN PLANNING.

We are proud to offer our own custom cabinets made in our own cabinet shop. When you deal with us, the motto is:

ONE CONTRACTOR—ONE RESPONSIBILITY

THIS SALE IS FOR THE NEXT TWO WEEKS ONLY! We hope to see you.

Figure 8.3.

A. ATTENTION

Letters are useless unless someone reads them. To encourage the reader, you must make your letter brief, clear, and interesting. Use the "you approach" and suggest immediately a specific reader benefit. Your letter may be long only if it is dramatic and interesting; generally use brief paragraphs. Rhetorical questions, jokes, cartoons, capitalization—any imaginative device—may be used to attract attention as long as they are in good taste and relevant to your message; don't use them simply for the sake of their own cleverness. Respect your reader's intelligence and don't allow gimmicks to distract him from your central message. Examples of distracting gimmicks include some of the sales promotion games and contests mailed out by companies wishing to sell magazine subscriptions; instead of stressing the possible savings, they encumber the reader with magazine stamps to be placed on giant cards for insertion into giant envelopes. Another poor gimmick is the "personalized" computer letter.

B. PERSUASION

You must first determine the proper sales appeal; marketing research, simple experience, or common sense psychology will help you here. In selling a sub-compact car for instance, you will probably place the greatest emphasis on its initial cost or gas mileage rather than on comfort or durability. With luxury cars, such as Cadillac or Lincoln Continental or Rolls Royce, your potential customers are concerned less about cost than prestige, dependability, and comfort. Remember too that profit and pleasure are the strongest motivations for action. Don't make outlandish claims or promises

If you are unhappy with your present investment program because of stock market conditions and inflation, and you are an investor with risk capital available, then consider the alternatives available through commodity futures trading. Compare opportunities for yourself:

> IF YOU PURCHASE 100 SHARES OF STOCK AT $36.00 PER SHARE AND SELL THE STOCK AT $40.00, YOU HAVE MADE A PROFIT OF $400.00 ON A $3,600.00 INVESTMENT.
>
> IF YOU PURCHASE 1 FUTURES CONTRACT OF CATTLE AT 46¢ PER POUND (ON A CONTRACT OF 40,000 POUNDS), AND SELL IT AT 50¢ PER POUND, YOU HAVE MADE $1,600.00 ON A $1,200.00 INVESTMENT.

For the unusual gains available in commodity futures trading, there are obvious risks. We know them and we want you to know them also, but the example above is not uncommon nor out of line to what's happening in almost all commodity markets today.

Helping people analyze and trade commodity futures has been our only business for years. We would like to provide you with the opportunity to learn more about commodity trading. Our booklet "Facts and Factors for Commodity Futures Traders" does help explain commodity trading to you. For your free copy of Facts and Factors, please return the enclosed card. No sales person will call.

We hope to work with you in planning your Commodity Market goals.

Figure 8.4.

that insult the reader's intelligence. ("Buy a Scott Sewing machine and never worry again about mechanical failures.") Simply describe in a direct, clear way the merits of your product or service.

C. ACTION

Conclude your letter in a positive, decisive manner. Avoid such tired formulas as "Awaiting your reply," or "Hoping to hear from you," or "Thanking you in advance for a possible order." Suggest more direct action:

> If you have any questions, call me (toll free) at (800) 848-1170.
>
> Reserve your time NOW—Return the enclosed postage paid reply card, or call (609) 665-4500.
>
> By sending in the enclosed order blank, you will be eligible for an additional 10 percent discount on these fine chairs.

Such conclusions are needed to stimulate the convinced or willing reader. It is usually essential to provide him with telephone numbers for direct ordering, order blanks, or postage paid envelopes, etc. You help insure the sale by providing such aids to action.

Frequently it takes more than one letter to achieve success. The first one generally makes the contact, while the later ones supply answers to possible questions bothering the reader. Follow-up letters must avoid being merely repetitious; they should supply new, persuasive facts or should present old facts in a fresh way. For our final examples, let's take a look at some successful sales letters (Figures 8.5, 8.6, 8.7, and 8.8) sent out by an insurance company.[3] The first letter, Figure 8.5, makes the contact:

3. Courtesy of E & E Insurance, Westerville, Ohio 43081.

$27.80			$14.00	$76.40	$45.80
	$33.00	$26.00			$34.60
$43.20	$104.60		$16.40	$90.80	$42.30
	$17.00	$22.00	$35.40	$53.76	

If money talks, the sums above are telling you about the savings on automobile insurance enjoyed by the good, responsible drivers who have discovered E & E . . . the automobile insurance company which services more than 180,000 policies direct from the home office by mail and phone.

And despite the fact that E & E automobile insurance generally costs less, E & E generally gives more in protection and service. And E & E is one of the very few companies which doesn't raise your rates when you have an accident.

If you'd like to explore fully what E & E has to offer, just complete the enclosed request for quotation card and give it to the mailman. You'll receive, by mail, complete details, including a personalized rate quotation which will enable you to make a coverage-by-coverage comparison of E & E against your present auto policy. How much you will be able to save depends on where in the state you live, the car you drive, who drives it, how it is used and with whom you are now insured.

If your present auto policy expires within the next 15 days, don't wait for the mailman. Just pick up the phone and give us a call. You can call toll free by dialing 800-282-8810 from any phone in Ohio or 800-848-8810 from all other states . . . service hours are 8 to 5 weekdays, 8 until noon on Saturday. If, on the other hand, you've just renewed your present policy, don't hold the card; send it in. We'll send you a rate quotation now and a reminder at the proper time.

Cordially,

Mike A. Hamlin
Vice President - Sales

MAH/RT

Figure 8.5.

The unconventional opening appeals directly to the reader's pocketbook. Buying E & E automobile insurance can save you money; this is the central point and it attracts the reader's attention. The "protection and service" are mentioned, but not elaborated on, for E & E simply wants the reader to send for a quotation. Thus the major portion of the letter stresses further action the reader should take.

Suppose the reader does send for a rate quotation. With it he gets the letter shown in Figure 8.6.

After this letter's effective opener (which uses ellipses and capitalization for visual emphasis), E & E elaborates on the services available to its policy owners. The reader already knows from looking at the rate quotation if the cost savings make it worthwhile for him to switch insurance companies, so the letter wisely concentrates on the question uppermost in his mind: "WHAT ABOUT

The enclosed rate quotation speaks for itself . . . so you're probably thinking:

"I KNOW YOU CAN SAVE ME MONEY, BUT WHAT ABOUT THE SERVICE?"

That's a reasonable question. A savings of $20 to $30 a year on your automobile insurance may be no bargain if you have to sacrifice on service.

But when you insure your car with E & E you can expect better service than you've been used to . . . better because that's the way we try to do everything . . . because you deal direct, not through a series of intermediaries.

When you change cars, change your address, or when anything else happens that requires service on your policy, you drop us a note or give us a call—toll free. It makes no difference whether you live across the street or across the state . . . we're as close as your telephone.

If you have an accident, you call the E & E claims representative nearest you . . . or, if you prefer, you can call the home office and we'll put him in touch with you. E & E has its own claims offices in many cities . . . and in others we work with the same network of independent claims adjusters used by most other auto insurers.

Another thing you'll like about E & E claims service is the lack of red tape. On minor claims under the comprehensive coverage . . . broken glass or a damaged aerial, for example, all you have to do is get it fixed at your own convenience, then send us the bill along with a simple note of explanation . . . no complicated forms, no running after estimates. We're proud of the fact that most claims under E & E auto policies are paid within 48 hours after proof of loss is received at the home office.

How can you be sure the service is all that we say it is?

Well, there are thousands of E & E policyholders who can testify to it. Or, consider this . . . a good price will sell a policy, but it takes good service to keep it sold. E & E's renewal percentage is among the very highest in the auto insurance industry.

As we said in the beginning, the enclosed rate quotation speaks for itself. Your exact savings will depend upon the car you drive, how you use it, where you live, and with whom you are now insured. But, if you can't save at least $10 a year . . . you're one of the rare exceptions. The typical E & E policyholder is saving from $20 to $30 a year per car.

There are two good reasons why we can give you so much for so little:

1. E & E specializes in insuring those who are good, responsible drivers, and thus entitled to lower than average rates.

2. E & E employs no salesmen, pays no commissions. Direct-to-policyholder service means lower sales and handling costs, and the savings are shared by every E & E policyholder.

E & E issues the same broad-form family auto policy written by most other auto insurers. And your rate quotation gives rates for each coverage separately and for various limits under the coverage

Figure 8.6.

so that you can make an accurate comparison with your present policy. But, if you have any questions about E & E coverages, rates or service, please don't hesitate to give us a call. You can reach us from 8 to 5 weekdays, 9 to 12 on Saturday. Just call the toll free number shown on the enclosed quotation. It's free . . . E & E pays for all calls.

Cordially,

Mike A. Hamlin
Vice President - Sales

MAH/RT

P.S.   The enclosed rate quotation is based on our current rates, but it may not be based on current information about you and your car. If you have changed cars or moved to a new home, if there are new male drivers under 25 or new female drivers under 21, or if the youngest male driver has had a 22nd or 25th birthday since the time of your original inquiry, please give us a call so that we may check the rates for you. You may be pleasantly surprised.

Figure 8.6. *(continued)*

THE SERVICE?'' The letter supplies persuasive details: E & E has claims offices in many cities, it has toll free telephone service, it pays most policies within 48 hours after proof of loss is received. The final paragraph suggests action to be taken if the reader still has any questions.

Suppose that despite this appeal our reader never responds. He either forgot about it or simply isn't interested. However, E & E has spent time and money supplying this reader with a rate quotation so it decides to try one more time. See E & E's letter in Figure 8.7, and the attached questionnaire, Figure 8.8.

E & E refuses to allow a desperate, impatient tone to creep into this final sales letter. It simply repeats earlier information, but in an imaginative, humorous way. It also suggests action the reader can take to receive a new quotation or another copy of the old one.

All of E & E's letters are effective. They employ sound psychology and sensible business practices.

IF YOUR BROTHER-IN-LAW HASN'T SWITCHED TO E & E

. . . it might be because he's never heard of E & E. Or it might be that he's heard all about us but just never got around to requesting the personal rate quotation which would show him exactly what E & E could do for him.

But you're different . . . you did hear about E & E . . . and you did request, and receive, a rate quotation. But you haven't yet made the switch! Where did we slip up? We know why people do make the move (it's because they can obtain quality auto insurance protection and superior service at a savings) . . . but we'd like to know more about those who don't, in the hopes that what you tell us now will help us serve you in the future.

Won't you take 60 seconds to fill out the enclosed questionnaire and return it to me?

If you don't recall the quotation you received several months ago, or if you'd like to have a current one, just complete the coupon at the bottom of the questionnaire. A new personal rate quotation will be sent to you by return mail.

Remember . . . there's no obligation. No salesman will call, because we have none. Direct-to-policyholder service, through the mails, is one reason why we can probably help you save $10 to $30 a year . . . or more . . . on your automobile insurance. We think that's reason enough for switching to E & E, but we would certainly appreciate your thoughts on the subject.

Thank you for your interest . . . and your help.

Cordially,

Mike A. Hamlin
Vice President - Sales

MAH/RT

P.S.   If your brother-in-law has made the switch and is enjoying all the advantages in savings and service that E & E offers, how come you've let him get one up on you?

Figure 8.7.

Mr. Mike A. Hamlin
E & E Insurance
Westerville, Ohio 43081

Dear Mr. Hamlin:

☐ I liked your rates, but E & E slipped my mind and I renewed the old policy. Please send a new rate quotation.

☐ I don't even remember receiving a rate quotation from E & E. Please send me a new quotation.

☐ I turned out to be one of the rare exceptions who couldn't save money by insuring with E & E. Or so it seemed. Maybe you quoted me the wrong rates. Send another rate quotation and I'll take a fresh look at it.

☐ I could have saved a little money by switching my insurance to E & E but I put it off because I lacked a complete answer to this question:

☐ Somebody goofed. I did switch and am now a happy E & E policyholder. My policy number is _____ .

☐ Other:

_____   _____
Name   (please print)   Telephone

_____
Address

Figure 8.8.

EXERCISES

A. SALES LETTERS

1. Rewrite the computer letter presented on page 85, Figure 8.2. The market for the home study course offered in the letter would be men and women in their 30's who wish either to begin a new profession or to make additional money part-time. Assume that you are Mrs. Kathy Harris, Director of Information for the Kassel Correspondence School, 8203 Plymouth Building, Washington, D.C. 20515. Use proper letter form (block or semiblock) in writing to Marlin Miller, 3804 Oak Lane, Philadelphia, Pennsylvania 19106 and Mrs. Linda Lauer, 19 Louella Drive, Bridgeport, Conn. 06328. Decide whether you should compose a different letter for women.

2. Robert Brent of 1617 Alabaster Drive, Santa Fe, New Mexico 87501 has subscribed to *Outdoors* magazine for the past five years, but has recently allowed his subscription to lapse. Assume you are Edith Steiner, Director of Sales Promotion for *Outdoors* with offices in the Regency Towers, 908 Bolton Drive, Akron, Ohio 44304. Write Mr. Brent a letter encouraging him to renew his subscription. As an inducement, indicate that while the newsstand rate for one year of *Outdoors* is $22, and the previous yearly subscription rate is $14, you are making a special offer of a $10 renewal rate. Remind him of the features that he has enjoyed over the years.

3. Buck Rondo, president of the Kayo Toy Company, 2104 Manning Street, Lexington, Kentucky 40507, makers of children's war toys, sends a toy catalogue each year to a list of toy store managers as well as to a group of individual families. The same catalogue goes to both groups, but the store managers also receive a code allowing them to determine wholesale as well as suggested retail prices. Mr. Rondo must compose a different letter for each group in which he praises the general quality of Kayo toys and indicates particular bargains. Help him write both letters.

4. Judith Cole, Director of Sales for Warehouse Imports at 804 Belcher Blvd. in Charleston, South Carolina 29411, is responsible for promoting the annual winter clearance sale. She knows from experience that there are two sets of customers—one preferring the sophisticated foreign imports, another group buying the "Early American" line. She also has a fairly complete list of former customers based on previous purchases. Using this list, should she write one letter for all or two letters depending on the customer's taste? Write the letter or letters she might send out.

5. An important part of any sales letter is good psychology. For instance, consider the case of CampusBake, a corporation which for $8 will deliver a birthday cake to your son or daughter who is away at school; they will at the same time guarantee that the delivery person will sing "Happy Birthday." Compose a letter to be sent to parents offering this service. What points do you stress? Be especially careful with your opening sentence.

6. A television store owner opened his sales letter (Figure 8.9) as follows:

Small aplience, rodeo, tv. cup it out.
Choose a friend or an accantince.
Convice him that he needs it or sell it to him.

Due Monday   Ruf dfinal Typed

Dear Customer:

The following notice recently appeared in the "Personals" column of a Wilmington newspaper:

> Thelma, since you left me, my heart has felt a great loss. The house is darker
> than before. No one to talk to me at mealtimes or in the evening. The warm
> glow that greeted me upon coming home is no longer there. Never had I
> realized how lonely life could be. Knowing how much this has hurt me, please
> stop my suffering and send the television back.
>
> Bud

Figure 8.9.

Is this an effective opening? If you agree, complete the letter. If not, compose a new letter.

ORDER LETTERS AND ACKNOWLEDGMENTS

A. ORDER LETTERS

The major characteristic of an order letter is accuracy. You need not concern yourself about the "you approach," or basic psychology, or any stylistic suggestions. You don't need to impress or convince anyone. You simply need to communicate as briefly and as clearly as possible what you wish to have sent to you.

Frequently a supplier makes clearly printed order forms available that enable you to check off the items needed and fill in the amount required. He may also provide return envelopes with his brochure or catalogue. If not, you will need to write your own letter. Make certain to include the following:

1. Quantity of items desired.
2. Name of product (with catalogue number if known) with relevant descriptive details (size, weight, color, price, material, grade, pattern, finish).
3. Information on payment. Indicate credit number if you wish to charge the order. Otherwise you should request c.o.d. (cash on delivery), or send a check (personal or certified) or money order (postal, express, or telegraph).
4. Information on shipment—how (if special requirements are needed), when (by what date is it needed?), and where (indicate in the body of the letter if item is to be sent to address other than that in the heading). You will usually know from the supplier's catalog or advertisement how much is charged for shipment and handling. If unknown, you can estimate the charge and submit a check. If the actual amount is less, you can ask for a refund; if it is more, you can be billed for the remainder (if this is agreeable to the supplier) or have the merchandise shipped c.o.d. The latter, however, will cost more.

Our first example, Figure 8.10, involves a hardware store owner who has an account with a major supplier. Notice the clear tabulation of items ordered and the detailed information given. Listing the prices helps avoid disagreement and possible ill will.

1819 Bartram Street
New Britain, Connecticut 06050
April 12, 197___

Reliance Distributors
3009 Bering Highway
Buffalo, New York 14214

Gentlemen:

　　Please ship me immediately by express the following items from your latest catalogue and charge them to my account (#83462-1):

6 CT9830 Crassen & Rohm 7¼ in. circular power saw, avocado 　　with optional safety shield @19.62	$117.72
4 CT6315 Belkett Engraver, Model 22SL @ $8.60	34.40
3 boxes CP812 Saw Combo @$15 a box	45.00
20 gal. C903 White Latex Paint, Smooth Texture @$8.99	179.80
	$376.92

Thank you.

　　　　　　　　　　　　　　　　　　　Sincerely,

　　　　　　　　　　　　　　　　　　　Earl T. Jones

Figure 8.10.

You need not tabulate the items if only one article is ordered, as in Figure 8.11.

Gentlemen:

　　Your recent catalogue advertised Peg Lasky's Home Repairs Made Easy for $8.95.

　　Please send me by parcel post four copies of this book and bill all charges to my account (#83462-1). Thank you.

Figure 8.11.

B. ACKNOWLEDGMENTS

When acknowledging order letters keep in mind, especially with first orders, that you have an excellent opportunity to solidify a potentially beneficial business relationship. First impressions are indeed lasting ones, so take the time to send a personal letter or a carefully worded form letter with personal details handled in a postcript. An example of the latter is shown in Figure 8.12.

Dear Mrs. Thomas:

Thank you for your recent order of DURABEST paints; it has been shipped and should reach you in a few days.

Thank you too for becoming a new customer. We welcome your business and hope to serve you in any way possible. We are proud of DURABEST paints and are certain that your customers will be pleased with the results once they use them. The very best color pigments, oils, and resins combine to make DURABEST paints remarkably durable, smooth, and easy to apply.

The enclosed pamphlet gives information on other DURABEST products, such as fine brushes, waxes, and wallpaper. To order any of these just use the order blank and postage-paid envelope in the back of the pamphlet.

Welcome again to the world of DURABEST!

Cordially,

James P. Cramer
Customer Service

P.S.   Thank you, Mrs. Thomas, for the $500 check. The total price, with the new customer discount, came to just $452, so our check for $48 is on its way. I have also sent you a credit application. Please complete it and return it in the attached envelope. Thank you.

Figure 8.12.

For normal acknowledgments, always respond promptly, even if you cannot fill the order immediately. Never keep your customer in doubt or make him feel that you are indifferent to his needs. Let him know of your actions, and let him know right away, even if you must use a form postcard to do so. A personalized letter would be better, but because of time and money this may not always be possible. A form postcard may simply say:

Dear Customer:

Thank you for your recent order. We are processing it now and you should receive it by May 20.

The date may be the only part of this postcard that is personalized, but at least you have been efficient and courteous in sending it. Just remember that such postcards, however, are but a minimum response. A personalized letter is preferable, especially for new and potentially important customers. It is also best to write a letter under any of the following conditions.

1. When the order is not clear.   The customer may have neglected certain details, or relied on an outdated catalogue.

Dear Mr. Kronos:

Thank you for your order of May 19. Eight barrels of unbleached white flour and one barrel of baking soda were shipped yesterday and should reach you within three or four days.

We would appreciate additional information regarding your third item: "one barrel of sugar." Last month we had the pleasure of sending you two barrels of granulated sugar, and in previous months we have filled various orders for brown sugar and powdered sugar.

What kind of sugar should we ship you on this order? We wish to serve you promptly and efficiently, so please reply in the attached postage paid envelope or call us (collect) at 215-687-1200. The correct barrel of sugar will be on its way the day we hear from you.

Thank you for your patronage.

2. *When all or part of the order cannot be filled.* In this case you must ask the customer whether he wishes his money returned or whether he is willing to receive the goods at a later date. You may also make suggestions on possible substitute items.

Dear Mr. Saunders:

Thank you for your order of March 18. We have sent the crystal vase, as you requested, to Mrs. Andrew Poston of Sioux Falls. We hope she enjoys it.

The brass candlestick holders, however, are presently unavailable. We expect a new shipment around April 1 and we will be pleased to send them to you at that time. Please let us know if this is agreeable.

Thank you for your patronage.

3. *When the delivery will be delayed.*

Dear Customer:

We are extremely sorry for the delay in getting our shipment of books to you. Frankly, the response to the sale was so overwhelming that even with additional personnel we were not able to maintain our usual pace in filling orders.

We sincerely hope you will accept our apologies. As a token of our appreciation for your order you will find below a certificate which will allow you a 10 percent discount on your next Marple Press order. Instructions for redemption appear on the coupon.

EXERCISES

B. ORDER LETTERS AND ACKNOWLEDGEMENTS

Kretzler's Department Store, 8904 Carson Drive, Knoxville, Tennessee 37921 sends out their summer 1976 catalogue of children's fashions. Some of the items listed include the following:

a) Apron party dress with signature embroidered on detachable lace-trimmed heart. In pink or light blue checked gingham polyester/cotton. Signature in color to match. 4-6x (8041). 15.00

b) Sailboat pullover, jacquard knit, ribbed trim. Skipper blue and white. 4-6 (8135) 10.00; 7-14 (8136) 11.00

c) Clover printed shift in polyester/cotton 4-6 (8193) 9.00; 7-14 (8194) 10.00

d) Oopsy Daisy halter, one piece pull-on nylon knit with daisies in lime/orange or royal/pink. 4-6 (8208) 7.00; 7-14 (8209) 9.00

e) Rag-stitch denim jeans with 2 front slip pockets under waistband. Navy polyester/cotton with contrasting zigzag stitching. 8-12 reg. or slim (8269) 10.00; prep 26-30 medium or long leg (8270) 12.00

f) Spring jacket with drawstring hood and waist, elastic cuffs, pockets. Bright pink or blue nylon with cotton flannel lining. 2-4 (8284) 6.00

g) V-neck pullover sweater in acrylic knit. Navy, yellow or light blue with white trimming. 4-7 (8306) 12.00; 8-20 (8307) 13.00

h) All-star football shirt in nylon mesh jersey. Red, navy or gold S (8), M (10-12), L (14-16), XL (18-20) (8324) 5.00

1. Order c.o.d. from Kretzler's items *a, c, f, g, h.*

2. You remember liking item *a,* but have since lost the catalogue. How would you order this item from the store?

3. A customer sends you an order for *b, d,* and *e.* You can send *b* and *d,* but item *e* is presently out of stock. You expect a new shipment in about two weeks. Communicate these facts to your customer.

4. Acknowledge the orders mentioned in *1* and *2.* Assume with *2,* however, that the customer neglected to indicate the color desired.

5. Compose a courteous form letter to be sent to all new customers.

6. Mrs. Robert Haggis, of 9316 Ramona Road, Waco, Texas 76703 orders *a, d, h.* She indicates in her letter that she is not a regular customer, but would like to establish a credit account. Meanwhile, she is sending a postal money order with another letter to pay for her order. Write a response.

7. You receive Mrs. Haggis' letter mentioned in 6, but no money order is enclosed. Write her a reply.

LETTERS OF ACCEPTANCE AND REFUSAL

Chapter 3 dealt in part with the psychological structure of Yes-No or Acceptance-Refusal letters. We feel the topic important enough to risk repeating ourselves here. By way of summarizing our previous discussion let's first examine the following illustration:

YES LETTER
(To a contest winner.)

Opening: Direct statement of what reader wants to hear—("Congratulations on winning . . . .")

Body: Necessary details—("You will receive . . . .")

Closing: Brief, but courteous punchline—("Congratulations again!")

NO LETTER
(To a scholarship applicant.)

Opening: Courteous greeting; mention of something you and your reader can agree on—("You are to be commended for your scholastic ambitions . . . .")

Body: Careful, tactful wording of refusal; be natural and avoid abruptness—("We support schools, but not individuals.")

Closing: Be pleasant and maintain friendly relations—("Best of luck in your future work.")

As we stressed earlier, you should place yourself in the position of the reader of your letter. If someone has good news for you, you want to hear it right away. If it's bad news, you don't want to hear it at all. But since you must, you at least want to have the blow softened and to feel that you are dealing with a compassionate person, not a machine. You will experience most difficulty in writing "No" letters, so we will concentrate on them.

Let's examine a series of letters from the Director of Professional Service at a large pharmaceutical company. Like the directors of our hypothetical foundations in Chapter 3, this man, Mr. Ted Hilton, gets numerous requests for medical school scholarships or grant support for research. Most requests must be refused, and Mr. Hilton must say "No" to individuals who directly affect his business—the doctors and future doctors who will develop and promote Alpha Drugs, Mr. Hilton's employer. Letters written now may significantly influence the profitability of Alpha Drugs in the future.

We'll suppose that one letter Ted Hilton receives (Figure 8.13) is from a high school senior who plans to enter a college pre-med program.

Mr. Hilton, who was just recently promoted to his position, checks the files for copies of letters handling similar requests. Basing his reply on an old letter, he formulates the response in Figure 8.14.

Now Ted may be pleased to clear his desk so quickly, but his letter is not a good one. It is not merely brief, but curt. Yes, you say, but Ted is a busy man with little time for writing such letters. Well, we agree, but remember the possible advantages to the company if he takes the time to compose one *good* letter that can be adapted to all such requests. He's relying on a form letter now; the only problem is that it's a bad one. Perhaps the only memory Miss Bullock will have of Alpha Drugs is the word "regret." Here's another approach:

Dear Miss Bullock:

We are happy to learn that you are considering a career in medicine, for it is an exciting and rewarding field. However, while Alpha Drugs does financially support the healthcare professions, we have no scholarship program for college students.

Information concerning financial aid for a high school graduate is probably available through the school guidance office, or the college of your choice.

---

49 Rogers Avenue
Lincoln, Nebraska 69508
July 8, 197—

Alpha Drugs, Inc.
P. O. Box 162
Boston, Massachusetts 02115

Dear Sir:

I am writing to your company seeking information concerning scholarships for deserving college students in pre-medical studies.

I graduated from Central High School this June and have been accepted at Northeastern University. My final term average was 97%, and I received final grades of 100% in Biology, 95% in Physics, and 98% in Mathematics.

My parents are not in a position to provide full financial assistance for my schooling, nor will my summer work provide the necessary funds. Does your Corporation presently have any programs which would provide me with such help, so that I may be of assistance to your organization in the future?

Thank you for considering my request.

Sincerely,

(Miss) Laraine Bullock

Figure 8.13.

Dear Miss Bullock:

In reply to your inquiry concerning the availability of scholarship grants we regret to advise you that we have no program authorizing expenditures of this type. We regret that we cannot be of service to you in this connection.

Sincerely yours,

Ted Hilton
Director of Professional Service

Figure 8.14.

Ted's second effort would be an improvement, but it still needs much work. Where is the "you approach," the psychological organization, the supporting information on grants that Alpha Drugs does provide, the more positive tone? Ted finally comes up with the following version. How does it compare with his earlier efforts?

> Dear Miss Bullock:
>
> Thank you for your letter requesting information on the availability of college tuition assistance programs from Alpha Drugs.
>
> First, I commend you on your well-organized career plans. Knowing what you want to do and where you want to go in life is, in many respects, having the most difficult problem of all solved. If your grades accurately indicate your potential (and most often grades do), you are well on your way to realizing those well-laid plans.
>
> Alpha Drugs provides considerable sums each year in support of continuing education programs for the healthcare professions. The assistance which we make available helps to finance meetings, symposia and conferences. Grants are awarded to hospitals, associations and schools of medicine, but not, unfortunately, to individuals. Our supportive efforts are based on the belief that many should share in our assistance on as fair a basis as possible and that, ultimately, patients should benefit.
>
> As you pursue your career in medicine, I trust that you will be among those beneficiaries of Alpha Drugs sponsored programs in continuing education.
>
> Please know that we support you in spirit and, on behalf of Alpha Drugs, I extend best wishes to you for many happy years in the profession of medicine.

This letter should leave Miss Bullock disappointed but nonetheless pleased. For Ted Hilton takes the time to compliment her on her plans and on her excellent academic record. He buries his "No" amid details supporting the assertion in his previous letter that Alpha Drugs does financially support the healthcare professions. Finally, the entire tone of this letter is impressive; the "you attitude" is present throughout and Ted personalizes his response through the use of "I" rather than "We." It is a courteous, human refusal that cannot damage Alpha Drugs' public relations.

THE INSURANCE CASE

Let's examine another case, that of Mrs. Myrtle Ransom, Box 311, Wilkesboro, North Carolina 28697. She writes the following letter to Regency Mutual Insurance Company.

> Dear Sirs:
>
> I received your check for the amount of $57.14 which I was proud to get for the days in the hospital. I also filled out a form and sent to you for the time I was off from work, when I went into the hospital March 17, and was discharged March 22. Now I had to go and stay with my daughter from the time I was discharged until April 22, which was four weeks I could not work, so I have been looking for some more pay while off from work. However I'm back at work now.

Mrs. Ransom feels entitled to additional compensation, but you know, as a claims examiner, that she is not eligible for home confinement benefits. How then to communicate the terms of her policy in language that she will understand and in a way that will not alienate her? This is the kind of problem faced by numerous professionals in any working day. What was Regency Mutual's first response to her? See Figure 8.15.

June 4, 197___

Mrs. Myrtle Ransom
Box #311
Wilkesboro, North Carolina 28697

RE: POLICY #987312

Dear Mrs. Ransom:

Thank you for your letter of May 28, 197___.

Upon reviewing your file, I find that we have paid the maximum benefit allowable for your
March 17 through March 21, 197___ hospital confinement. On May 1, 197___, we approved your
benefit for four days at $100.00 a week or $57.14. However, we could not approve benefits under
your Convalescent Rider because this Rider states that when injury or sickness confines a person
to a hospital for not less than seven consecutive days, and upon termination of such hospitalization
the covered person is immediately subjected to home confinement while this Rider is in force, we
will pay a home confinement benefit of $50.00 a week for the period of home confinement, but
not to exceed the period of the immediately preceding period of hospitalization for which the
hospital confinement benefits are payable under the policy to which this Rider is attached. Benefits
reduce 50% at the age of sixty-five. You were only confined to the hospital four days, thus, we
could not approve benefits under this Rider.

I hope that I have clarified your questions. If you should have any further questions, please feel
free to call on me.

Sincerely,

MELBA MOORE
Claims Services Representative

MM:tr

Figure 8.15.

Can Ms. Moore's letter possibly be satisfactory? One method of evaluation is our triangle of
Tone, Information, and *Organization*. The opening is fine, but the remainder of the letter is a little
cold in tone. Look at the opening of the second paragraph. Instead of being positive and mention-
ing the fulfillment of past obligations, Moore suggests immediately that the company is not going
to pay any more. This is both poor tone and faulty organization, for the reader will probably not
be receptive to the reasons for the decision. Why not start with: "We were happy to approve benefits of $57.14 for your recent hospital stay"? (Avoid the word "confinement"; it connotes a stay
in an asylum.) This sentence, with the positive word "happy," complements the courteous "thank
you" of the opening sentence.

The information (or reason for the rejection) then begins with the word "However," and runs
to the end of the paragraph. It is absurdly difficult to read. Mrs. Ransom will never be able to

understand it. Read Mrs. Ransom's letter again to get a sense of her educational background. Then read the company response to see how inadequate it is to her needs and education. Think of ways to revise portions.

We hope you did some mental editing of Ms. Moore's letter as you read it, because an "explanation" like hers will cost the Regency Insurance Company money. It is too long and too complicated; it may well cause Mrs. Ransom to write another letter, which could have been avoided had Ms. Moore taken the time to translate the policy for her and not merely recite its confusing provisions. Also, it is very bad psychology to tell a policyowner or customer what she *could* have gotten had she been eligible. Never dangle cash and then pull it away; you'll only frustrate your reader.

Here is the way we would have answered Mrs. Ransom:

> Dear Mrs. Ransom:
>
> Thank you for your letter of May 28, 197__.
>
> We were happy to approve benefits of $57.14 for your four days in the hospital. However, please refer to your policy. Under the Convalescent Rider, you are not eligible for home benefits unless you had a hospital stay of at least seven days. Since you were in the hospital only four days, I could not approve home benefits. I am happy, Mrs. Ransom, that you are now well and back at work. Please call or write if you have any other questions.

This letter, briefer than the original, has, we believe, a warm human tone, a clear statement of information, and effective organization. It informs without confusing; it rejects without alienating.

EXERCISES

1. As Vice-President of Sanders College in Seattle, Washington 98105, Dr. Marie Altman is conducting a search for a new Dean of the Business School. Over eighty people apply for the position. Write a form rejection letter to be sent to 79 of these applicants. Send an acceptance letter to the new Dean.

2. Martin G. Zagel, administrative assistant to Dudley Wynn, a State Senator from Baltimore, Maryland 21229, usually handles all office mail. He sends out most letters from the Senator's office in Annapolis, Maryland 21402. The Senator is entitled under state law to award four state scholarships each year. These scholarships, worth around $11,000 over a four year period, enable a student to attend his choice of seven state colleges and universities. The intense competition for these awards results in four pleased families and many disappointed ones. Compose announcement letters to both groups.

3. As Personnel Director for the Limeblast Construction Company, 13 Granite Run, Portsmouth, New Hampshire 03801 you have a problem. There are two candidates for the position of equipment salesman: Bart Natoli of 3108 Prudence Boulevard, a bright, personable young man with five years of sales experience; and Andrew Coughlin of 63 Jefferson Way, an indifferent, singularly unpleasant young man who happens to be Mr. Limeblast's favorite nephew. Write Natoli an acceptance letter, and Coughlin a rejection.

ADJUSTMENT LETTERS

We have separated our discussion of "Acceptance and Refusal Letters" from "Adjustment Letters," but it should be obvious that this is merely an artificial division. Both writing situations are similar and potentially troublesome. In either situation you must usually place great stress on tone and organize your letters in terms of the "Yes-No" psychology. Remember, "adjustment" is just a neutral word for "claim" or "complaint."

Imagine yourself in the position of seeking an adjustment or responding to a customer's demand for one. If you are the person seeking an adjustment, concentrate on the person receiving your letter. Remember that another person is on the receiving end, not some nameless, faceless machine that will simply spin a few magnetic tapes to solve all your problems. Remember too that most people appreciate common courtesy, so don't be rude or sarcastic at your reader's expense. Simply communicate your basic grievance in as clear and direct a way as possible. Marshall all the facts (order number, date of purchase, price, condition, etc.) and, if necessary, assist your adjuster by supplying copies of relevant documents. For instance, examine the following letter in Figure 8.16 to a credit card center. Communications like this that are complete with details of purchase, account number, etc., are likely to hasten the adjustment process.

Now let's reverse roles and make you the receiver of an adjustment letter. As you might guess, these can be sarcastic, vehemently angry, even crudely obscene. Your reply, however, should never attempt to match blows. No matter how angry or offended you are, it does little good (and possibly much harm) to display such feelings, and difficult though it may be, you should be courteous, tactful, and helpful. We might heed the advice of Sir Ernest Gowers, an authority on communication: "If he [the writer] is rude, be specially courteous. If he is muddle-headed, be specially lucid.

If he is pig-headed, be patient. If he is helpful, be appreciative . . . . But never let a flavour of the patronising creep in."[4]

Be reasonable in your attitude toward customer complaints. You can't assume that all claims are valid and immediately comply with the customer's wishes; neither should you suppose that every author of an adjustment letter is a foolish, lying cheat. Regard each letter as an opportunity—an opportunity to discover and remedy defects in your goods or services, and an opportunity to build or reinforce good will among your customers. Assume too that the customer has a legitimate problem; otherwise he would not have taken the time to write. Even if he is mistaken or misinformed or (in a small percentage of cases) lying, always be tactful and patient. Nothing is gained by your losing your temper or being in any way less than diplomatic and pleasant.

Dear Sir:

    I would appreciate your checking the attached bill for December 8, 197__. You indicate that I owe $17.20 for a purchase of 34 gallons of gasoline at Harbison's Auto Center on Richardson Highway. The original statement (copy attached), however, indicates that in fact I purchased but 14.4 gallons for $7.20 (a more realistic amount for my 1973 Valiant).

    I look forward to hearing from you regarding this matter.

                                 Burt Wolfson

                                 Account #120-391-876

Figure 8.16.

In order to save money, some firms send out obvious form letters to complaining customers, while others send form letters that are not so obvious (see Figures A.13 and A.3 in the appendices for examples). As we have stressed before, there is nothing wrong with formulas. It's smart to formulate openings and closings and set paragraphs that you can apply to various situations, and many companies have such formulas on computer tapes and use them frequently. Yet you must be certain that the formula is a clear, courteous one, and one that applies to the particular situation you're dealing with. If it doesn't, the reader will know you are using a routine letter and may well resent the fact. After all, his letter to you is personal and in no way canned. To suggest that you are casual or indifferent toward the customer's needs may result in future billing statements being folded, spindled, and mutilated.

Let's now apply our theories to particular cases. In our first one (Figure 8.17), a distraught elderly customer writes to Margaret Adams, Director of Quality Control for the Omega Packaging Company.

Well, anyone who has struggled with safety caps on medicine bottles can sympathize with Mr. Halsted. But Omega is not totally to blame. Under Title 15, section 1473b of the United States Code, the Federal Government requires safety packaging of drugs to avoid the possible poisoning of small children. However, this same law allows for "noncomplying packages," usually for elderly or infirm patients, in homes where there are no small children.

Mrs. Adams should be aware of these facts, yet nevertheless she sends Mr. Halsted the reply shown in Figure 8.18.

---

4. Sir Ernest Gowers, *Plain Words: Their ABC.* New York: Alfred A. Knopf, Inc. 1957.

Dear Mrs. Adams:

The operator gave me your name when I called the other day, but you weren't around, so I am writing this letter. I am 67 and my arthritis hurts real bad, especially on rainy days, and Dorinol, which my Doctor gave me, helps a lot. But I have the darndest time gittin those fool caps off the bottle. Can't you people fix things better than this. I had to break the bottle to get some relief the other day. The old caps were fine, so why did you change them? I don't see any damn use in buying pills I can't get at. Please do something.

Art Halsted

Figure 8.17.

Dear Mr. Halsted:

I am in receipt of your letter in which you claim to have had difficulty with our safety caps on bottles of Dorinol.

While I regret your difficulty, I must point out that the cap with which you have struggled is a result of recent legislation which requires a child resistant closure for any prescription product which may be dispensed to a consumer for use in the household in its original container. The purpose, of course, is to reduce risk of child poisonings.

The packaging industry was not fully prepared to meet the new federal regulations. Closures such as the one in discussion were the only ones approved for use at the time. Conversion of packaging procedures to comply with this closure requirement created problems such as you have described. As you can see, the problem has been caused not by us, but by the federal government. We are sorry you were dissatisfied, but we can only say that we are working on the problem. Realistically it may be several months before a solution can be effected which will relieve the difficulties in all pharmacies.

We regret the situation and ask you to be patient.

Margaret Adams

Figure 8.18.

Mr. Halsted will probably find this letter offensive—and for good reason. In fact, it is a model of how *not* to write an adjustment letter. Consider the implication and tone of some of Mrs. Adam's words and phrases shown below. (Phrases in parentheses indicate similar negative expressions commonly found in adjustment letters.)

"You claim . . ."   Implies that he is a liar or is very confused.
(You allege; You assert; You state)   A possible substitute: "we understand that . . ."

"regret;" "dissatisfied" (neglected, failed, hereby deny)	Negative words that only intensify the customer's unhappiness.
"I must point out . . . "as you can see" (I am sure you will agree; I am not certain I understand)	Offensively patronising.
"caused not by us, but by . . ." (although we are not responsible . . .)	Buck passing.

Such expressions are hardly designed to create a cheerful, positive tone.

The alternative letter in Figure 8.19 would correct these and other problems:

Dear Mr. Halsted:

Thank you for taking the time to write and tell us about the difficulty you had opening our safety-closure caps on bottles of Dorinol.

We are very sorry that you had this experience with our package. Learning that there was a problem disturbed us, and prompted by your letter, we reviewed our production and packaging procedures to find out why there was a problem. That analysis has been fruitful and we expect to correct the situation in future production.

Until newer production lots reach your pharmacy, the following information may be useful: Title 15 of the United States Code, section 1473b allows pharmacists to dispense medication such as Dorinol in "noncomplying packages" (for instance, using a closure like the "old caps" mentioned in your letter) when a doctor directs or when requested by the purchaser. Please remember, however, that this should be done only in homes without young children.

We would like to send you a replacement package of Dorinol. If you will send us in the attached postage-paid envelope the name and address of your pharmacist, we will forward the package to him for delivery. Since this is a prescription item, we cannot send the Dorinol directly to you.

Again, we apologize for the difficulty you had, Mr. Halsted. We appreciate your bringing the problem to our attention. Improvements often depend on the type of constructive comments that you were thoughtful enough to share with us. Thank you again.

Margaret Adams

Figure 8.19.

In addition to being courteous, this letter takes the extra step of seriously trying to resolve Mr. Halsted's problem. It indicates how he might order containers without the safety caps, while at the same time warning him that this should not be done if young children are in the home. The letter also attempts to make Mr. Halsted feel good about writing. It suggests that he is not a bother, but an asset, for he has brought a serious problem to the attention of the company. Notice too that it is a sound policy to send him a new bottle of Dorinol. The cost to the company is minimal, and the public relations benefit is worth the cost. There is little likelihood that Mr. Halsted is writing merely to get a free bottle of pills (as some customers do). His complaint is a reasonable one and should be dealt with accordingly.

Of course, it is always easier to handle letters such as Mr. Halsted's where adjustments *can* be granted. It is more difficult to say "No," as must be done in the following situation (illustrated by Figure 8.20).

Policy Number ___883907___

Date ___5-24-7___

Dear Policyowner:

Your request to discontinue your plan has been referred to me for a reply.

However, as the request to cancel was not signed by you, our records have not yet been adjusted. Please sign the bottom portion of this letter and return the instructions to our office. We will give this matter our prompt attention.

Thank you for this opportunity to be of service.

Sincerely,

Tony Maynard
Special Services Division

Please make the necessary adjustments to discontinue plan ___A___.

Date *May 30, 1975* ___   Signature *Mrs Valerie Patton* ___

Please send back our premium of $21.80 for the month of April or the $133.32 in benefits we have coming. We have not paid for April because of the non-payment of benefits we have coming. We don't want to discontinue our insurance with you, but we think our claim was valid and you are mistaken. We can't continue with this kind of insurance that doesn't live up to what it says

Figure 8.20.

In response to an earlier request from her, the Titan Health Systems Corporation has sent Mrs. Valerie Patton a letter requesting her to sign a cancellation form. She signs and returns it with a handwritten note at the bottom, indicating that she is canceling her coverage because she is so upset over the company's failure to pay a previous claim. Titan's response to her complaint will be very important. If it sends her a courteous, informative letter, one which speaks directly to her grievances, she may well decide to continue with her insurance. She herself says "We don't want to discontinue our insurance," but she feels that the situation warrants this drastic move. Even if Titan can't get her to continue as a policyowner, it should attempt to restore her confidence in the company by being courteous and clear. An angry, dissatisfied policyowner is the worst kind of advertisement.

Assume that you are Charles Dougherty, a claims examiner handling this case. Checking the status sheet, you find that the reason Mrs. Patton's former claim was not paid was because she had wanted to collect on bills incurred in the treatment of a condition that had existed prior to the effective date of her policy. Therefore you write her the following letter, Figure 8.21.

Mrs. Valerie Patton
Telford Mobile Village
Tarkio, Missouri 64491

Re: Policy 883907

Dear Mrs. Patton:

Mr. Maynard has recently referred your letter to my attention. I am writing in reference to the claim that was submitted for your April 7, 1975 hospitalization.

Mrs. Patton, you may be aware that your policy has a contestable period of two years. This means that conditions that existed prior to its effective date can not be covered until your policy has been in effect for a period of two consecutive years. Your policy's effective date was March 12, 1975. On the claim form both you and your physician stated that your condition had been present since 1964. Furthermore, you stated that the tumor on your chest had been growing larger during that time. As you can see, your condition did exist prior to the effective date of your policy and therefore we are unable to extend benefits for this hospitalization.

I am sorry we were unable to help you at this time. If you should have any further questions regarding this matter, do not hesitate to notify me.

Sincerely,

Charles Dougherty
Supervisor
Claims Examining Department

CD/ak/1165

Figure 8.21.

In the insurance business failure to pay because of a pre-existing condition is common, and as a claims examiner you may write this kind of letter hundreds of times, but you must remember that this is the first time Mrs. Patton has ever received one. You must beware of allowing a bored, routine tone to creep into your communication. Treat every case as you would want it treated were you the claimant.

In general, Dougherty does a good job, but his letter could use some revision. Read it over again in order that you might offer some constructive criticism.

How about that first paragraph? We have encountered a similar situation before. Remember how we handled it? A better formula would be: "Thank you for your letter to Mr. Maynard; he has asked me to give it my personal attention." This is preferable to the exaggeratedly cold and formal "I am in receipt of," and it is more personal than Dougherty's original, which implies that Mr. Maynard is passing the buck.

Dougherty improves with his second paragraph, especially in its psychological structure. Rather than immediately beginning with "we are unable to extend benefits," Dougherty attempts a clear explanation of the reasons for the denial of the claim. This "Slow No" is designed to convince Mrs. Patton of the rationale for the rejection. If she sees the "No" immediately she will probably discard the letter or read on in an upset state. Dougherty also personalizes his letter by referring to the policyowner by name. Then he explains "pre-existing condition" clearly without relying on a great deal of jargon. His only problem is that he doesn't go far enough, doesn't take the extra step to insure a complete, careful answer. Therefore, we have to recommend some changes.

After his sentence, "Your policy's effective date was March 12, 1975," we would revise his original in the following manner:

> . . . Your policy's effective date was March 12, 1975; therefore, no condition that existed prior to March 12, 1975 can be covered until March 12, 1977. On the claim form both you and your physician stated that your condition has been present since 1964. Furthermore, you stated that the tumor on your chest had been growing larger during that time. Thus your condition did exist prior to March 12, 1975.

> Of course, all conditions not existing before March 12, 1975 were covered, and it is for this reason that we are unable to return your payment. I am sorry we were unable to help you at this time, but would remind you that this fine policy will cover future claims on this condition after March 12, 1977. I hope you will reconsider canceling your policy.

Our revision deals with the matters that Dougherty originally completely overlooked—Mrs. Patton's cancellation request and her request for the premium payment. She might have thought that Titan Health Systems was dodging those matters and have been prompted to send in another angry letter. Also, we added a few sentences to clarify the "pre-existing condition" problem. You must be certain that no confusion will result from your letters, even if it takes a few extra sentences to be sure everything is perfectly clear. Better to take the extra time at first than to have to write again.

EXERCISES

D. ADJUSTMENT LETTERS

1. Thomas Quigley, 82 Johnson Avenue, Muncie, Indiana 47306 orders a pair of size 11-C tennis shoes from Babson's Sporting Goods P. O. Box 313, Knoxville, Tennessee 37916 for his vacation which starts on July 20. The shoes arrive on July 19, but they are size 9-B. Write a letter of complaint to Babson's. Compose the adjustment letter from Babson.

2. As Richard Finneran, 8 Calmar Drive, Houston, Texas 77004, write to Techtron Systems, Inc., 43 Hilldale Road, Norman, Oklahoma 73069. The picture tube on your $950 color TV just burned out for the third time in fourteen months. The first two failures were corrected by the local shop (Coleman's Radio and Television Store, 93 Jackson Heights, Houston, Texas 77004), but the year's warranty has now expired and Coleman refuses to be responsible for the repairs; he suggests instead that you write Techtron.

3. In the previous case, write a response to Mr. Finneran. Assume you are Elaine Fromm, Director of Customer Service for Techtron. Indicate that a wiring problem has caused the picture tubes to burn up and that the company is working to correct this flaw. Suggest that he return his set to Coleman's and that Techtron will be responsible for all repairs.

4. Carl F. Samuelson of 83 Cedar Drive, Cleveland, Ohio 44118 is so upset over the condition of a T-38 pocket calculator that he ordered by mail for $49.50 that he returns it to Carson Electronics, 651 Terrence Boulevard, Flushing, New York 11367, with the following note: "This damn thing stinks. Send my money back!" While the manufacturer did advertise the item with a money-back guarantee if not completely satisfied, Mr. Robert J. Carson would like to discover exactly why Mr. Samuelson disliked the calculator; the item returned seems to be in good condition. Write a letter from him to Mr. Samuelson.

5. Thomas Youngblood is the Vice President of Consumer Relations for the Better Taste Baking Company at Merchandise Mart Circle in Flint, Michigan 48503. How should he handle the following letter?

> Dear Sir:
>
> I am not a very happy consumer of your Better Taste Chocolate Chip cookies. I refer to the fact that the individually sealed packages in which the cookies are wrapped tend to fall apart easily in use or come unsealed in the box. The result is that the cookies tear out of their cellophane and tumble to the bottom of the box, thus making them stale. This has been the case with the last two boxes of these cookies that I have purchased. I would appreciate your looking into this matter.

Mr. Youngblood must explain that this is the first such complaint he has received. He asks the customer to send future packets that are similarly troublesome. The company will repay the customer for any cost involved. Write his letter to the customer, Mr. Hal Wyatt, 318 River Road, San Francisco, California 94132.

6. Woodruff Color Laboratories P. O. Box 4289 in Parkersburg, West Virginia 26104 specializes in rapid, low-cost film processing. Their business is 98 percent mail-order. Andrew DaCrema, 18 Kindall Lane, Charlottesville, Virginia 22903 has been dealing with this firm for five years, but on his last order Woodruff failed to make prints of five different pictures requested by Mr.

DaCrema, who noted them on his original order form. Write a claim letter from Mr. DaCrema and an adjustment letter from Thomas Woodruff.

7. Use the following facts in seeking an adjustment from Wittenberg's Hardware Store, Reboth Road, Kalispell, Montana 59901: on October 25 you purchased a can of antifreeze for $5.79 in their Glendive store and subsequently returned it for credit on October 27 (credit voucher #962726). The November credit statement charged you for the $5.79 and you paid it (check #815, Montana National Bank). You are writing on January 20 because neither your December or January statements have recorded the credit.

8. Assume the customer in the previous case is Caroline Dawson of 97 Olive Lane in Glendive, Montana 59330. As Beverly Johnson, Credit Department Supervisor for Wittenberg Hardware, respond to Ms. Dawson's letter. The credit was never recorded because of a computer break-down. It will be adjusted on the February statement.

COLLECTION LETTERS

We have not yet achieved a cashless society, but we are not too far from it. More and more we have less need for cash, especially when making substantial purchases. We have American Express, Carte Blanche, BankAmericard, Diner's Club, Master Charge, and individual credit cards for hundreds of airlines, hotels, restaurants, service stations, and department stores. We can direct our bank to pay automatically a variety of bills—from home mortgages to electric rates. We can use food coupons, drink coupons, gasoline coupons, store coupons. These conveniences of modern commerce mean that most purchases involve not a cash transfer, but a signing of one's name. And since many people are not paying on the spot for goods or services they buy, credit has become an important industry.

Most credit accounts are billed monthly—often on the first of the month. Paying the entire account when it comes due prevents monthly service charges, but otherwise one remits a portion of the balance and pays a service charge, usually ranging from 15 to 18 percent per annum. In some cases, especially those involving orders from manufacturers and wholesale houses, the full amount must be paid when the bill comes due.

People who fail to pay their bills generally fall into one of the following categories:

1. Those who did not receive or neglected to notice their bill;
2. Those who because of a financial setback or other misfortune are unable to pay;
3. Those who can pay but are slow doing so;
4. Those who can pay but must be forced to do so;
5. Those who never intended to pay.

The majority of collection letters will be sent to those in categories 2, 3, and 4. Only in rare instances do customers fall into categories 1 and 5.

A good collection letter must collect money while retaining the customer's good will. Besides being diplomatic and persuasive, the writer must employ sound psychology. Remember that embarrassing people alienates them, angering them incurs their wrath, threatening them makes them defensive and hostile. You may be angry because your books do not balance at the end of the month, but don't vent your frustration on the customer and regard him simply as a source of disorder in your life. Good reasons may exist for his failure to pay and, if so, you should attempt to understand them. Before writing, try to place yourself in the customer's predicament; then you will be less likely to corner him. Give him room to maneuver and save face; give him options instead of ultimatums.

Of course, there are limits to one's patience. Good business practice (as well as good psychology) dictates that you must eventually be firm and forceful in demanding your money. After all, you have your own bills to meet, and too many delinquent accounts will seriously reduce your cash flow and undermine your own financial position. But always remember to move by stages in the collection process and to allow your customer enough time and freedom to settle his own debts.

A. STEP I: REMINDER

The reminder need not even be a letter. You can simply send a duplicate of the bill with "Second Notice" or "Reminder" or "Account Overdue" stamped on it. Often a number of the large credit companies send a brief billing sheet listing the present balance, the amount to be remitted, and a few sentences, such as:

> YOUR EAGLE CREDIT PAYMENT HAS NOT BEEN RECEIVED
> Please insure that your credit rating is protected. Remit the amount due as soon as possible.
> Thank you.

Somewhere on the sheet you will usually find a note saying, "Please disregard this notice if payment has been made."

B. STEP II: FOLLOW-UP

Again, policy differs from company to company. Some may simply send another duplicate of the bill with "Third Notice" or "Final Reminder" stamped on it. Others may send a brief note. In either case be friendly and imply that the customer has merely overlooked the payment.

> Overdue bills can create awkward situations. Why not send us your payment today?
>
> Please keep your credit record perfect by remitting the overdue charge.
>
> Your check for $91.17 will be very welcome. Please send it as soon as possible.
>
> We know you will want to order more goods from our fall catalogue. So please clear your present account by sending us today your check for $109.13.
>
> Just a friendly reminder that your check for $67.50 due September 9 has not yet reached us.
>
> You will sleep better knowing that your check for $35.86 is in the mail to us.
>
> Help us clear up our records. Please send your check for $73.50 today.

The tone of the above notices is friendly and positive. They tactfully point out that money is overdue, while suggesting to the customer that it is to *his* benefit to pay as soon as possible. They imply not that "costs of handling overdue bills lose the company a great deal of money," but rather that "prompt payment helps reduce the cost of our merchandise to our customers." Notice though that there is an implied threat in these otherwise pleasant letters: credit ratings may be damaged, future orders will not be honored, embarrassment will result, sleep will be lost. The reader should be able to read between the lines. You need not be blunt or sharp with him—just provide a gentle nudge. Then if your nudges are insufficient motivation, you must move on to the next stage (remembering that it becomes increasingly more difficult to collect money as time passes).

C. STEP III: STRONGER FOLLOW-UP

You still should be courteous, but much more forceful and direct. Try to spell out the facts as clearly as possible:

> Your account is now two months past due. We provided quality merchandise that apparently pleased you, so please send us your check for $97.50 in today's mail.

> You agreed to pay all account balances on the first of every month. We sent you your bill for $164.29 on April 1 but received no response. We then sent you notices on April 15 and May 10. Still no response. We dislike bothering you this way, so please send us your check immediately.

> It has been four weeks since our second reminder about your overdue balance of $37.50. We have been patient and fair. We ask you to be the same and send us your check today.

D. STEP IV: POSSIBLE COMPROMISE

As we suggested earlier, you must always be reasonable. But at this stage you may be angry. You've wasted time and postage sending nice reminders to someone who hasn't sent either money or an explanation. "Well," you decide, "that shiftless no-good had time enough. On to the courts." But before that final, drastic step, try one more approach. Perhaps the customer has not simply ignored your pleas. Perhaps he has been distracted by a terrible family disaster or financial setback, or both. Give him a chance to explain and offer to work out a payment schedule. This way you may not get all of your money immediately, but at least you might get part of it.

Possible compromise letters might be written along these lines:

> I am worried that you have failed to answer our previous letters. Knowing your past payment record to be excellent, I feel that you may have encountered some difficulty. Why not call or come by to see me? I am certain we can make some reasonable arrangement regarding your unpaid bill.

> Please write or call to tell us why you have not met your obligations. We are open to suggestions on a new payment schedule.

> Undoubtedly, there is a good reason for your overdue account. Why not pay a portion of it now and indicate when you can send us the rest?

> Many of our best customers have encountered financial difficulties in the past. We have worked together to help resolve such problems. Why not drop by to talk things over? Perhaps we can do the same for you.

E. STEP V: LAST CHANCE

Finally, if even the calm reasonableness of Step IV proves ineffectual, then you have no other recourse than to offer an ultimatum. You have exhausted your patience. Now, while still being forceful without being rude or hostile, you become more open in your threats. Phrases should appear in your writing such as "stern measures," "action will be taken," "no recourse but," etc. It is also imperative to set a precise course of action—the "pay by this date or else" approach.

> We regret that our previous letters have gone ignored. Unless we receive $57.19 from you by March 18, we will be forced to resort to legal action.

> We dislike filing a bad credit report to the Central Credit Commission, for it means that you will be unable to secure future credit at most stores. However, your failure to pay the $116.98 you owe us leaves us no alternative. Unless this money is in our hands by December 4, we must file this report.

> Your failure to live up to a valid contract and pay us the $186.49 due on your account is very disturbing. Unless this money reaches us within the week, we will turn the matter over to our attorneys, Henchman & Taggart. They will advise you when suit has been commenced.

Let's see how the steps outlined above can be applied in a particular situation. Mr. Clendon Thomas had been a good customer of Kroger's Department store for the past three years, and he agreed to make three monthly installment payments of $250 each on a new refrigerator. He made his February and March payments but missed his April payment. Over the period of the next two months he will receive the five collection letters shown in Figures 8.22, 8.23, 8.24, 8.25, and 8.26.

I.

April 15, 197___

Dear Customer:

Just a friendly reminder that your installment payment is now past due. We must receive your payment immediately to protect your fine credit rating.

Sincerely,

Henry T. Putnam
Credit Director
Time Payment Accounts

Figure 8.22.

II.

May 1, 197___

Dear Sir:

Everyone overlooks matters, and it is especially tempting to neglect those bills that come due each month. We have the same temptations, but we must meet our obligations or go out of business.

You can help prevent that. Please submit your April payment, which is now a month over-due. You will be glad you did (and so will we).

Sincerely,

Henry T. Putnam

Figure 8.23.

III.

May 15, 197__

Dear Mr. Thomas:

On January 10, 197__ you agreed to pay us three straight monthly payments of $250 in return for the delivery of a new Benson Refrigerator-Freezer. You received this merchandise on January 15, but have since made only two payments. You received two previous notices regarding this oversight, but took no action. We would appreciate your sending us the third payment of $250 as soon as possible.

Thank you.

Henry T. Putnam

Figure 8.24.

IV.

June 1, 197__

Dear Mr. Thomas:

I have sent you notices on April 15, May 1, and May 15 regarding the amount due on your account.

I realize that customers sometimes are unable to meet obligations for various important reasons. This must be the case with you since you have always been an excellent customer. Kroger's tries to be reasonable. Why not do one of two things:

1) Submit in the attached postage-paid envelope a portion of the amount overdue and a schedule of when you can pay the remainder;

2) Arrange to see me to discuss this matter.

I look forward to hearing from you.

Henry T. Putnam

Figure 8.25.

V.

June 15, 197__

Dear Mr. Thomas:

    I had hoped you would take the advice in my letter of May 15. But, since I received no word or payment from you, I am forced to hand the entire matter over to our legal department. Unless we receive $250 by June 22, our lawyers will commence suit.

    I regret taking this action, but you leave me no alternative.

Henry T. Putnam

Figure 8.26.

EXERCISES

1. Tillman's Shoe Warehouse, 8975 Rodman Way, Lafayette, Indiana 47907, supplies shoes to local stores. They have a well-earned reputation for speed and reliability. Thomas Barger, owner of Barger's Shoes, 112 Seltzer Drive, Lafayette, Indiana 47907, has been a customer of Tillman's for three years. His account allows him to charge all goods with full payment in thirty days. On January 15 he receives a shipment of brown loafers, black wing-tips, and tennis shoes; the total charge is $472.86. Five days before the bill is due, Tillman's sends Mr. Barger a standard reminder. February 15 passes with no payment made. Robert Tillman becomes concerned around March 1 and sends a friendly reminder, but still no response. Compose the letter that Mr. Tillman should send around April 1. Assuming no response, what letter should be sent on April 25?

2. Miss Eileen Short, the Credit Manager for Bomar Oil Company, 83 Sunset Boulevard, Miami, Florida 33054, finally receives a response from Mr. Curt Ellis, who has been overdue on his account for two months. Owner of Curt's Service Station, he owes Bomar $873 for gasoline shipments. Miss Short has sent two reminder letters, the first on March 18—one month after the bill was due—and the second on April 3. Mr. Ellis writes on April 18. He apologizes for the delay, encloses a check for $250 and requests a new shipment of fuel. Compose Miss Short's reply.

3. You are business manager for Tomlinson's Sweater Company, Carson Circle, Birmingham, Alabama 35333. Mr. Morris Kibler owns the Goodwear Clothing Store, 380 Regent Road, Bristol, Tennessee 37622. He has ordered sweaters from Tomlinson's for the past twenty years and has paid all charges within thirty days. Yet he has suddenly become delinquent in his payments. You have already sent him two notices, but have received no response. It is now four months since the bill for $659.41 was due. Remember that Mr. Kibler has been an excellent customer for the past twenty years. How would you handle this problem in a third letter?

4. In the previous situation, you write Mr. Kibler a courteous, straightforward third letter, but still receive no response. Compose a fourth letter. Stress your desire to arrange an easier payment schedule. Point out your friendly business relationship over the years.

5. Mr. Kibler still fails to communicate with you, and the bill is now six months overdue. Compose a final warning, but keep in mind that he may still have a good reason and that you would like to retain his business.

6. *Creditor:* Klassen's Candy Company, 816 Ridge Avenue, Burlington, Vermont 05401. *Client:* Singer's Sweet Shop, 201 Paramus Road, Vineland, New Jersey 08360. Klassen's is a young company. Attempting to build up a volume of sales, it is offering attractive discounts and easy credit terms. Singer's takes advantage of this by ordering on credit a $452 supply of butter creams, chocolate eggs, peppermint sticks, and peanut brittle. Klassen's sends Mrs. Helen Singer a routine reminder when the bill comes due on September 9. One month later you must compose a second letter. Try to discover if Mrs. Singer was not satisfied with her first order.

7. Mrs. Singer does not answer this second letter. Compose a third response in which you diplomatically suggest that if she pays immediately you will still honor her future credit purchases. Stress too the advantages of dealing with Klassen's; they offer good products at a reasonable price.

Chapter 9

THE ART OF DICTATION

Mend your speech a little, lest it may mar your fortunes.

—King Lear

More than twenty years ago a magazine called *Advertising Age* estimated that letter writing was costing businesses around $12,000,000 each day. In 1962, the Federal Government estimated that the cost involved in having a GS-14 executive (then making around $15,000 a year) plan, dictate, and sign a 175-word letter ran to around $4.81. Allowing for even a mild inflation, much less the leaping, bounding inflation we have experienced in some years, you can understand why it is necessary to learn to write letters effectively in order to reduce or keep such costs under control. The art of careful dictation also provides one such control.

As a person in business, you will dictate most of your letters either to a secretary or to a machine. Try to remember which you're dealing with! Also keep in mind the three essential stages in effective dictation.

A. BEFORE DICTATING

1. Make sure you are able to write a clear letter with good tone, information, organization, spelling, and grammar before attempting dictation. You should not depend on your secretary's ability to revise and organize your random thoughts; thus a quick outline on paper—even just a listing of thoughts in proper sequence—will facilitate the actual dictation. This is especially important if you want your first dictation to be the finished one. Otherwise it might be helpful to dictate spontaneously and then rework the rough draft at your leisure. We especially recommend the latter procedure for those people frightened by the dictaphone or tape recorder. Only continual practice will make you confident with these machines. As a Navy pamphlet on the subject once noted, "dictating a letter is a little like driving a car or kissing a girl: once he gets a little experience, every operator thinks he's an expert."

2. Have the incoming letter at hand (with marginal notes) if you are responding to one. Also, have available any additional figures, reference material, diagrams, etc. you might need. Finally, make certain that the dictation equipment is ready to use.

B. WHILE DICTATING

1. Be certain to give adequate instructions concerning the communication you are dictating. Is it an interoffice memo or a formal letter? Do you desire a rough or finished copy? How many copies will be necessary, and to whom should these carbons be sent?

2. Specify correct spelling and punctuation. Spell out names and addresses, indicate where capitalization is required, and where there is unusual punctuation. Be certain also to indicate when you are correcting earlier dictation. Indicate where new paragraphs are needed.

3. Try to be as natural as possible when dictating. Speak clearly without being too fast or slow, loud or soft. Don't dictate while eating, smoking, drinking, or fumbling with papers.

4. Don't allow the machine to run while you are thinking of what to say. This causes long pauses on the tape. The machine may also pick up disconcerting background noise that may confuse your secretary.

5. Dictate complete thoughts rather than a disordered collection of words and phrases. THINK before speaking!

C. AFTER DICTATING

1. Turn off the machine, or dismiss your secretary.

2. Check carefully all copies that are returned for your signature. Remember that you are responsible for what you sign. If corrections are necessary, make them clearly and be considerate. Remember that time, money, and your secretary's good humor are saved if she does not need to retype the entire letter. Give verbal instructions regarding minor mistakes or pencil them in lightly.

DICTATION CHECKLIST

I. Preparation
   1. Is this letter really necessary?
   2. What is its purpose?
   3. Do I have a clear sense of my reader?
   4. Have I briefly outlined what I wish to say?
   5. Are my notes or other reference materials readily available?
   6. Is my dictating equipment in working order?
   7. Am I certain I know how to operate it?

II. Delivery
   1. Is this to be a rough draft or a finished copy?
   2. Are there additional instructions?
      a. type of communication?
      b. recipients?
      c. additional copies?
      d. special stationery?
   3. Am I speaking naturally and clearly?
      a. too fast or too slow?
      b. too loud or too soft?
      c. enunciating clearly?
      d. running words together?
      e. smoking, eating, etc. while speaking?
   4. Do I give precise instructions as I dictate?
      a. precise spelling of names, addresses, medical terms, other difficult words?
      b. corrections?
      c. special punctuation?
      d. paragraph divisions?
      e. proper salutation?
   5. Do I dictate complete thoughts?
   6. Do I turn off the machine when not dictating?

III. Corrections
   1. Do I read the final version carefully?
   2. Am I considerate when only minor corrections are needed?
   3. Does my signature match the heading in tone?
   4. Did I compliment my secretary for doing a good job?

Part III
A WRITER'S HANDBOOK

Chapter 10

INTRODUCTION

Back in Part I we suggested that most people are either nervous or routinely careless about writing when they should be creatively relaxed. Think for a minute about playing baseball or tennis. In both games the object is to propel a ball from point A to point B. But, when you're at bat or preparing to serve, if you worry about your ability to perform the series of movements necessary to connect with the ball, you are likely to strike out or double fault. The trick in these sports is to have enough confidence so that you can relax and concentrate on the ball rather than on your execution of the movements. So, in sports the solution to nervousness is practice, and in writing, too, the answer is practice. Practice builds your confidence, and allows you to relax and redirect your major concern from the mechanics of producing a message to the nature of the message itself. The main barrier to creatively relaxed writing is, we think, an excessive concern with mechanical correctness, notably with grammar and punctuation.

A few years back, Carl Reiner and Mel Brooks had a comedy routine featuring Mel as "The Two Thousand-Year-Old Man." Carl played a news reporter. Carl asked the Two Thousand-Year-Old Man if he had known the great writer Shakespeare, and Mel replied that he had known him, but he hotly denied that he was a good writer. Carl was incredulous and pressed for an explanation; whereupon Mel calmly explained that Shakespeare had had very sloppy penmanship and got ink blots all over the pages of his manuscripts. The best comedy is firmly rooted in reality, and like The Two Thousand-Year-Old Man many people are so preoccupied with mere correctness that they have little awareness of and no skill with the more sophisticated techniques of communication.

Many would-be writers undergo a kind of creative paralysis worrying about grammar and punctuation. Very often they verbalize their fears by saying something like "I don't know any *grammar.*" But what they really mean is that they have experienced difficulty with the ticklish points of *formal usage,* such as whether to say "I don't mind *him* using my car" or "I don't mind *his* using my car." (The correct version is "his using" and the formal rule is that one should use the possessive case with a gerund.)

The truth is that people who complain about not knowing any grammar really know an enormous amount. Linguistics experts estimate that the average person follows five or six grammar rules during every second of normal, fluent speech.[1] How can this be? Well, grammar can be defined very basically as the conventional rules governing the way we put words together to make coherent statements. There is a good deal of grammatical expertise required even to formulate a simple statement like "I see the cat." How many other ways can these four words be rearranged and still form a coherent statement?

1. I the cat see.

2. See I the cat.

3. See the cat I.

4. Cat I the see.

The first version makes sense, but anyone whose mother tongue is English would reject it as being too stilted and unnatural. The second combination might, by a very charitable stretch of the imagination, be said to make a kind of sense, but it is more than simply unnatural—it is positively bizarre. Versions three and four are completely incoherent, and it would take a mathematician to calculate just how many more incomprehensible combinations of these four words are theoretically possible. To combine these four words in a *comprehensible* sequence, however, does require following rules of grammar, and so it is that anyone who can order a cheeseburger or ask the way to city hall has to know "grammar." The few rules that really give people trouble represent no more than the tip of an iceberg when you consider how many conventions of language logic you began, painlessly and unconsciously, to learn from the first moment you heard English spoken. So take heart in the vast knowledge you already have.

In Chapters 11 and 12 we will discuss the most troublesome points of grammar, and how to master the difficulties they present. You've probably been hearing about these problem areas ever since you started school. They include sentence construction, phrases, clauses, and parts of speech, and if you are like most people, you are still a little hazy about them. However, if you want to be confident of your ability to handle these persistent grammatical trouble spots, you must eventually come to grips with the basic ways in which the parts of an English sentence—like an automobile transmission—mesh and function together. But once again, take heart, for you already have a vast subconscious knowledge of grammar, and consciously learning the grammar you need for relaxed writing is a lot easier than reassembling a transmission.

The speed and ease with which people learn things increase in direct proportion to their need to know. Therefore, the reason you may still be a little vague about the difference between an adverb and an adjective is that you never really had a gut-level conviction that you needed that bit of knowledge. But if you climb up the promotional ladder to the point where you must write frequently, you will very quickly acquire the necessary grammatical expertise. Necessity is the mother of facility.

Punctuation is another facet of correctness that inhibits the creative relaxation necessary for effective written communication. Chapter 13 will, we hope, clarify most of the important punctuation rules. Just about everything we've said about grammatical correctness applies to punctuation too, including the fact that to be at ease with the problem you must understand the elements of sentence construction. We do, however, have a couple of practical tips on the subject we want to present here.

The first is that punctuation marks are not decoration; they are indispensable signposts to aid your reader in understanding your writing. Though there are many finicky rules about punctuation, the most important rule is simply that punctuation is designed to help your reader grasp your meaning.

---

1. Martin Joos, "Language and the School Child," *Word Study,* XL (December, 1964), p. 4.

The second thing to remember about punctuation is that, while it is designed to convey meaning, it does so through the technique of silence. Consider that written communication is in a sense an unnatural act: man spoke for thousands of years before he wrote. You have only to listen to your friends' conversation to realize how important such things as gestures, facial expressions, tone shifts, and pauses are to oral communication. Punctuation marks are like musical notations indicating pauses of one duration or another, and these pauses convey meaning. If you're ever in doubt about whether you should use a comma at a certain point in your writing, and you can't bring to mind the particular rule that applies, just try reading the sentence in question aloud. If you find yourself pausing at any given point, it is likely that you should have a comma there. If, on the other hand, you find yourself passing smoothly over the spot in question, you probably don't need a comma. (Note: This applies only if you're a fairly normal reader. If you're a speedreader, or one who pauses after every couple of words, forget this tip immediately!)

Finally, Chapters 14 and 15 relate to style and usage. By themselves they may not instantly transform you into a capable writer, but taken together with the rest of this text they offer a number of hints on how to improve your writing style and your use of language. We have a friend, for instance, who evaluates a person's intelligence simply by how that person uses "imply" and "infer." Any confusion in their use, he feels, constitutes enough evidence of language laziness or incipient cretinism to brand someone a dullard. Our Chapter 15, "Word Problems," will help you avoid being so labeled. Chapter 14, "Style Points," elaborates on some issues of style that were mentioned earlier in the text—transitions, parallel structure, etc. The section on "Wordiness," for example suggests ways to reduce a complex, formidable report of twenty pages into a clear, readable one of ten pages. Most bosses, if they must read reports, would rather read a ten- than a twenty-page one. So take heed!

To help you determine your major areas of strength and weakness in grammar, punctuation, and usage, we have designed the Diagnostic Test that follows. Take the test and then begin working to strengthen yourself in those areas you find difficult.

Chapter 11

In Chapter 10 we defined grammar as "the conventional rules governing the way we put words together to make coherent statements," and we went on to give you the good news that we've all managed easily and unconsciously to learn most of these rules. We've got more news about grammar now and some of it's good and some of it's bad. The good news is that we believe that there are only four major problem areas in grammar:

1. *Number*—distinguishing between the singular and plural forms of words.

2. *Case*—indicating whether words are to be regarded as *subjective* (sometimes called *nominative*), *objective,* or *possessive.* Fortunately, in English only pronouns are declined for all three cases.

3. *Agreement*—establishing a correspondence in gender, number, person, or case between words—chiefly between verbs and their subjects, and pronouns and their antecedents.

4. *Tense*—indicating the time in which the actions of verbs take place or are completed.

Now the bad news is that these four areas comprise only the *major* areas of grammatical trouble. If we restricted our study to these four areas, we would still fail to give you a grasp of the overall theory of English grammar, for you do need overall theory to solve problems in number, case, agreement and tense with any confidence. In fact, you may have already been troubled by certain terms we have used to designate and define the basic problem areas. What, you may have wondered, does *decline* mean? What the devil is an *antecedent*? We'll come to that, but in this chapter we're going to review some of the overall theories of grammar. Those four specific problem areas are going to wait. We'll get to them in Chapter 12, but for now let's take first things first.

We wish that we, like the matchbook ads that promise to teach you how to perform brain surgery at home for fun and profit, could tell you that we have a surefire formula for mastering a complex subject overnight. We have no such formula. We are going to require you to do quite a bit of work in the following pages—to master quite a few definitions, to grasp a number of word relationships, and to perform a good many practical exercises, all of which relate to overall theory. We do, however, promise to keep this chapter as simple as possible. We'll concentrate only on those points that, in our experience, are needed to make you not a theoretical grammarian, but a writer who is reasonably confident of his grammar.

Everything we are going to cover reviews familiar material. Of course, there is a difference between being familiar with something and knowing it well. We hope you do know the basic theory and terminology of grammar, but even if you do, a little review can do you no harm. The very best golf and tennis professionals consistently work on their basic strokes. And, if you never have learned this basic material, to be able to troubleshoot your own communications difficulties it's important that you learn it now.

Knowing the elementary terminology of any craft is one good sign of its mastery. Would you trust your car to a mechanic who didn't use the term *carburetor,* but instead kept referring to the "thing that shoots gas into the system"? If you were a manager would you entrust any important communications responsibility to someone who couldn't distinguish between a noun and a verb? No? Then let's start learning some grammar.

To begin with, the subject of grammar can be broken down into two basic considerations—*syntax* and *inflection.* **Syntax** is the way in which groups of words are put together to form coherent units of thought, or the way in which phrases and clauses fit together to form sentences. **Inflection** comes from the same root as *flex* (to bend) and it describes the ways in which individual words are bent or changed to indicate different meaning relationships. On a practical level, we may be said to inflect a word when we change the way it's spelled in order to indicate different grammatical relationships: we *decline* pronouns, (**I, me, my**); we *conjugate* verbs (**I go, you go, he goes**); we add apostrophes and letters to words to make them plural or possessive (**Tom's tomatoes**). These are all examples of inflection.

When we speak of syntax, we are concerned with the part of grammar which deals with the way groups of words fit together to form meanings. When we speak of inflection we are concerned with the grammar of individual words. Which part of the subject should we take up first? Like the question about the chicken and the egg, this is a hard question to answer. It would be nice if we could tell you everything you need to know about syntax before going on to talk about inflection. Or vice versa. The trouble is that it is impossible to study either aspect of grammar in a vacuum, just as it would be impossible to talk rationally about a carburetor without referring to how that one part fits into the whole internal combustion system. Since this chapter is a review of grammar for you, we feel that you probably won't be too baffled if we presume a little knowledge of inflection while we first discuss syntax. Anyway, you have probably already noticed that this chapter is titled Syntax and the next one is called Inflection.

WHAT IS A SENTENCE?

So we have decided to begin with syntax (the chicken) and leave inflection (the egg) for later. Syntax, you will recall, is the way groups of words work together to form units of meaning. The basic unit of meaning in English, and almost every other language for that matter, is of course the *sentence.*

What makes a sentence? You could define a sentence by saying that it is a group of words that begins with a capital letter and ends with either a period, a question mark, or an exclamation point. You could say that, but you shouldn't, because actually *a sentence is a group of words that makes a coherent, independent statement.* To do this it must have—in addition to an initial capital letter and a terminal punctuation mark—a *subject* and a *predicate.* A **subject** is a word or a group of words about which something is said. A **predicate** is a word or group of words which says something coherent about the subject. Invariably, the predicate is a verb.

Here are two basic sentences:

He dreams.

I see.

These are the stripped down economy models, but they are complete sentences. Though they have only two words each, those two words are the essential ones—a subject and a predicate. Actually, it's possible to have an even shorter sentence than those two. For example:

Stop!

This is an example of an *elliptical* sentence, that is, a sentence in which a vital part is left out but understood. In this case, the subject (**you**) is understood.

Most sentences are, of course, a good deal longer than these examples we've been considering. In reality, most sentences contain, in addition to the essential subject and predicate, words and groups of words which generally fall into two categories:

A. Modifiers

B. Complements

A. MODIFIERS

In a little while we're going to get down to the practical business of reinforcing our theory with some exercises in which we dissect various sample sentences and name their parts. But, for now, we're going to stay with theory and definitions. *A **modifier** is a word or group of words that changes—or modifies—the meaning of another word or group of words. Adjectives and adverbs* are called modifiers, you'll recall. We'll have more to say about adjectives and adverbs when we get to Chapter 12 on inflection, or the grammar of individual words, but for the moment we'll remind you of the familiar grammar school definitions of adjectives and adverbs: "adverbs are words that modify verbs, adjectives, or other adverbs; adjectives modify nouns." To this we would also add the by-now-familiar admonition that *groups of words can function adverbially or adjectivally.*

Now let's translate our definitions into practical language. The word **apple**, by itself, can refer to green apples, yellow apples, even purple apples, but if we *modify* its meaning with the adjective **red,** we change its reference to something more specific. There are any number of ways in which a person can be said to walk, but if we modify the verb **walk** with an adverb like **quickly** we have changed, rendered more specific, the meaning of the verb. That's really what *modify* means.

Remember the basic sentences we looked at earlier? Let's add a few modifiers to them.

He dreams often. (**Often** is an adverb.)

I see very poorly. (**Poorly** is an adverb modifying **see** and **very** is another adverb modifying **poorly**.)

Let's take another sentence:

The tired man sat down.

This basic sentence consists of the simple subject and predicate "The man sat." But we make the statement more precise by adding an adjective, **tired**, and an adverb, **down**.

So far we've been using individual words to modify basic parts of sentences. Next we'll use groups of words acting together as adjectives and adverbs, but first another definition: *A group of words without a subject or a predicate that acts together to perform a function in the syntax of a sentence is called a phrase.* Most phrases are used as modifiers, that is, as adjectives or adverbs.

The man sat **in the chair**.

Walking home, he saw the accident.

In the first sentence the bold face group of words is a phrase that modifies **sat**. Technically, it is an adverbial prepositional phrase. In the second sentence the bold face group of words is a phrase that modifies **he**. Technically, it is a participial phrase used adjectivally. We'll have more to say in Chapter 12 about prepositions and participles, but for the time being we just want to demonstrate how groups of words, as well as individual words, can be used to function as modifiers.

B. COMPLEMENTS

Let's look again at that second sentence above. If **he** is the subject, **saw** is the predicate, and **walking home** is a modifying phrase, what is the syntactical function of the word **accident**? If you remember, we said that, in addition to the subject and predicate, most sentences contain *modifiers* and *complements*. "Accident" is a complement.

O.K., so what is a complement? *A **complement** is a word or group of words that is used to complete the statement (the predication) of a verb.* Let us say, for example, that we have the two basic sentence requirements—a subject and a predicate—but what they say doesn't make complete sense, as in:

> He hit.
>
> or
>
> He was.

Obviously these two "sentences" need something to complete them, something to help the verb make a logical statement about the subject's actions or being.

> He hit the **ball**.
>
> He was **old**.
>
> or
>
> He was **chairman**.

In these sentences, **ball**, **old**, and **chairman** are complements; they complete the predication of the verb to form a coherent unit of thought, a sentence.

There are six different types of complements, but before we tell you what they are, we want to define another very useful, timesaving grammatical term you should know—*substantive. A substantive is a word or group of words that acts as a noun.* The term applies to nouns, pronouns, verbals (about which more later), and phrases and clauses (about which more soon). Any words or word which can be used as the subject of a predicate is a substantive. But back to complements. As we said, there are six types.

1. Direct object. A substantive that receives the action of the verb is a direct object, as in this sentence, "He hit the ball."

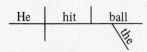

Ball receives the action of the verb **hit**.

2. Indirect object. A substantive that names the person or thing *to whom* or *for whom* the verb's action is performed is an indirect object. **To** and **for** are prepositions, but they never are actually stated in connection with indirect objects. They are implied. Another way of describing an indirect object is as an adverbial prepositional phrase used without benefit of a preposition. Consider this sentence: "He gave me the ball."

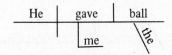

The word **me** is the indirect object of the verb **gave**. Note that the verb also has a direct object—**ball**. You can't have an indirect object unless you have a direct object as well.

3.   *Predicate nominative.*   This is a noun or pronoun that follows a special kind of verb called *an intransitive verb of incomplete predication.* These verbs are more commonly and simply called *copulative* or *linking* verbs. To be able to recognize this type of verb constitutes one of the more important and troublesome aspects of grammar.

   The predicate nominative, unlike the direct object, does not receive the action of the verb. Nor can it be said to somewhat modify the verb like an indirect object. Instead, the predicate nominative completes the predication of the verb and refers back to the subject, as in the sentence, "He was chairman." **Was** is the linking verb and **chairman** is the predicate nominative.

```
He  |  was  \  chairman
    |
```

Think of the linking verb as an equal sign:

   He = chairman.

4.   *Predicate adjective.*   This too follows a linking verb. It completes the predication of the linking verb and refers back to and modifies the subject. For example: "He was old." In this sentence **was** is the linking verb and **old** is the adjective. The adjective does not directly modify the subject, but completes the statement of the verb before referring back to the subject.

```
He  |  was  \  old
    |
```

   These first four types of complements are the most common. The most difficult ones for the average student of grammar to recognize are the last two—the *predicate nominative* and the *predicate adjective.* The trick is to learn to recognize linking verbs. These are usually forms of the verb *to be,* and verbs like **appear, seem, become,** as well as verbs referring to the physical senses, like **taste** and **look.**

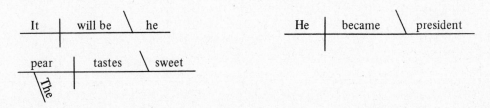

   We're a little dubious about bringing up the subject of the last two types of complements. They're fairly rare and there is not much practical advantage in knowing about them. Nevertheless, for the sake of completeness, here they are:

5.   *Retained object.*   This is a substantive that follows a verb in the passive voice, as in: "He was told the tale." **Tale** is the retained object.

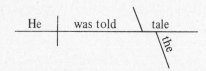

6. Objective complement. A substantive or an adjective which at once completes the predication of a verb and qualifies its direct object is an objective complement, as in the sentence, "They dyed the cloth red." **Red** is the objective complement. Likewise, **governor** is the objective complement in the sentence, "They elected him governor."

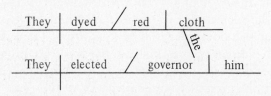

The *objective complement* invariably designates some change in the nature of the direct object that is brought about by the predicate.

You may have noticed that we've been using a system of lines to illustrate the syntactical relationships among the various words in our examples. This is called *diagramming*. You probably recognized it. Diagramming used to be a passion among earlier generations of English teachers, who delighted in calling on luckless students to diagram sentences of incredible complexity on the blackboard. The results often looked like the basic blueprint for a nuclear reactor. Many teachers overdid diagramming and made it an end in itself. Nevertheless, it is a useful way of illustrating the way sentences work, and we'll continue to use it in our discussion of syntax. We'll also assume that the principles of this illustrative technique either are or will become self-evident as we move along.

So far in our study of *syntax* we've observed how individual words and phrases mesh together to form basic units of thought, i.e., sentences. The sentences we've used as examples have been very basic, while in reality most sentences are not only longer, but more complex as well. The reason for that complexity is that many sentences have *compound* subjects, predicates, complements, and modifiers, and they contain *clauses*. Now, having checked ourselves out on the basics of syntax, let's run through the most elementary manner of complicating sentence structures, compounding elements.

C.   COMPOUNDING

Compounding actually is just another way of saying that *a simple sentence can have two or more subjects:* "John and I caught a cab."

It can have two or more predicates: "John and I ran and caught a cab."

Note that one of the predicates has a direct object while the other does not. *Or it can have two or more complements:* "John and I ran and caught a cab and a bus."

Even any combination of the above is possible!

Compounding elements is a relatively easy way to form complex sentences. However, before we tackle even more complicated sentence structures, those formed by adding clauses, we want to pause to do two things. The first thing is to ask you whether you've asked yourself, "What's the use of learning all this business about indirect objects and predicate nominatives? What's in it for me?" If you haven't asked yourself this question, you're a poor student. A good student always keeps in mind the practical applications of theory he's asked to learn. Actually though, we already answered that question a few pages back. We told you that if you want to troubleshoot your own writing, if you want to be reasonably confident about the coherence of your written communications, you must master basic theory—just as a mechanic has to master the basic terminology of his craft.

The second thing we want to do at this point is to ask you to work through a few practical exercises that reinforce the basic theory we've been discussing. Please don't skip these exercises, no matter how simple they may seem. Don't tell yourself that you've already learned all this theory and can skip on to the next section. What have you got to lose? If you really have mastered this basic material, it won't take you more than a few minutes to do the exercises and you'll have the satisfaction of proving to yourself how smart you are. On the other hand, if you're puzzled by some of the exercises, this may be an early warning to you that you should go back over the previous material, and perhaps ask your instructor to clarify some of the points that escape you. Remember, it's best to get it right before you get in over your head.

CLAUSES—INDEPENDENT (MAIN) AND DEPENDENT (SUBORDINATE)

We saw how compounding provides one way to give the meanings of sentences greater complexity, but another complicating element in the structure of sentences is the use of clauses. Clauses involve more intricate concepts.

*A **clause** can be defined as a group of words having a subject and predicate and acting together to perform a function in the complete sentence.* Here some confusion may arise. We already defined a *phrase* as a group of words which act together to fulfill a function in a sentence. So what's the difference between a *clause* and a *phrase* if they're both groups of words? The difference is that, in addition to being a group of words with a specific syntactical function, *the clause also has a subject and a predicate.* For example, consider the following sentences:

> He spoke to the man **with a hat.**

> He spoke to the man **who wore a hat.**

In the first sentence **with a hat** is a group of words which fulfills the adjectival function of modifying the substantive **man.** A substantive within the group of words itself, the noun **hat,** could conceivably be a subject, but the group of words has no verb to predicate something about **hat.** Therefore, **with a hat** is a phrase—technically, an adjectival prepositional phrase.

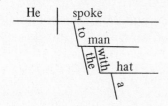

In the second sentence, **who wore a hat** is a group of words which also modifies **man,** but this group of words has a subject, **who,** and a predicate, **wore.** It is, therefore, a clause—technically, an adjectival clause.

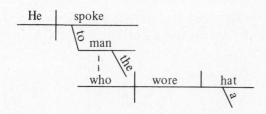

Why is it of practical importance to be able to recognize clauses? Let us answer this with a specific case. Choose the right form of the pronoun in the sentence below:

> I will give it to (whomever, whoever) asks for it.

Have you made your choice? Did you pick **whomever**? Can you give a reason for your choice other than "it sounds right"? You might have reasoned that the pronoun follows the word **to,** which, as all the world knows, is a preposition. Therefore, since pronouns that are objects of prepositions are in the objective case, the right form must be **whomever.**

But if you made that choice, you were wrong, because in this case the pronoun is *not* the object of a preposition. It is the *subject of a clause,* and the function of the whole clause is to be the object of that preposition. The pertinent rule is that the case (subjective, objective, possessive) of a pronoun is governed by its function in a clause, not by its simple proximity to a preposition or a verb. Diagrammed, the sentence would look like this:

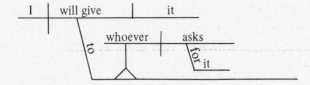

So now you may begin to appreciate why we have made such a big deal about all this theory. As we said, one of the most persistently troublesome problems in day-to-day grammar is choosing the correct case of pronouns. The only way you can choose with any certainty is by having confidence in your understanding of the basics of syntax.

To get on with clauses, however, essentially there are two kinds—*independent* clauses and *dependent* clauses.

A.   INDEPENDENT CLAUSES

Independent clauses are sometimes called *main* clauses. *They are clauses that can make a logically complete statement when they are separated from the rest of the sentence.* They are often connected to the complete sentence by words known as *coordinating conjunctions,* but sometimes their connection to the complete sentence is indicated only by a punctuation mark, i.e., the semicolon (;). The major coordinating conjunctions are *and, but, or, nor, for,* and *yet.*

> I picked up my paycheck, and Mr. Harris told me to take the day off.
>
> I picked up my paycheck; Mr. Harris told me to take the day off.
>
> She brought an umbrella, yet rain was not forecast.
>
> I will get the promotion, or I will quit.

Each of the four sentences above is composed of two independent clauses; in three of the sentences the clauses are joined by coordinating conjunctions. In the second sentence (as in the one you've just finished reading) the clauses are joined only by a punctuation mark. You could change that semicolon to a period and have two separate, independent sentences:

> I picked up my paycheck. Mr. Harris told me to take the day off.

B.   DEPENDENT CLAUSES

Sometimes called *subordinate* clauses, *dependent clauses are related groups of words which have their own subject and predicate, but do not make a coherent statement if they are separated from the complete sentence.* For example, let's take a sentence we looked at earlier:

> I will give it to **whoever asks for it.**

Whoever asks for it is a dependent clause; it has a subject and a predicate, but it just does not make sense by itself. It is obviously a subordinate element in the complete sentence.

So much, then, for the basic distinctions between *independent* and *dependent* clauses. Theoretically, there's no limit to the number of independent clauses you can string together. However, sentences composed of too many independent clauses have a choppy, mechanical effect:

> I see the cat and the cat sees me. The cat is easy to see; the cat is on fire.

Clusters of independent clauses like these not only lack grace, but are logically offensive as well.

They suggest that each clause contains an idea of equal, or *coordinate* importance. More sophisticated writers tend to indicate the logical relationships of ideas by using dependent clauses, suggesting that one idea is subordinated to another:

> I see the cat who sees me. Because he is on fire, he is easy to see.

While independent clauses can make sense by themselves, dependent clauses can make sense only in terms of their syntactical function in the main sentence. Any given dependent clause must fulfill one of three functions in the sentence:

1. It can act as a *substantive,* that is, as a subject, a complement, or an object.
2. It can act as an *adjective,* modifying a substantive.
3. It can act as an *adverb,* modifying a verb, an adjective, or another adverb.

Let's look at some diagrammed examples of the first of these functions of *dependent* clauses, the substantive function. Clauses of this type are sometimes called *noun clauses.*

1. Substantive clauses. A substantive or noun clause may be used as the subject of a sentence, or as the direct object, an object of a preposition, a predicate nominative, or an appositive. Here are some examples.

A.   Subject: "Whatever he wants is good enough."

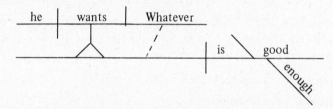

In this case, as in many others, you have to rearrange the word order of the sentence to see the true syntactical functions of its parts. Even though **whatever** comes before the verb, it is not the subject; it is the direct object of the noun clause's predicate. **Whatever** is a special kind of pronoun known as a *relative pronoun.* It not only has a function in the dependent clause, but it *relates* or *connects* that clause to the whole sentence. Other types of words that relate dependent clauses to the main sentence are *subordinating conjunctions* (*since, if, unless, although, before,* etc.) and *relative adverbs* (*when, while, where, how,* etc.).

B.   Direct object: "He thought that Lamar Philips had jammed the stapler."

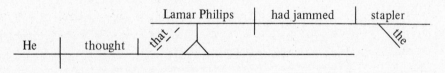

We have another relative pronoun here, **that** (others are *who, which* and *whose*), but this time the pronoun merely *relates* and does not play a role in the syntax of the dependent clause.

C.   Object of a preposition: "He collected a dollar from whoever came to his office."

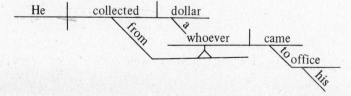

D.   Predicate nominative: "A dollar was what I gave."

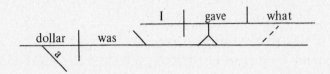

E.   Appositive (an *appositive* is a word or group of words that stands next to another word and means the same thing): "Mr. Philips, who is our efficiency expert, is late.

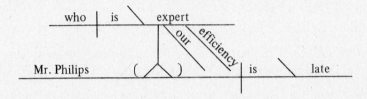

It's fairly easy to see how substantive clauses work. But before we move on to discuss the other two functions of dependent clauses—adjectival and adverbial—let's reinforce our concept of substantive clauses with some exercises.

MORE CLAUSES—ADJECTIVAL AND ADVERBIAL

We examined the ways in which dependent clauses can be used as nouns. Now let's look at the other two uses of dependent clauses.

2. Adjective clauses. One word or a phrase can be used to modify a substantive; so can a clause. *Adjectival clauses modify substantives.* Here are two diagrammed examples.

A.   The sales technique **which was most productive** was the veiled threat.

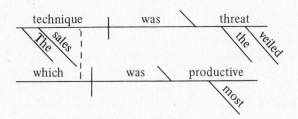

B.   I have the invoice **that he wanted**.

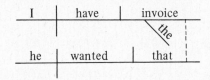

Adjectival clauses are very often introduced by *relative pronouns* (*which, that, who, whom, whatever, whichever, whoever,* etc.) or by *relative adverbs* (*where, when, while,* etc.). But sometimes the relative element is left out, or merely understood. For example, Sentence B might just as correctly have been phrased, "I have the invoice he wanted."

C.   This is the town **where they opened a branch**.

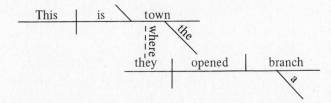

One practical problem with adjective clauses concerns punctuation. This is the question of whether the clause is used *restrictively* or *nonrestrictively*. What do these terms mean? A *restrictive* element in a sentence is a clause (or a word or phrase) which restricts the meaning of the word preceding it in such a way that it cannot be left out without severely altering the meaning of the sentence. *Nonrestrictive* elements, on the other hand, are not vital to the essential meaning of the sentence, though they may add interesting information.

The point to remember here is that restrictive clauses (or other elements) are *not*, we repeat, *not*, set off by commas. *Nonrestrictive* clauses *are* set off by commas. Here are a couple of examples:

Employees **who have not reported their Social Security numbers** will not get paid.

The employees, **who were mostly men**, took their vacations in August.

The italicized clause in the first example is restrictive. If we left it out, the sense of the statement would be radically altered. The sentence doesn't mean that "employees will not get paid"! Because the clause is necessary to restrict the meaning of **employees**, it is not set off by commas. But the italicized clause in the second sentence is not vital to the sense of the sentence. It is not needed to restrict the meaning of **employees**. It is, therefore, nonrestrictive. It gives additional, but logically unnecessary information. We could leave it out, but instead we indicate its relative unimportance by setting it off with commas. We could, if we wanted to dramatize its supplemental nature, enclose it in parentheses—"The employees (who were mostly men) took their vacations in August." It may help you in distinguishing between restrictive and nonrestrictive clauses (and other elements) to think of the commas used with the nonrestrictive ones as mild parentheses.

Here are two more examples that may help you with this exasperating restrictive vs. nonrestrictive distinction.

> RESTRICTIVE, no commas: The man **who works near the window** is her secretary.

> NONRESTRICTIVE and set off by commas: Mr. Clark, **who works near the window**, is her secretary.

3. Adverb clauses. The adverbial clause is used, like a single adverb, to modify a verb, an adjective, or another adverb. Adverbial clauses are ordinarily introduced by *subordinating conjunctions* (*because, before, after, as, if, unless, until, although,* etc.) and *relative adverbs* (*when, where,* etc.).

A.   Lamar left **when the auditors arrived**.

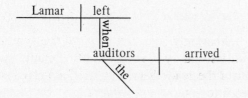

B.   I arrived late **because I was delayed by Lamar**.

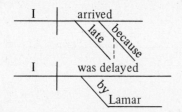

With a little concentration all this is simple enough.

At this point we have just about finished our review of *syntax*. Beginning with the most basic, subject-plus-predicate, type of complete sentence ("I see."), we've demonstrated how syntactical formulas can be built up and extended by adding *modifiers* and *complements, compounding* elements, and incorporating various types of *phrases* and *clauses* into the sentence.

We'd like to add a word of caution though, and that is that *all the various components of the sentence should fit together coherently*. When an element of the sentence—a word, phrase, or clause —does not connect logically with the structure of the overall sentence it is said to *dangle*.

A.   DANGLING ELEMENTS

Dangling elements are usually clauses or verbal phrases. The dangling element is almost invariably intended to modify some other part of the sentence, but trouble comes when a writer neglects to provide an obvious connection between the modifier and what it is intended to modify.

Certain types of phrases called *verbal phrases* (we'll discuss verbals more fully in Chapter 12) are said to *dangle* when they do not clearly refer to (or modify) a substantive in the main clause of a sentence. In the examples below, dangling modifiers are in bold face.

By glancing at the balance sheets, a clear assessment of the situations was reached.

Who was glancing at the balance sheets? The only answer the sentence provides is **a clear assessment** and that answer is illogical.

While eating our lunch, the train pulled out of the station.

Who was eating lunch—the train?

Driving from Central Park to Greenwich Village, many apartment houses can be seen.

By whom can the apartment houses be seen? Who or what was driving to Greenwich Village?

Dangling phrases, which crop up in our speech very frequently, and which occur in our writing more often than we may realize, can be repaired in one of two ways: 1. By inserting a subject in the main clause that the dangling phrase logically modifies.

While eating our lunch, WE watched the train pull out of the station.

2. By converting the phrase into a dependent clause, thereby giving it its own subject.

While WE were eating our lunch, the train pulled out of the station.

Sometimes writers composing dependent clauses deliberately leave out some of the syntactical elements, believing that these elements will be easily understood by the reader. Such clauses, as has been mentioned earlier, are called *elliptical clauses.* But if the reader cannot easily perceive how the elliptical clause modifies the subject of the main clause, it too is said to dangle.

Dangling elliptical clauses can also be repaired in two ways. The "understood" element can be reinserted in the dependent clause, or the subject of the main clause can be changed so that the elliptical dependent clause can readily be seen to modify it. In the example below, the bold face clause is elliptical and dangling.

While making his annual inspection, a number of improper procedures appeared.

Either of the following sentences correct the dangling condition.

While HE was making his annual inspection, a number of improper procedures appeared. (The "understood" elements have been replaced in the dependent clause.)

While making HIS annual inspection, HE discovered a number of improper procedures. (The main clause has been changed to show more clearly how the elliptical dependent clause modifies it.)

Finally, there is one other special type of structure, called the *nominative absolute,* that appears to dangle in the technical sense in that it does not modify any *one* element in a sentence. The nominative absolute, however, modifies the *whole* sentence. It closely resembles the type of verbal phrase known as the participial phrase, but unlike that construction, the nominative absolute has its own subject.

All the evidence being in, the jury relaxed.

The music having stopped, the dancers sat down, except for Lamar Philips.

That's pretty much it for our review of syntax. We're going to ask you now to put your theoretical grasp of the subject to the practical test of a few exercises. Then we'll move on to the grammar of individual words, or *inflection.*

Chapter 12

INFLECTION

In the preceding chapter we discussed *syntax,* or the grammar of the sentence taken as a whole. Now we'll concern ourselves with the rules (or grammar) governing the way individual words operate within the sentence—*inflection.*

You'll recall that earlier we said that *inflection* comes from the same root as *flex* and is concerned with the way words are changed or flexed to indicate different meaning relationships within sentences. Practically, this means we will be concerned with such matters as conjugation and declension, and the classification of words in terms of parts of speech.

The various parts of speech—and they could just as well be called the parts of writing—are not something to be memorized in the abstract like a list of the successive wives of King Henry VIII. There can be no such thing as a *noun,* or a *verb,* or a *preposition* in the abstract. These are simply terms that we use to describe the function of a particular word in a particular sentence. You cannot name a word's part of speech until you see it functioning in an actual sentence. For example, let's take the word **dream**. What part of speech is it? It can be a noun, or it can be a verb. Its meaning depends on the way it functions, not on its form.

I **dreamed** about it last night. (Here **dream** is a verb.)

I had a **dream** last night. (Here **dream** is a noun.)

Traditionally, there are eight parts of speech:

1. Nouns ⎫
2. Pronouns ⎬ Substantives
3. Verbs (and Verbals)
4. Adverbs

5. Adjectives
6. Conjunctions
7. Prepositions
8. Interjections

For all practical purposes we can forget about interjections since, by definition, they are "interruptors," words that have more to do with emotional tone than with the logic of a sentence. Words like **Oh, aha, Wow, alas,** and many others that we all know but are afraid to print are examples of interjections. If we put interjections aside, we are left with only seven parts of speech, and two of these seven, nouns and pronouns, can both be classified under the single heading, substantives. Let's now go on to individually define and discuss these seven parts of speech in terms of their functions.

SUBSTANTIVES—NOUNS AND PRONOUNS

A. NOUNS

Nouns are words that are used to name people, things, ideas, qualities, or acts. There are two basic kinds of nouns—*common nouns* and *proper nouns.* **Common nouns** are used to name one or all of the members of a class. For example, **city, books, mountains, person.** *Proper nouns* are used to name special, individual members of a class. They are always capitalized. For example, **Chicago,** *War and Peace,* **Mount Washington, John.** There are also some other descriptive terms applied to nouns, notably *collective* nouns, *compound* nouns, *concrete* nouns, and *abstract* nouns.

1. Collective nouns. Collective nouns are names applied to groups; like **army, family, senate,** and **audience.** They may be either proper or common, and they are usually, but unfortunately not always, considered to be singular.

If the collective noun is thought of as a single unit with all of its parts acting together, it is regarded as being singular and requires a singular verb.

> The army *is* marching toward us.
>
> The family *is* vacationing in Florida.

But sometimes we use the collective noun in a way that indicates that we think of the members of the group as acting separately:

> The family *are* going to spend their vacations in Florida, New England, and Death Valley.

In a case like this the collective noun takes a plural verb.

2. Compound nouns. These are proper or common nouns made up of two or more words. The practical difficulty with them is that sometimes they are written as one word (**grandmother, football**), sometimes as two or more separate words (**Great Britain, post office**), and sometimes they are hyphenated (**mother-in-law, self-indulgence**). There does not seem to be too much rhyme or reason governing these differences, so when in doubt as to how to write a compound noun, consult a dictionary.

3. Concrete nouns. Concrete nouns name things that can be physically perceived (like **rock, desk, star,** or **room**).

4. Abstract nouns. Ideas or qualities (like **bravery, intelligence, multiplicity**) are named by abstract nouns. All things being equal—though they rarely are—concrete nouns are stylistically preferred over abstract nouns. Jargon specialists delight in abstract nouns.

B. PRONOUNS

A pronoun is a word used as a substitute for a noun. If we didn't have pronouns, we'd have to keep repeating specific names of people, places, things, and concepts. Pronouns can be broken down into seven basic subdivisions.

1. Personal Pronouns. Examples are **I, you, me, they.**

2. Intensive or Reflexive Pronouns. These always end with **-self** or **-selves**. Examples are **myself, himself, ourselves.** *Intensive pronouns* are used to increase the effect of another noun or pronoun, as in the sentence "John, himself, did it." **Himself** is used *intensively. Reflexive pronouns* are a little more difficult to define; they are used as direct objects of reflexive verbs. Fine, but what's a reflexive verb? A reflexive verb is a verb that has an identical subject and direct object, as in the sentence "John hit himself." The subject and object are one and the same, and **himself** is used reflexively. A practical tip: don't, in an attempt to be elegant, make the mistake of using an intensive or reflexive pronoun when you should use a plain old personal pronoun.

> WRONG: John and **myself** are not in favor of that.
>
> RIGHT: John and **I** are not in favor of that.
>
> WRONG: He gave it to Mary and **myself**.
>
> RIGHT: He gave it to Mary and **me**.

3. Relative Pronouns. The function of relative pronouns is to connect (or relate) dependent clauses to independent clauses. Examples are **who, which, that, whom.** Take the sentence "I will give it to whoever wants it." **Whoever** is a *relative pronoun.* It relates the dependent clause, "**whoever wants it,**" to the main clause, "**I will give it.**" Note the use of **whoever,** not **whomever.** In the sentence above the pronoun **whoever** is not the object of the preposition **to.** The whole clause is the object of the preposition, and the pronoun is the subject of the clause. Moral: Just because a pronoun lies smack up against a preposition, it is not necessarily the object of that preposition.

4. Interrogative Pronouns. Interrogative pronouns are used in asking questions. Examples are **who, what, which.**

5. Demonstrative Pronouns. Pronouns used to point out something are demonstrative. Examples are **that, this, these, those.**

6. Reciprocal Pronouns. Reciprocal pronouns combine two pronouns into one term, suggesting a mutual relationship. Examples are **one another, each other.**

7. Indefinite Pronouns. An indefinite pronoun is a pronoun that is not very specific about the noun it stands for. Examples are **all, another, any, anybody, both, each, everyone, few, many, none, one, some, someone.**

Taken together, nouns and pronouns can be called by the collective term *substantives.* And we'll now go over the major grammatical problems substantives present.

C. PROBLEMS WITH SUBSTANTIVES: NUMBER

The first problem is that of *number,* or, more plainly, whether or not a given substantive is regarded as singular or plural. Especially with nouns, part of the problem is also how to spell the plural form. There are some formulas governing the spelling of plural nouns, but there are so many exceptions, and the rules are so difficult for the average writer to remember, that our best advice is just the familiar admonition, consult a dictionary. Here, however, are a few tips concerning substantives, and number:

1. Collective nouns (**family, army, jury**) *are usually regarded as singular.* Company names are usually regarded as collective nouns and follow the rule that if the company name ends with a singular word, the collective noun is considered singular; if the name ends with a plural word, the collective is considered plural.

PLURAL: Charles Smith and Sons **have called** in all **their** representatives.

SINGULAR: Caustic Unguent, Inc. **pays its** bills on time.

2. *Units of measure are customarily treated as singular.*

> **Fifty dollars** is too much to pay.
>
> **Thirty-six years** was the time allotted.

3. *Compound nouns are made plural by pluralizing the most logically important part of the compound.* It is often a philosophical question as to which part is more important.

> attorneys-general
>
> boom towns
>
> mothers-in-law

4. *Foreign plural forms follow no precise rules.* Most substantives in English have been absorbed from other languages. Sometimes they retain their foreign plural forms, sometimes they become naturalized and are pluralized like English substantives, and sometimes they can have either foreign or English plurals. Here are some examples of all three types:

SINGULAR	FOREIGN PLURAL	ENGLISH PLURAL
appendix	appendices	appendixes
virtuoso	virtuosi	virtuosos
memorandum	memoranda	memorandums

Generally, if an accepted English plural form exists, it is preferred. But remember that certain words use *only* their native plural forms.

SINGULAR	PLURAL
alumna	alumnae
datum	data
phenomenon	phenomena

Note that **data** and **phenomena** are plural forms. One **data** is a **datum** and one **phenomena** is a **phenomenon**.

5. *Indefinite pronouns are, for the most part, treated as being singular.* Such indefinite pronouns as **anybody, anyone, nobody, each, someone,** and **nothing** are regarded as singular; that is, when they are used as subjects they take singular verbs, and when they are used as antecedents they are referred to by other singular pronouns.

> **Anyone is** welcome.
>
> **Each is** responsible.

However, there are a few indefinite pronouns that are plural: **many, several, others, both, few.** Fortunately, they not only are plural, but they sound plural.

> **Both have completed** their jobs.
>
> **Many are called** but **few are chosen.**

6. *Compound subjects require special attention.* We recall from our study of syntax that when substantives are connected by conjunctions, they form compound elements of the sentence. When they are compound subjects the problem is raised as to whether they should be considered singular or plural. Our choice of correct verb forms depends on the outcome of that decision.

When two or more subjects are joined by **and**, the compound is considered *plural,* regardless of whether the individual substantives are singular or plural in themselves.

> Lamar **and** his debtors **are** having a pre-bankruptcy conference.

> The date **and** time of the hearing **have** not been arranged.

There is one exception to this rule about compound subjects formed with **and**: it is that when two or more singular *indefinite* pronouns are connected by **and** the compound is treated as being singular.

> Anything **and** everyone **is** grist for his mill.

However, if the substantives in the compound element are joined by the conjunctions **or** or **nor**, then we have a more complicated situation when it comes to deciding whether we ought to use a singular or plural verb. The basic rule is to consider these compound subjects as singular when the component parts are singular.

> Either he or I **is** going to be promoted.

> Her brother or her sister **is** likely to be there.

But, when you have singular *and* plural parts of a compound subject joined by **or** or **nor**, the rule is to make the verb agree in number with the element of the compound subject that is closest to it.

> Either the auditors or Lamar **is** wrong.

> Either Lamar or the auditors **are** wrong.

D. PROBLEMS WITH SUBSTANTIVES: CASE

Another basic grammatical problem connected with nouns and pronouns is that of *case.* *Case* has to do with the way substantives are inflected to express meanings within sentences. We have good news for you about case in English, and that is that English has essentially only three cases—*subjective, objective* and *possessive.* (You may have heard these same cases called *nominative, accusative,* and *genitive.*)

More good news about case is that in English, as opposed to many foreign languages, we don't inflect (decline) nouns as their case changes. The noun **bird** for example, is spelled the same way whether it is used as a subject or an object. And we indicate the possessive case of nouns, not by radically changing their spelling, but through variations of the apostrophe and the letter **s**. (See Chapter 13 for more on the apostrophe.) For all practical purposes, we are concerned with only three cases in English, and with those only insofar as they affect pronouns.

Pronouns *are* declined for case.

SUBJECTIVE	OBJECTIVE	POSSESSIVE
I	me	my, mine
he	him	his
she	her	hers
it	it	its
you	you	your, yours
who	whom	whose
they	them	their, theirs

There is however, one type of pronoun that forms its possessive as nouns do, by adding an apostrophe and **s**. This is the indefinite pronoun: **one's, another's, someone's, everyone's, no one's.** When the word **else** follows one of these indefinite pronouns, we also treat it as part of the pronoun and add an apostrophe and **s** to it to form the possessive case: **no one else's, someone else's.**

What are the major considerations concerning case in English? The basic sentence situations governing *Case* are shown below.

1. When a pronoun is the subject of a verb, use the subjective case.

> **I** talked to Lamar's lawyer.
>
> Lamar and **he** will return soon.
>
> When did **she** leave?

In the examples above, the pronouns **I, he,** and **she** are the subjects, respectively, of the verbs **talked, will return,** and **leave.**

Watch out for pronouns in *compound* subjects! People are sometimes inclined to put such pronouns in the objective case.

> WRONG: Lamar and **him** were both demoted.
>
> RIGHT: Lamar and **he** were both demoted.
>
> WRONG: **Him** and **me** applied for the same promotion.
>
> RIGHT: **He** and **I** applied for the same promotion.

When in doubt in situations like this, drop all the words in the compound but the pronoun and see which sounds most natural, the subjective or objective case. You would never say, for example, "**me** applied for the same promotion." Nor would you say, "**Him** was demoted."

Use the same test when you use a pronoun followed immediately by a noun (**we** salesmen). Drop the noun and read the sentence. Your ear will tell you that the subjective case is the correct case.

> **We** salesmen have penetrated the market.
> (You would never say "**Us** have penetrated . . . .")

2. When a pronoun is the complement of a linking verb, use the subjective case. We treated the subject of complements and linking verbs earlier, during our discussion of syntax in Chapter 11. We'll have more to say about linking verbs later in this chapter. For the present, however, remember that linking verbs are chiefly forms of the verb **to be.**

> I am **he.**
>
> It was **she.**

3. When a pronoun is the direct or indirect object of a verb or the object of a preposition, use the objective case.

> Direct object: I left **him** this morning.
>
> Indirect object: He gave **him** the order.
>
> Object of preposition: He gave the order to **him.**

Here too, trouble may arise when the pronoun is used in a compound situation or is immediately followed by a noun. As we mentioned above, drop the distracting elements from the construction and try saying the sentence with just the preposition.

> Lamar gave it to **us** accountants.
> (You would never say "Lamar gave it to **we**"!)
>
> Have you seen Lamar and **him**?
> (Your ear wouldn't permit you to say "Have you seen **he**.")

4. When a pronoun is part of a dependent clause, its case is determined by its function in that clause. We treated this subject too in our discussion of syntax. But this may be a good time to go back and again quickly review and reinforce your knowledge of dependent clauses. To decide the correct case of the pronoun, separate the dependent clause from the rest of the sentence and determine how the pronoun functions within that clause—as a subject, as an object, as the object of a preposition, or as an indirect object.

> The supervisor, **whom** I met today, was recently hired. (**Whom** is in the objective case because it is the object of the verb **met**.)

> The supervisor, **who** comes from Peoria, is a friend of Lamar's. (**Who** is in the subjective case because it is the subject of the verb **comes**.)

Be on the lookout for pronouns in *elliptical clauses,* or clauses in which parts are left out and said to be understood. Most frequently these situations involve comparisons.

> I am taller than **he**. (**He** is subjective because it is regarded as the subject of the understood construction **than he is tall**.)

> Lamar makes less money than **she**. (What is understood here is the construction **than she makes** or **than she does**.)

5. When a pronoun is used as an appositive (a word or group of words standing next to another word and meaning the same thing), it takes the same case as the word to which it is in apposition.

> The delegates, Lamar and **I**, went to the meeting. (**I** is in apposition to **delegates**. **Delegates** is the subject of the sentence and **I** must therefore be in the subjective case.)

> This concept **is** important to **us** market analysts. (**Us** is in apposition to **market analysts** which is in turn the object of the preposition **to**. **Us** must, therefore, be in the objective case.)

These are the basic grammatical considerations concerning case. We will postpone considering one problem of the case of substantives. That problem regards a special class of words called *verbals.* We will consider verbals later in this chapter.

E. PROBLEMS WITH SUBSTANTIVES: REFERENCE

The third major—and for our purposes, final—problem area connected with substantives is *reference,* and this is a problem that primarily concerns pronouns.

Pronouns, as we know, are words which take the place of other substantives. Our readers should never be confused about what person, place or thing any given pronoun is referring to. To put it in formal terms, pronouns should clearly *refer* to their *antecedents.* The major problems to be avoided are *ambiguous reference, generalized reference,* and *weak reference.*

1. Ambiguous reference. This situation occurs when a pronoun seems to refer to two or more possible antecedents.

> Lamar delegated John Smith to do the job because he was convinced of its importance. (Who was convinced of the job's importance—Lamar, John Smith, or both?)

> The letter is on the table that was delivered Monday. (What was delivered Monday—the table or the letter?)

To avoid ambiguity, place the pronoun as close as possible to its intended antecedent. Our last example could be rewritten this way:

> The letter that was delivered Monday is on the table.

2. Generalized reference. This occurs when a pronoun has for its reference a general idea that is vaguely stated. **This, that, which,** and **it** are pronouns which are frequently used in a generalized manner. This situation can be remedied by completely revising the sentence, or replacing the pronoun with a specific noun.

GENERALIZED: Lamar wore sequins to meetings which upset management. (What upset management—the sequins or the meeting?)

CLEAR: Lamar's wearing sequins to meetings upset management.

GENERALIZED: The meeting was a disaster. Lamar fell asleep, the air conditioning broke down, and the sales figures were incomplete. This disturbed the chairman. (What disturbed the chairman—one of the above, some of the above, or all of the above?)

CLEAR: The meeting was a disaster. Lamar fell asleep, the air conditioning broke down, and the sales figures were incomplete. All of these things disturbed the chairman.

3. *Weak reference.* This occurs when a pronoun has no expressed antecedent, only an implied one.

WEAK: Lamar spent his vacation hunting but didn't bag a single one. (**One** refers to nothing in this sentence.)

CLEAR: Lamar spent his vacation hunting robins but didn't bag a single one. (**One** now clearly refers to robins.)

WEAK: Lamar computed his taxes on the assumption that he was entitled to use a schedule applicable to the head of the household, which is in error. (Who or what is in error—Lamar's assumption or the head of the household?)

CLEAR: Lamar computed his taxes on the assumption that he was entitled to use a schedule applicable to the head of the household. His assumption was in error. (Here we have replaced the weak pronoun **which** with the specific noun **assumption**.)

A final tip on the clear use of pronouns is to avoid the impersonal use of **it, they,** and **you.** The examples given below are not, strictly speaking, wrong, but they are wordy and vague:

In the letter it says to fill the order promptly. (Why not say "The letter says to fill the order promptly"?)

In the last scene they suggest that the heroine will live. (Who are they? Better to say "The last scene suggests that . . . .")

They say that it will rain tomorrow. (Once again, who are they? This probably should read "The weatherman says . . . .")

Let's sum up now the basic grammatical concerns you must remember in dealing with substantives.

1. Do I know the correct plural form?

2. Do I know whether a given substantive should be regarded as plural or singular in order to agree with verbs and pronouns?

3. Do I know how to determine the case of a pronoun?

4. Do I know how to make pronouns clearly refer to their antecendents?

Some exercises to help you answer these questions follow.

VERBS

A *verb* is a word that asserts (or predicates) something about the subject of a sentence. *Verbs either state what the subject is doing or what is being done to it*. There is always a quality of *action* implicit in a verb. The action may be very obvious and physical (**hit, run, dance**) or it may be more subtle and abstract (**exist, analyze, conceive**), but all verbs are action words.

Verbs are perhaps the most important part of speech and are certainly the most complicated. Fortunately, most people unconsciously mastered the main complexities of the verb as they grew up. Here we will quickly review the overall subject and then zero in on problem areas where instinctive reactions are likely to be a little unsure.

When we *inflect* substantives, we call the process *declension;* when we *inflect* verbs, we call the process *conjugation. Conjugating* a verb means simply to take its basic, or *infinitive* form (**to see, to walk, to be**) and, by changing its spelling or combining it with various other words called *auxiliaries,* make it express relationships of meaning. There are five main categories of verb meanings. They are traditionally called properties. The five verb properties are: 1. *Number*—has to do with how many people, things or concepts are involved in the action of a verb. 2. *Person*—regards who is performing the action—the first person (**I**), the second person (**you**), or the third person (**he, she, it, they**). 3. *Mood*—indicates the viewpoint of the writer (or speaker) regarding the activity. If the writer simply makes a statement the verb is in the *Indicative mood:* "He is here." Indicative is the most common mood. If he makes a command or request, the verb is in the *Imperative mood:* "Come here." If he expresses a wish or a condition that is contrary to fact then the verb is said to be in the *Subjunctive mood:* "I wish he were here." 4. *Voice*—tells whether the subject is acting ("He hit it.") or being acted upon ("He was hit."). If the subject is acting, the verb is in the *Active voice;* if it is acted upon, the verb is in the *Passive voice.* 5. *Tense*—tells at what time (past, present, or future) the activity is taking place.

We dealt with the properties of *number* and *person* in the preceding section where we were concerned with the problem of subject/verb agreement (a verb must agree in number and person with its subject). So we'll concern ourselves now with the last three properties of verbs: mood, voice, and tense. We'll also discuss transitive and intransitive verbs.

A. MOOD

We'll give the subject of mood very short shrift. There are no special problems relating to the *indicative* or *imperative* moods. Our instincts operate smoothly when we want to use an appropriate verb to express a simple statement or give a command. Unfortunately, our instincts don't operate so smoothly when we use the *subjunctive* mood; that is, when we want to express something conditionally, wishfully, etc. But, fortunately, so many people have had so much trouble with the subjunctive that its use is gradually phasing out of the language, except in the most formal kinds of writing or speech. Rather than become involved with a full-scale exploration of the mysteries of this special, formal inflection, let us simply point out that it usually involves the verb **to be**. We'll also give you some examples of its use:

INDICATIVE:	He **was** here.
SUBJUNCTIVE:	I wish he **were** here.
INDICATIVE:	He **was** chairman of the board.
SUBJUNCTIVE:	If he **were** chairman, he would fire Lamar.
INDICATIVE:	He **was** promoted.
SUBJUNCTIVE:	Lamar insisted that his nephew **be** promoted.

B. VOICE

Voice, as we said earlier, is the property of the verb which determines whether the subject is acting or being acted upon. If the subject is acting, the verb is in the *active voice:* "**I gave** him the promotion." If the subject is acted upon, the verb is in the *passive voice:* "**I was given** the promotion."

One thing to remember about verbs in the passive voice is that they always use some form of the verb **to be** as an auxiliary: **was given, will be given, am given, is given.**

Another thing to remember about verbs in the passive voice is that they should not be overused. We are *not* saying that you should avoid using the passive voice. There are some ideas that can only be expressed in the passive voice. However, an *excessive* use of passive voice constructions is the hallmark of vague, wooly, abstract prose. Writers who, consciously or unconsciously, want to avoid being direct, or avoid responsibility, find the passive voice their favorite refuge.

C. TENSE

Tense is the property of the verb concerned with the *time* in which an action takes place. In English we have six basic tenses: *present, past,* and *future* tenses; and *present perfect, past perfect,* and *future perfect* tenses. The three perfect tenses not only designate actions that take place in a certain time phase, but also emphasize that the action is *completed* in that time phase.

PRESENT:	I pay.
PRESENT PERFECT:	I have paid.
PAST:	I paid.
PAST PERFECT:	I had paid.
FUTURE:	I will pay.
FUTURE PERFECT:	I will have paid.

Most of the time, we casually and instinctively negotiate our way through the various inflections of tense without difficulty. From time to time, however, all of us have problems with certain troublesome or *irregular* verbs. Anyone who has studied a foreign language knows the trouble irregular verbs can give. We can ease our troubles, however, if we remember that we only need to know three things about any English verb in order to inflect it correctly in any way we want. The three things we need to know are the *principal parts* of verbs.

The principal parts of verbs—from which we derive all other forms of the verb—are the *infinitive* (**walk**), the *past* tense (**walked**), and the *past participle* (**has walked**). We used **has** with the past participle to point out the fact that this form is ordinarily used with an auxiliary verb, like **is, was, shall, have, had,** etc.

We only have to know the same *three* things about an irregular verb to properly inflect it. Any good dictionary will tell you the three principal parts of an irregular verb. However, for reference purposes we have provided Table 12.1, a list of common troublesome verbs and their vital principal parts; some verbs, as you will see, have alternative forms.

Before we abandon the subject of verbs, we want to introduce you to a basic distinction between two kinds of verbs. We will show how these two categories can be further broken down into sub-categories, and we'll point out the practical value of being able to make these distinctions. Finally, we'll pull all this together for you in a handy-dandy patent Verb Chart that will, we hope, sum up the essential distinctions you need to make among verbs.

D. TRANSITIVE AND INTRANSITIVE VERBS

All English verbs are classified as either *transitive* or *intransitive.* The key to understanding the distinction lies in that root word *trans* which in Latin means *across,* as in Trans World Airlines.

TABLE 12.1. PRINCIPAL PARTS OF TROUBLESOME VERBS

INFINITIVE	PAST TENSE	PAST PARTICIPLE
arise	arose	arisen
awake	awoke, awaked	awaked
bare	bared	bared
be (am, are, is)	was	been
bear (carry)	bore	borne
bear (give birth)	bore	borne, born
begin	began	begun
bid (command)	bade	bidden
bid (offer)	bid	bid
bind	bound	bound
bite	bit	bitten
blow	blew	blown
break	broke	broken
burst	burst	burst
buy	bought	bought
catch	caught	caught
choose	chose	chosen
come	came	come
creep	crept	crept
deal	dealt	dealt
dive	dived, dove	dived
do	did	done
drag	dragged	dragged
dream	dreamed, dreamt	dreamed, dreamt
draw	drew	drawn
drown	drowned	drowned
dwell	dwelt	dwelt
drink	drank	drunk
drive	drove	driven
eat	ate	eaten
fall	fell	fallen
flee	fled	fled
fling	flung	flung
flow	flowed	flowed
fly	flew	flown
forget	forgot	forgotten, forgot
forsake	forsook	forsaken
freeze	froze	frozen
get	got	got, gotten
give	gave	given
go	went	gone
grow	grew	grown

TABLE 12.1. *(continued)*

INFINITIVE	PAST TENSE	PAST PARTICIPLE
hang (suspend)	hung	hung
hang (execute)	hanged	hanged
hide	hid	hidden
hold	held	held
know	knew	known
lay	laid	laid
lead	led	led
lend	lent	lent
lie (recline)	lay	lain
lie (falsify)	lied	lied
light	lighted, lit	lighted, lit
loose	loosed	loosed
loosen	loosened	loosened
lose	lost	lost
mean	meant	meant
meet	met	met
mend	mended	mended
pay	paid	paid
prove	proved	proved, proven
raise	raised	raised
reach	reached	reached
read	read	read
rid	rid	rid
ride	rode	ridden
ring	rang	rung
rise	rose	risen
row	rowed	rowed
run	ran	run
say	said	said
see	saw	seen
seek	sought	sought
set	set	set
shake	shook	shaken
shed	shed	shed
shine (beam)	shone	shone
shine (polish)	shined	shined
show	showed	shown, showed
shrink	shrank	shrunk
sing	sang	sung
singe	singed	singed
sink	sank, sunk	sunk, sunken
sit	sat	sat

TABLE 12.1. *(continued)*

INFINITIVE	PAST TENSE	PAST PARTICIPLE
slay	slew	slain
slide	slid	slidden, slid
slink	slunk	slunk
sow	sowed	sowed, sown
spew	spewed	spewed
speak	spoke	spoken
spring	sprang, sprung	sprung
steal	stole	stolen
sting	stung	stung
strive	strove, strived	striven, strived
swear	swore	sworn
swim	swam	swum
swing	swung	swung
take	took	taken
teach	taught	taught
tear	tore	torn
tell	told	told
throw	threw	thrown
wake	waked, woke	waked, woken
wear	wore	worn
weave	wove	woven
win	won	won
wring	wrung	wrung
write	wrote	written

Transitive verbs are verbs whose action is carried across to some other part of the sentence. That other part of the sentence to which the action is carried is either the *subject* of the verb or the *object* of the *verb*. **Intransitive verbs**, on the other hand, are verbs whose activity is *not* carried across to another part of the sentence; the activity remains self-contained within the verb itself. Here are some examples of transitive and intransitive verbs:

TRANSITIVE: Lamar **rifled** the petty cash **drawer.** (Here the action of the verb is carried across the sentence to the object, **drawer.**)

The petty cash **drawer was rifled** by Lamar. (Here the action of the verb is carried across the sentence to the subject, **drawer.**)

INTRANSITIVE: Poverty still **exists.** (The verb **exists** makes a statement about the subject, but its action does not directly affect any other part of the sentence.)

Lamar **appears** furtive. (Here again the action remains static within the verb.)

Now, what's the practical value of making this transitive/intransitive distinction? Well, the value is in the fact that there are six verbs in English that seem to cause more trouble than all the others combined. They are: **sit, set; rise, raise; lie, lay.** You cannot use any one of these troublesome and—unfortunately—common verbs with accuracy unless you can resolve the transitive/intransitive question; that is, whether or not the activity of a verb is directed toward its object or its subject.

The first three of the above verbs (**sit**, **rise**, **lie**) are intransitive:

> I will **sit** quietly.
>
> My brother is **lying** down.
>
> The sun will **rise**.

The second three (**set**, **raise**, **lay**) are transitive verbs; their activity is directed toward an object or a subject.

> Lamar **set** the box in the floor.
>
> The box **was laid** on the platform.
>
> Lamar **raised** the box above his head.

If you can remember the transitive/intransitive distinction in regard to these six verbs, you'll be at least one jump ahead of most English-speaking people.

Transitive verbs can be subdivided into two further categories. And these you already know—active voice and passive voice. But remember that voice applies only to transitive verbs; there is no such animal as an intransitive verb in the active or passive voice. By this time you know the practical advantage of being able to distinguish between the two voices of the transitive verb: you will be able to avoid a vague, impersonal style.

Now, intransitive verbs can also be broken down into two subdivisions. These are (1) intransitive verbs of *complete* predication and (2) intransitive verbs of *incomplete* predication. What is the basis for this distinction? *Intransitive verbs of **complete** predication need only a subject and, perhaps, a modifier or two to make sense*—to make a logically complete predication. Here are some examples:

> Lamar **lives** quietly.
>
> He **sits**.
>
> Lamar **dreamed**.

Note: If we were to say "Lamar dreamed it." then **dreamed** would not be used intransitively. It would have an object, **it**, and it would be a transitive verb in the active voice. Many verbs can be used transitively or intransitively.

*Intransitive verbs of **incomplete** predication need more than a subject to help them make a complete predication.* They need in addition a complement, either a *predicate nominative* or a *predicate adjective*. We encountered these verbs before in Chapter 11 (see p. 139). There they went under the less pretentious name of *linking verbs*. Look at the examples below:

> I am.
>
> He is.
>
> She seems.

These verbs can't make sense by themselves. When we read them, we find ourselves asking "I am **what**?" or "He is **who**?" They need complements, either substantives or adjectives, to complete their predication and, in the process, refer back to the subject:

> I am he.
>
> I am exhausted.
>
> He is the supervisor.
>
> He is worried.
>
> She seems tall.

You'll recall from our discussion of complements in Chapter 11 that the chief linking verbs are forms of **to be**, and **appears**, **feel**, **seem**, **look**, **taste**, etc. We hope you also recall why it is of practical importance to recognize these intransitive verbs of incomplete predication. The reason is that if the complement of one of these verbs should happen to be a pronoun, that pronoun must be put in the subjective case ("I am he." Not "I am him."). What is more, we can use this distinction to avoid the common error of confusing adverbs with adjective complements. (We'll discuss this last point when we take up adjective and adverbs a little later in this chapter.)

In summary, the following chart, Table 12.2, should pull the four distinctions between verb types together for you.

TABLE 12.2.

TRANSITIVE	INTRANSITIVE
ACTIVE VOICE	PASSIVE VOICE
I **laid** it down.	It **was laid** down.
He **hit** the ball.	He **was hit** by the ball.
She **took** the letter.	The letter **was taken** by Miss Kline.
I **set** it over there.	It **was set** over there.
COMPLETE PREDICATION	INCOMPLETE PREDICATION *
Lamar **dreams** often.	Lamar **is** narcoleptic.
Lamar **lies** down.	Lamar **seems** sleepy.
Lamar **will rise** for dinner.	It **was** he who woke Lamar.

* Needs a complement (noun, pronoun, or adjective) to make sense.

VERBALS

Verbals are words that are derived from verb forms but do not act as verbs; that is, they do not make statements about subjects. What they do, however, is to act like other parts of speech. Verbals can, and do, act as *substantives* (nouns or pronouns), *adverbs,* or *adjectives.* There are three types of verbals: (1) *gerunds*, (2) *participles*, and (3) *infinitives:*

A. THE GERUND

*The **gerund** is a form of a verb that always ends in **ing** and functions as a substantive.*

> **Jogging** is good for you. (**Jogging** is derived from the verb **jog** and is used as the subject of the sentence.)
>
> I want to talk to you about **jogging**. (Here the gerund is used as the object of the preposition **about**.)

B. THE PARTICIPLE

*The **participle** is a form of a verb that sometimes ends in **ing** and is used as an adjective: that is, it modifies substantives.* Verbals are enough like the verbs they are derived from to have tenses. Present participles end in **ing** but past and perfect participles do not.

> The **wandering** men explored the cave. (**Wandering** is a present participle formed from the verb **wander** and modifying the substantive **men**.)
>
> They marked the **explored** cave on the map. (**Explored** is a past participle modifying **cave**.)

C. THE INFINITIVE

The *infinitive* is an all-purpose verbal. *Infinitives are formed from verbs and can function as nouns, adverbs, or adjectives.* Unfortunately for our ease of diagnosis, they are not always preceded by **to**. Let's look at the various ways the infinitive can be employed: 1. Infinitives used as Nouns—**To review** this report will take a while. (**To review** is the subject of the verb **will take**.) He wants **to review** the report. (**To review** is the object of the verb **wants**.) 2. Infinitives used as Adjectives—Lamar has time **to kill**. (**To kill** modifies the substantive **time**.) We saw him **walk**. (**Walk** modifies the substantive **him**. Note that **to** is understood here.) 3. Infinitives used as Adverbs—I am ready **to review** the report. (**To review** modifies the adjective **ready**.) It did not help **to have talked** to Lamar. (**To have talked** modifies the verb **help**. Note that the infinitive is in the perfect tense.)

Now, what is the practical advantage of being able to recognize verbals? It helps us escape confusion, that's what! There are special problems connected with verbals, and we'll deal with them now.

Although they are not verbs, verbals are derived from verbs and may, like verbs, have subjects, objects, and complements. Therefore, the case of substantives used with verbals can be a problem.

A noun or pronoun preceding a *gerund* is considered to be the gerund's subject, but is customarily put in the possessive case.

> He objected to **Lamar's drinking** all the champagne.
>
> I don't like **his drinking** all the champagne.

The subject of an *infinitive* is, paradoxically, put in the objective case.

> I don't want **her to sing**. (Neither the pronoun **her**, nor the infinitive is the object of the verb. Both the infinitive *and* its subject comprise the verb's object.)

The infinitive **to be** presents special problems of case. We know that the subject of the infinitive is in the objective case. We should also remember that the complement of a linking verb takes the same case as the subject of the verb. The infinitive **to be** can be regarded as a *linking verbal,* and any complement it has should be in the same case as its subject. So, confusingly enough, the complement of the *linking verbal* **to be** should be in the objective case. Thus:

> Lamar was confused and thought her **to be** him (Not "Lamar thought she to be he.")

Earlier, in Chapter 11 on syntax, we talked about dangling modifiers (pp. 154-155). Verbal phrases, especially participial phrases, are the most frequent danglers. Whenever we use a verbal construction, we should take special care that the phrase modifies some *specific* part of the main sentence.

> DANGLING: Hurrying to meet the deadline, many errors were committed. (Who or what was hurrying?)
>
> CORRECTED: Hurrying to meet the deadline, Lamar committed many errors. (Here the participial phrase has been given something specific and logical—**Lamar**—to modify.

The last problem connected with verbals has to do with infinitives. Actually it is thought by many not to be a problem at all. This is the matter of *split infinitives*. A split infinitive occurs when a word, usually an adverb, crops up between the two parts of the infinitive.

> SPLIT INFINITIVES: to quickly walk
>
> to softly approach
>
> to quietly come

Some traditionalists believe that these split constructions should be avoided at all costs:

> REPAIRED INFINITIVES: to walk quickly
>
> softly to approach
>
> to come quietly

But there is no logical reason why we should not split infinitives, and we have undoubtedly split a few in this text. However, remember that the construction still does disturb some people.

ADJECTIVES AND ADVERBS

Adjectives and *adverbs* are the next parts of speech we'll take up. We encountered these terms in our discussion of syntax when we reviewed the subject of modifiers (pp. 137-138). Adjectives and adverbs should not detain us for long. We'll simply repeat that **adjectives** *modify (or restrict the meaning of) substantives, and* **adverbs** *modify verbs, adjectives, and other adverbs.*

Now to the practical point. What problems may arise with adjectives and adverbs? We'll cover a few.

A. COMPARISON

One problem with adjectives and adverbs has to do with the *comparison* of these words. If substantives are *declined* and verbs are *conjugated,* adjectives and adverbs are inflected through the process known as *comparison.* Just as there are three cases for substantives, there are three degrees of comparison for these modifiers—*positive, comparative,* and *superlative.* To illustrate this, we'll put some adjectives through their paces of comparison. (Adjectives are the most troublesome in this respect.)

POSITIVE	COMPARATIVE	SUPERLATIVE
red	redder	reddest
many	more	most
beautiful	more beautiful	most beautiful
full	more full	most full
full	fuller	fullest

Looking at the examples above, you can see the potential problems. Some adjectives are compared by simply tacking **-ed** and **-est** on the end. Others—like **beautiful**—can be compared only by using **more** and **most**. Some others, like **full**, can be compared by using either **more/most** or **-er/-est**. The point is to pick one method of comparison and stay with it; don't combine two. In *Julius Ceasar* Shakespeare could write about "the most unkindest cut of all," but modern practice demands that we avoid such double comparison. Finally, there are other adjectives as well—like **many**—that don't use either the -er/-est or more/most method of comparison, but instead radically change their spelling when they are inflected. These are said to be *irregular adjectives,* and when in doubt about these, you should, as with irregular verbs, consult your dictionary.

Another difficulty with comparison stems from having to remember to use the superlative form when comparing more than two things, and the comparative form when comparing only two things. Thus:

> This is the **tallest** of the **three** trees.
>
> This is the **taller** of the **two** trees.

Still another problem with comparison is that there are some modifiers, which, to use the technical phrase, do not admit of comparison. In other words, these words already represent some quality to the fullest degree, which, technically at least, cannot be improved. Some common examples of incomparable adjectives and adverbs are:

complete	exactly	square
completely	perfect	supreme
dead	perfectly	total
exact	round	unique

The last issue of comparison involves what is known as *incomplete comparison.* When you compare two things, be sure that your reader knows exactly what you are comparing. When in doubt about the clarity of your comparison, you should explicitly name all or both items in question.

INCOMPLETE:	I enjoy this sort of thing better than Alice.
COMPLETE:	I enjoy this sort of thing better than Alice does.
INCOMPLETE:	Lamar's report outlines the difficulties better than Alice.
COMPLETE:	Lamar's report outlines the difficulty better than Alice's (or Alice's does).

B. ADJECTIVE-ADVERB CONFUSION

The second major cause of problems with adjective and adverb modifiers has to do with distinguishing between predicate adjectives and adverbs. Usually we have no problem instinctively putting an adjective instead of an adverb after a linking verb:

That report is **correct**. (We would never use the adverb **correctly**.)

The report appears **accurate**. (We would not say **accurately**.)

But, when we use certain linking verbs that denote senses, our instincts may waver. Usually verbs like **feel, taste, look,** and **sound** are followed by a predicate adjective, but sometimes they are directly modified by an *adverb*.

I feel **bad**. (Here the verb is complemented by a predicate adjective. The speaker means that he is ill.)

I feel **badly**. (Here the verb is modified by an adverb. The speaker means that, like a surgeon working in mittens, his sense of touch is out of order.)

The steak looks **tender**. (**Tender** is a predicate adjective.)

Lamar looked **tenderly** at the steak. (**Tenderly** directly modifies the verb.)

People who know a little grammar and want to appear more knowledgeable than they are, often make a great show of using an adverb when they should use an adjective. They seem to think it more elegant to say "She looks badly." rather than the simpler and correct "She looks bad."

C. ARTICLES

The third and last basic kind of problem with modifiers is the correct use of those modifiers called *articles.* There are only three articles in English: the *definite* article **the**, and the *indefinite* articles **a** and **an**.

One difficulty with articles stems from a rule that states that we must use **a** before words beginning with a consonant sound, even if the sound is spelled with a vowel (as in **a university**); and we must use **an** before words beginning with a vowel sound or a silent **h** (**an hour**). There is a mild controversy about whether **a** or **an** should be used before words beginning with a pronounced **h** (like **hotel** or **historian**). Most American writers, however, use **a** with words like these.

Also, remember that if you use an article before each of two or more connected nouns or adjectives, you are signalling to your reader that you are referring to two separate items:

We elected **a** president and **a** vice-president. (Two distinct offices were filled.)

He has **a** black and white automobile. (He has one automobile with two colors.)

Finally, never use either **a** or **an** after **kind of, sort of, manner of, type of,** etc.

INCORRECT:	What type of a car did you buy?
CORRECT:	What type of car did you buy?

CONJUNCTIONS

*A **conjunction**, as the term itself implies, is a joining word; it connects words, phrases, and clauses.* There are three common types of conjunctions: (1) *coordinating,* (2) *subordinating,* and (3) *correlative.*

1. Coordinating conjunctions join elements of equal syntactical importance. The five basic coordinating conjunctions are **and, but, or, nor, for, yet,** and (sometimes) **so.**

2. Subordinating conjunctions are particularly important to recognize since their chief use is to begin subordinate (or dependent) clauses. In Chapter 11 we discussed subordinate clauses (pp. 149-150) and how important their recognition is to understanding sentence construction. Some common subordinating conjunctions are:

after	because	since	unless
although	in order that	than	until
as	inasmuch as	though	when

3. Correlative conjunctions are conjunctions that always work in pairs. Some common correlative conjunctions are:

either . . . or	not only . . . but also	both . . . and
neither . . . or	if . . . then	since . . . therefore

Correlative conjunctions emphasize words or ideas that are parallel.

Very few problems arise with respect to conjunctions, but most have to do with punctuation. These will be covered fully in Chapter 13. But we will touch on one problem here.

Many people have problems with *conjunctive adverbs.* Conjunctive adverbs are words like **however, therefore, consequently, moreover, nevertheless,** and **still.** These words at once connect and show relationships between clauses. A clause introduced by a conjunctive adverb is considered to be grammatically independent, but it still logically depends on the preceding clause to make complete sense. Don't confuse conjunctive adverbs with *coordinating conjunctions.* Clauses joined by a conjunctive adverb are not as closely related as those joined by a coordinating conjunction. Therefore, clauses joined by a conjunctive adverb must be separated by a semicolon or a period and not by a comma.

> The police beat on the door, **but** Lamar remained cool.
> (These are independent clauses joined by a *coordinating conjunction.*)

> The police beat on the door; **nevertheless,** Lamar remained cool.
> (These are independent clauses joined by a *conjunctive adverb.*)

Note: Phrases like **on the other hand, for example, in fact,** and **in the first place** are also regarded as conjunctive adverbs.

PREPOSITIONS

The final part of speech we will discuss is the *preposition*. Prepositions are *relating* words; that is, **prepositions** *are used to relate substantives to other parts of the sentence.* Generally, prepositions are one word (**at, by, upon, into, in**, etc.), but sometimes a group of words may function as a preposition (**in spite of, on account of**).

There are two notable problems connected with the use of prepositions—*case* and *idiom.*

A. CASE OF PREPOSITIONS

Prepositions are customarily used to form phrases (**at the store, into the car**), and a substantive which is the object of a preposition is in the objective case. This becomes a potential problem only when the object is a pronoun, which (you will recall) is the only substantive that changes its spelling as it changes its case:

> into **me** (objective case)
>
> to **her** (objective case)
>
> upon **me** (objective case)

But, do not make the mistake of thinking that just because a pronoun follows a preposition, it must be its object. Remember that it might play another, different role in a clause, in which case its function in the clause determines its case (see pp. 165-167).

> Take it from **whoever** can pay. (**Whoever** is in the subjective case because it is the subject of a noun clause. The whole clause is the object of the preposition.)

B. IDIOMATIC USE OF PREPOSITIONS

The word *idiom* comes from the Greek *idios* which means "special or peculiar." In grammar, an *idiomatic* usage is a way of speaking peculiar to a certain language. Idiomatic usages are governed by custom and tradition rather than logic.

If you've ever studied a foreign language you have probably been puzzled by various idiomatic customs governing the use of certain words and phrases. The French, for example, do not say "It is cold." Instead they say "*Il fait froid,*" or literally, "It makes cold." This may seem illogical to English speakers, but it is a perfectly good French idiom. English also is full of idiomatic usages that puzzle foreigners but seem natural to us. However, even native-born speakers of English occasionally have trouble with the correct idiomatic uses of certain prepositions with verbs and substantives. By custom, there are certain prepositions used with certain words and there seems to be no rhyme or reason for their interdependence. It just *is.* For example, we always say that we have the "knack *of*" doing something, not a "knack *for*". In English, people idiomatically "die *of*" a disease, they don't "die *from*" it. Furthermore, one is "employed *for*" a certain job, "employed *at*" a given salary, and "employed *in, on,* or *upon*" a specific task or business.

In the "Glossary of Usage" at the end of Part III we have provided a brief list of some of the more common idiomatic uses of prepositions. But, as with irregular verbs, spelling, and many other matters, a good dictionary is invaluable for solving vexing problems of prepositional idioms. We hope it may help a little just to be aware that the problem exists.

Finally, there are two more minor areas of difficulty with prepositions we'll mention here. One of these is a false difficulty caused by the old axiom "Never end a sentence with a preposition!" Like many old axioms this is untrue. There is no more logical reason for avoiding prepositions at the end of sentences than there is for not splitting infinitives. Again, just be aware that split infinitives and terminal prepositions still offend a few traditionalists.

The other area of difficulty, however, has to do with *unnecessary prepositions,* and it is a real problem. All we can say is try to avoid unnecessary prepositions:

> off **of**
>
> where **at**
>
> continue **on**
>
> near **to**
>
> divide **up**

In the phrases above, *all* the prepositions are unnecessary, and lucid, economical writers omit them.

Chapter 13

PUNCTUATION AND MECHANICS

CAPITALIZATION

The term *capitalization* comes from the Latin *capitalis*, meaning "chief or principal." It has the ring of money and importance, and is an appropriate mechanical device for highlighting both the beginnings of sentences and importance of certain words. In addition to helping us distinguish **grand rapids** from **Grand Rapids** and **intercourse** from **Intercourse, Pa.**, capitalization helps order our prose movement by indicating where sentences begin. Remember that capitalization can be an arbitrary process (either **senator** or **Senator** is correct, for example, though one should be consistent in using one or the other), but that the following rules are fairly standard.

1. Capitalize the first letter of sentences, sentence fragments, and lines of poetry. Also capitalize the first letter of direct quotations except when they are fragmentary.

"What is written without effort is in general read without pleasure," said Samuel Johnson.

I wish I had a horse. My kingdom for a horse!

You write with ease to show your breeding
But easy writing's curst hard reading. [Richard B. Sheridan]

Like other great men, Henry Ford took "the road less traveled by."

2. Capitalize all proper nouns and their derivatives, including all references to religious sects, deities, and sacred books. Do not capitalize common nouns.

Paris, Parisian, plaster of paris

Villanova University, university, Villanovan

Mother's Day, day

Bible, Protestant, Christ, Shakers, Quakers, Jewish, New Testament

3. *Capitalize the days of the week and months of the year, but not the seasons.*

> Thursday   summer
>
> January   winter

4. *Capitalize the names of specific courses and the names of languages.*

> I enjoy American Literature I, but dislike geometry and Spanish.

5. *Capitalize the names of streets, cities, regions, geographical features, etc., but not terms of direction.*

> San Antonio, Texas   equatorial climate
>
> The Middle East   north, northern, south
>
> Equatorial Africa   Pacific Ocean
>
> Central Park   The North Pole
>
> Lake Erie   the South
>
> the Midwest   Delancey Street

6. *Capitalize titles when used with proper names or when clearly referring to an individual.* Do not capitalize titles used in a general sense.

> President Johnson lived in Texas.
>
> The President will address the nation on television.
>
> Our club has a president, two vice-presidents, a treasurer, and a secretary.
>
> Ambassador Hunt will become an ambassador-at-large.

7. *Capitalize the names of local, national, and international buildings and organizations.*

> National Association of Manufacturers
>
> the Federal Government; the Government
>
> World Health Organization
>
> Kiwanis
>
> Knights Templar
>
> Department of Agriculture
>
> Chamber of Commerce

8. *Capitalize the first letter of all the words in a title, except articles, prepositions of less than five letters, and conjunctions.* The same rule applies to subtitles except that the first letter of the subtitle is always capitalized.

> Title of book with subtitle: *Factories Through the Ages: A Tour with a Camera*
>
> Title of an essay: "The Capture of the Embezzler"
>
> Title of a poem: "I Wandered Lonely as a Cloud"
>
> Chapter title: Background to Wills and Trusts

9. *Capitalize abbreviated titles following a name.*

> Ph.D., M.D., Esq.
>
> U.S.A. (Ret.), B.S.

There is no definitive rule on the capitalization of some abbreviations:

> AM, A.M., a.m.,
>
> mph, MPH, Mph, m.p.h.

10. *Capitalize salutations in letters and the first letter of signatures.*

Dear Mr. Knowles	Affectionately yours
To Whom It May Concern	Sincerely yours
Dear Aunt Margaret	Yours truly

COMMAS

Although it is true, as we suggested in our Introduction to Part III, that common sense can help you decide when to use a comma, you should also keep the following points in mind.

A. THE COMMA SPLICE

The comma is not as strong a punctuation mark as a period or semicolon. Thus, using it to join (or splice) two main clauses can lead to confusion. You may use a comma to separate clauses only when the clauses are brief and you are certain no confusion will result. Or you may use a comma when clauses are connected by the coordinating conjunctions **and, but, or, for, nor, yet**, and (sometimes) **so**.

> WRONG: Mr. Timmons decided that the monthly report on penicillin production did not contain enough details about direct expenses, I, on the other hand, felt the report was clear, detailed, and comprehensive.

Some possible corrections are:

1. Use a period and begin a new sentence: . . . direct expenses. I, on the . . . .
2. Use a semicolon: . . . expenses; I, on the . . . .
3. Use a coordinating conjunction preceded by a comma: . . . expenses, but I, on the . . . .
4. Rewrite the sentence to make one main clause subordinate:

   While I felt the report was clear, detailed, and comprehensive, Mr. Timmons decided that the monthly report on penicillin production did not contain enough details about direct expenses.

Here are some acceptable comma splices:

> RIGHT: We liked the report, he disliked it.
>
> He likes New York, she likes Maryland.

B. RESTRICTIVE AND NONRESTRICTIVE MODIFIERS

You must decide whether additional information about a noun is essential (restrictive) or nonessential (nonrestrictive), that is, whether or not the phrase or clause restricts the meaning of the noun (see also pp. 153-154). Examine the following sentences:

> WRONG: Men in the office, who wear blue shirts, are usually accountants.
>
> RIGHT: Men in the office who wear blue shirts are usually accountants.

The adjective clause modifying **men** is **who wear blue shirts**. It is essential to the meaning of the sentence since it gives necessary information about **men**. Therefore this clause cannot be set off by commas; it is restrictive. Here are some examples of nonrestrictive modifiers that do require commas.

> Peter Drucker, who often addresses conferences on management, is the author of *The Practice of Management*.
>
> Mark Twain, the famous American humorist, once said that the difference between the exact word and the nearly exact word is the difference between "lightning and the lightning bug."
>
> Some business consultants, who are often well paid, dislike the constant need to travel by airplane.

C. DATES AND ADDRESSES

Use a comma to separate the year when it follows the day of the month (except when using the military form where the day is given first). The comma is optional between the month and year.

Also, if the sentence continues, place a comma after the date of the month or year. No comma separates a zip code from the name of a state.

> On October 12, 1974, our new branch office opened.
>
> The military junta expropriated the oil fields on 7 May 1969.
>
> The company will mark its 125th anniversary on Tuesday, March 11, 1976.

Use a comma to separate a street address from the name of a city, and the city from the state. A comma after the state is optional.

> We moved on October 12, 1973, to 1801 Woodgrove Lane, Radnor, Pennsylvania.
>
> The address on the invoice was National Products, 8205 Belzer Circle, Clemson, South Carolina 29631.
>
> Employees in Boston, Massachusetts get additional pay.

D. COMMAS IN A SERIES

Coordinate words, phrases, and clauses in a series are separated by commas. This applies even though many current writers drop the final comma before the *and* in an a, b, and c series. Except for obvious compounds (bread and butter), avoid any possible confusion by retaining the comma before *and*.

> Bill, Tom, and Harry were asked to direct our Miami office.
>
> I took the accounting course, Mary took the broker's license course, and Ralph took the communications course. (Note: It is not a comma splice to separate coordinate main clauses in a series. But use semi-colons if there is any danger of confusion.)
>
> President Winthrop promised to increase profits, to cut overhead, and to change our image.
>
> For breakfast we all had milk and cereal, coffee, toast, bacon and eggs, and buns.

Coordinate adjectives can sometimes cause problems too. How would you punctuate the following?

> He found three small yellow pens in her desk.

No commas are needed here because the elements are not coordinate and could not be coherently rearranged (small yellow three pens?). However, this is not the case in the following sentence:

> You have never met a more upright, honest, thoughtful young man.

Note that adjectives denoting size or age are usually not set off. Also, do not put a comma between the last adjective and the noun it modifies.

> He assumed a happy, carefree attitude toward his job.
>
> The spry old man was happy and healthy and wise.

Commas are not used when series members are connected by conjunctions.

E. OTHER USES FOR COMMAS

1. Parenthetical elements. These are words, phrases, or clauses that interrupt the movement of the sentence in order to emphasize, clarify, or qualify some point being made. They should be used with commas.

> Hospital insurance, **of course**, will be paid by your employer.
>
> There are, **I am certain**, a variety of computer languages.
>
> **However,** he does make a good case for a national advertising campaign.

However, also, indeed, instead, likewise, moreover, nevertheless, still, then, therefore, thus, etc. are conjunctive adverbs which link statements to previous ones. Generally these conjunctive adverbs are placed between commas. But when they join two main clauses in a compound sentence, they must be preceded by a semicolon:

> WRONG: I am worried about the large expense, **however**, he does make a good case for a national advertising campaign.

> RIGHT: I am worried about the large expense; **however**, he does make a good case for a national advertising campaign.

2. Appositives. Expressions which redefine a preceding noun or pronoun are called appositives and require commas.

> The company treasurer, **J. C. Martin**, wisely invested the year's profits.

> My business seminar, **Marketing 103**, helped me to understand the value of good advertising.

3. Words Used in Direct Address.

> You, **Thorndike**, are the best typist we ever had in the office.

> "Come here, **Simpson**," the editor said, "and check this copy."

4. Introductory elements. Here one must be careful to use good sense. Introductory phrases and clauses that are long and nonessential are often set off by commas. Otherwise you must simply read the sentence and ask yourself: "Will this be clear to my reader?"

> Having looked for the Bargess papers in nine different filing cabinets, we finally found them in the desk.

> After a long day, I want to go home and go to bed.

> From above, the cars and people looked very small.

> Not wishing to hurt his feelings, I remained quiet during the meeting.

> Yes, we have no bananas for lunch.

(Note: The third sentence would be confusing without the comma.)

5. Interruptions in Direct Quotations. Commas are used to set off interruptions in quotations, usually speaker designations, unless the quotation ends with an exclamation point or a question mark.

> "Well, I never in my life," she said, "heard of such a thing."

> "How dare you question my figures!" the accountant snapped.

> "What should I do about the Hobson account?" Tim asked.

> "Well, running a snowball stand certainly can be a demanding task," Mr. Hobson agreed, "but do you have any other job experiences?"

ITALICS AND QUOTATION MARKS

A. ITALICS

The major portion of this text is printed in ordinary typeface known as *roman* (here italicized), while the slanted typeface used to emphasize certain words is called *italic.* Italics and underlining (its equivalent in typescript) are both used for emphasis.

1. Italics are used to indicate titles. Italics are most commonly used to indicate the titles of books, films, plays, long poems, newspapers, works of art and music, and names of ships and aircraft.

> *Paradise Lost*
>
> the Philadelphia *Bulletin* (Notice that the place of publication is generally not italicized.)
>
> *Playboy*   Michelangelo's *Pieta*
>
> *Waiting for Godot*   Lindbergh's *Spirit of St. Louis*
>
> *How Things Work*   Handel's *Messiah*
>
> *The Titanic*   *Gone With the Wind*

2. Italics denote foreign words and phrases. Recently the French Government was growing very concerned over the introduction into French language of many American and British terms, such as *le hot-dog, le drugstore, le jazz.* But we Americans are less chauvinistic in semantic matters and have through the years both expanded and enriched our language with many foreign words and expressions. The greater their use the less likely we are to see them italicized in print—no hard rule exists. You should consult the latest dictionaries for the exact usages of italics and foreign words.

> NO ITALICS: The soccer team members displayed a rare esprit de corps.
>
> The legislature must weigh the pros and cons before passing the bill.
>
> ITALICS: There was a certain *jeu d'esprit* in his manner.
>
> *Zeitgeist* literally means "time spirit."

3. Italics are used for emphasis. The use of italics to emphasize certain words becomes less effective if overused. Use italics sparingly to avoid such rhetorical bludgeons as the following:

> *I* like *this* slogan *very* much.

4. Italics indicate a word spoken of as such.

> The word *democracy* suggests different things to different people.

You may also use quotation marks for this same purpose.

5. Italics denote technical Latin titles of certain botanical and zoological species.

> sweet pea (*Lathyrus odoratus*)
>
> moonflower (*Calonyction aculeatum*)
>
> the mallaid (*Anas platyrhynchos*)

B. QUOTATION MARKS

Double quotation marks are generally used to indicate direct remarks and titles of brief works.

1. Use double quotation marks (" ") to enclose direct quotations. Include within the quotation marks all quoted material except explanatory expressions.

> International Widgets announced recently that it is "searching for an experienced, aggressive individual to head up its California operations."

"Without doubt," he explained, "the best person for the job is Peters."

"Where do I park my car?" she asked.

In the last two examples notice that when the full quotation is interrupted, a comma is used after the first part unless the quotation ends in an exclamation point or a question mark. Also, when quoting material longer than six or seven lines, use a *block quotation* in which each line is indented at least the length of a paragraph indentation. The lines are generally single spaced. You may omit the quotation marks when using block quotations or when you typographically set off the quoted material in some other way.

> The HEW pamphlet entitled "Your Social Security" answers your question in this way:

>> If you become disabled before 65, you and certain members of your family may be eligible for benefits. Do not wait too long after you are disabled to apply for benefits; if you wait more than a year, you may lose benefits. Payments may begin with the seventh full month of disability. If you are found eligible for disability insurance benefits, you will remain eligible as long as you are disabled. When you reach 65, your benefit will be changed to retirement payments at the same rate.

2.   Use quotation marks to enclose titles of articles, songs, essays, short stories, brief poems, and parts of works. Chapter headings of reports are not placed in quotation marks.

> "Pisanus Fraxi, Pornographer Royal" is an interesting chapter in Steven Marcus' *The Other Victorians*.

> Read that *Harvard Business Review* article by Wendell Farnum on "ITT and Transactional Analysis."

> Sinatra's "Strangers in the Night" is one of his best songs.

> James Joyce's "The Dead" is a story with too many symbols.

> "The Ballad of Danny O'Hagan" was written by an old Irish woman in Northern Ireland.

3.   Use quotation marks to call attention to words, but (as with italics) don't overuse them for ironic effect.

> He calls his jerky movements a "serve," but I don't feel that he is telling the truth.

4.   Use quotation marks (or italics) to designate words used as words, but be consistent in the method you choose.

> The term "feedback" occurs frequently in evaluation techniques.

> His rate scale is based on a "piecework" system.

5.   Use single quotation marks to enclose a quotation within a quotation.

> Our treasurer recently remarked; "I feel confident that before August the 'mild recession' recently predicted by the Manhattan Bank economists will have become a reality."

6.   Apply the following rules when using quotation marks with other marks of punctuation:
   a. All commas and periods go inside quotation marks.

> "Tim Evans," said the secretary, "is writing this month's report."

   b. Colons and semicolons go outside quotation marks.

> There are two major criticisms of the "American Cancer Society Report on Smoking":
> 1) it is wrong; 2) it does not go far enough.

> He said that "Samuelson has the most sensible approach to the wage control policy"; I said that Gill made more sense to me.

   c. Question marks and exclamation points go inside or outside quotation marks, depending on whether or not they are a part of the quotation.

He asked, "Are you going to the regional conference?" (Here the question mark belongs to the quoted part, not the rest of the sentence.)

Are you going to the "Indianapolis 500"? (Here the question mark belongs to the entire sentence, not just the quoted part.)

d. Only *one* terminal punctuation mark should be used at the end of a sentence.

Did she ask you: "What are your feelings about her work?" (Only one question mark is needed after this double question.)

THE APOSTROPHE

Use the apostrophe ('): (1) to indicate possession; (2) to mark omissions; and (3) to form plurals.

A. POSSESSION

All nouns, singular or plural, that do not end in s form the possessive by adding 's. Plural nouns ending in s form the possessive by adding just the apostrophe. The indefinite pronouns (*anybody, anyone, each, everybody, nobody,* etc.) also form their possessive with 's, but personal pronouns (his, ours, yours, whose, etc.) remain unchanged.

> The secretary's typewriter had a gash in its ribbon.
>
> Some men's egos are wrapped up in their jobs.
>
> That car is not his; it's ours.
>
> The girls' coats were left on the desk.
>
> It is anybody's guess as to how he got promoted.
>
> The cat's mother lost its tail.

Singular nouns of one syllable ending in s form their possessive by adding 's; singular nouns of more than one syllable ending in s form their possessive by adding just the apostrophe. This is the general rule, but not one that is rigidly followed. Usage allows either form in some cases.

> Yeats's (or Yeats') poetry is the best.
>
> Thomas's pay increase was held up by the Board. (Even though Thomas contains two syllables, the second *s* sound is expected.)
>
> Moses' leadership in the desert saved his people.
>
> James's (or James') hat fell into the can.

In compounds the possessive designation is added to the last word. But, if separate possession is indicated each noun takes the possessive.

> Mark and Susan's plan proved to be the best. (joint possession.)
>
> Mark's and Susan's plans proved to be the best. (separate possession.)
>
> My father-in-laws's business went bankrupt.
>
> Anyone else's job could go, but the boss's son-in-law's position had to be saved.

B. OMISSIONS

In contractions apostrophes replace an omitted letter or letters.

> Weren't (were not) you a member of the class of '76 (1976)?
>
> The other driver didn't (did not) see him coming.

Be especially careful though to distinguish between contractions and possessive pronouns. Failure to do so is a sure sign of either illiteracy or utter carelessness.

POSSESSIVE PRONOUN	CONTRACTION
its	it's (it is)
theirs	there's (there is)
their	they're (they are)
whose	who's (who is)
your	you're (you are)

C. PLURALS

Use an apostrophe to form the plurals of numbers, letters, symbols, and words or letters used as words or letters.

> I don't want to hear any **if**'s, **and**'s, or **but**'s.
>
> Spell that with two **t**'s and two **s**'s.
>
> Your **4**'s look like my **9**'s.

EXERCISES

THE APOSTROPHE

D. In the following sentences, place apostrophes where you feel they are needed, and eliminate needless ones. Also, look for and repair confusions of possessive pronouns and contractions.

1. Whose going with us to the meeting?

2. Bob's and Mike's plan conflicted with that of the architect.

3. Your sure your secretary is going with us?

4. Keep in mind that "embarrassed" has two *r*s and two *s*s.

5. The janitors lunch was left on the desk.

6. Steve Sickles car was not large enough to hold his various promotional material.

7. From our office window we could see the three trees leaves falling onto the ground.

8. It was nobodys fault except his own that he lost his position.

9. James work on the paper won him a promotion.

10. Its no wonder that the mens lockers were robbed.

11. Very often his *r*s' sound like *w*s'.

12. The class of 52 gave as its gift three girls bicycles for the dormitory counselors.

13. Managers feelings are too often ignored; the boss attitude seems to be that his word is final.

14. The Alexanders cats tail is shaped like the figure *9*.

15. In the 1950s you're fathers politics were the same as theres.

16. The secretarys' pad contained some damaging information.

17. In the alleys behind our home their is very little trash.

18. He is nobodys' fool when it comes to the *c*s and *n*s of contract negotiation.

19. His *maybes* and *buts* cost him his reputation as a decisive executive.

20. He has'nt been terribly successful with our case; how about your's?

OTHER MARKS OF PUNCTUATION

A. THE COLON

The colon indicates a longer pause than the comma. It is thus an excellent punctuation mark to introduce material.

Use the colon to call attention to a quotation, a formal list, or an explanation, and to set it off from the rest of the sentence.

> There are two classical incentive wage systems: Taylor's Differential Piecerate System and Gantt's Task and Bonus System.
>
> Max Amsterdam has a good definition of "business": "the art of extracting money from another man's pocket without resorting to violence."[1]
>
> I suggest you send your proposal to three government agencies: Department of Labor, Department of Defense, and Department of the Interior.

Note that the first letter of a statement following a colon need not be capitalized unless, in the case of a quotation, it is capitalized in the original or unless it is a complete sentence.

Also, the colon can be used to punctuate the salutation of a business letter, to separate hours and minutes in telling time, to separate subtitles from titles, and to separate chapter and verse in Biblical references.

> Dear Mr. Tims:
>
> At precisely 12:20 p.m. he read to us from Matthew 28: 16-20.
>
> Her new book was *Fashion Marketing: A Woman's View.*

B. THE DASH

The dash, or two hyphens (- -) on your typewriter, is generally used to indicate abrupt changes of thought.

> Henri Fayol's contributions to classical organization theory might be—and here I admit my own uncertainty—the best ideas we have.

C. PARENTHESES

Use parentheses to enclose numbers or letters which indicate items in a series, and to set off relevant but not absolutely necessary material.

> Fayol's first principle (division of work) applies best to us.
>
> There are two ways to cope with these grievances: (1) meet the demand for a pay increase, or (2) fire all the workers.
>
> His earlier statement (here I refer to the one made on July 12, 1972) made much more sense.

Dashes and parentheses can become substitutes for sound organization. Don't overuse them.

D. THE SEMICOLON

Go back to our remarks on "Commas" for more information, but here we'll repeat some of the points made there.

---

1. From Leonard Lewis Levinson, *The Left Handed Dictionary.* (New York: Macmillan, Collier Books, 1963), p. 34.

Use the semicolon to separate two main clauses not joined by a coordinating conjunction.

> We waited all day to meet the head of Purchasing; he never showed up.

> Never berate a worker in front of other workers; take him aside and quietly explain the problem.

Also use a semicolon to separate main clauses joined by conjunctive adverbs and transitional phrases.

> The notice advising a lapse of contract was sent to the client; however, he disregarded it.

> R. C. Davis is a firm believer in "executive span"; in other words, he feels that a top or middle manager should only supervise from three to nine individuals.

Finally, semicolons separate elements in a coordinate series when those elements are equal and have internal punctuation.

> There are three possible reasons for their failure to pick up the option: (1) they feel that current profits, though large, are based on a diminishing market; (2) they can not raise the money; (3) they are interested in another company.

EXERCISES

OTHER MARKS OF PUNCTUATION

E.   Where needed, insert appropriate marks of punctuation or change existing marks in the following sentences.

1.   The leaves of the white oak *quercus alba* are usually deeply lobed and broader near the apex than the bottom.

2.   The 8 30 a.m. train left later than usual, around 9 10 a.m.

3.   He has three principles of door-to-door selling always dress conservatively speak in a firm positive voice about the merits of your product and always look your customer directly in the eye.

4.   If you feel weary, please read Psalms 95 1-7.

5.   At the luncheon we heard him read selections from *The Lines of Life My Career with the Telephone Company.*

6.   The previous bill August 3, 1974 did not contain the service charge you have added to the last one August 14, 1974.

7.   Please check with the following Alice Thomas, Director of Purchasing, Gil Thorpe Personnel Director and Jake Whitlow, Employee Development Office.

8.   I have grave reservations about opening a new branch in Alaska however he will probably do it anyway.

9.   I call your attention to Proverbs 2 21-22 "For the upright will inhabit the land, and men of integrity will remain in it; but the wicked will be cut off from the land, and the treacherous will be rooted out of it."

10.   Do not I was certain he said that use this machine it needs to be repaired.

11.   He wanted to pick up the option but I advised strongly against it.

12.   The new wage agreement provides important new benefits a six percent wage increase effective immediately a cost-of-living provision and increased pension benefits.

13.   I do not like him personally therefore I have no desire to work for his company.

14.   So you can see why he applied such pressure he simply felt it was necessary to win the deal.

15.   The pipe shipment did not arrive until Tuesday hence there will be a delay of two weeks in renovating the office.

16.   His *sang froid* a French word meaning self-possession helped our side during the negotiations.

17.   I feel and I do mean *feel* great pain in announcing this decision.

18. Contact the Bureau of the Budget, the Federal Reserve, and First National Bank then if you still need more information give me another call.

19. An adverb has been called "an adjective with a tail on it."

20. He suggested three possible solutions 1 try to talk to the president of the company 2 try to work with the manager 3 try to find a new position.

ABBREVIATIONS AND NUMBERS

A. ABBREVIATIONS

If you have ever puzzled over **KCB, DSC,** or LL.D. following a person's name, you can appreciate our general rule for abbreviations: *avoid them*! The above—Knight Commander of the Bath, Distinguished Service Cross (or Doctor of Surgical Chiropody), and Doctor of Laws—are conventional abbreviations and you will find their meaning in any standard dictionary. But you may only confuse your reader by using them. Of course there are exceptions to the general policy of avoidance, and the following should be abbreviated in most cases:

1. Titles Preceding Names: **Mr., Mrs., Ms., Messrs., Dr., St.** (Saint)
2. Titles Following Names: **Sr., Jr., Esq., M.D., Ph.D., M.A., B.A.** (Do not use **Mr., Mrs.,** etc. in conjunction with other titles or abbreviations for academic degrees: Charles P. Stanton, M.D.; not Dr. Charles P. Stanton, M.D.)
3. Terms of time and measurement preceded by a number: **2:30 A.M., 1:00 P.M., 118 B.C., 36 ft., 250 hp., 15 lb.** (not *lbs.*), **8 in.**
4. Names of certain agencies of the government and widely known organizations: **FBI, ROTC, NATO, CIA, AFL-CIO, AAUP**

The names of recognizable groups such as those above may be abbreviated without periods. Also, in formal writing, and wherever confusion may exist, give a reference in full at least one time before using the abbreviation:

> The American Association of University Professors (AAUP) dealt with over fifty serious cases of tenure violation during the year. Chief among AAUP's cases was Shelton vs. Potomac University.

Also, you may abbreviate addresses (**St., Blvd., Dr.**), states (**Calif., Me.**) names (**Geo., Chas.**), some titles (**Pres., Gov.**), and company names (Hutzler Bros., **Inc.**); but it is more polite to use full references unless a company's letterhead indicates abbreviations or you are specifically requested to use them.

A handy reference guide to abbreviations follows.

Common Latin Phrases and Standard Scholarly Abbreviations

acct.	account	COD	cash on delivery, collect on delivery
anon.	anonymous	colloq.	colloquial
app., apps.	appendix, appendices	corp.	corporation
bal.	balance	dir.	director
BBB	Better Business Bureau	ed., eds.	editor (s), edition (s) edited by
bibliog.	bibliography	e.g.	*exempli gratia* (for example)
biog.	biography	env.	envelope
bro., bros.	brother (s)	equip.	equipment
c	copyright	esp.	especially
C	centigrade	esq., esqr.	esquire
ca. or c.	about (with dates only)	est.	established, estimated
cap.	capacity, capitalize	et al.	*et alia* (and others)
cf.	compare	etc.	*et cetera* (and others; and so forth)
ch., chs.	chapter (s)	ex.	example
chg.	charge	exec.	executive
co.	company	F	Fahrenheit
c/o	care of	f., ff	and the following (page (s))

fn., n.	footnote, note		pct.	percent
fwd.	forward		pl. pls.	plate (s)
ibid.	*ibidem* (in the same place)		pref.	preface, perferred
id.	*idem* (same)		prin.	principal
i.e.	*id est* (that is)		prob.	probable, probably, problem
ill., illus.	illustrated, illustration		prs.	pairs
introd.	introduction		pseud.	pseudonym
ital.	italic, italicized		q.v.	*quod vide* (which see)
l., ll.	line (s)		re	reference, regarding
loc. cit.	*loco citato* (in the place cited)		recd.	received
ltd.	limited		ref.	reference
MS, MSS	manuscript (s)		seq.	*sequens* (the following)
N.B.	*nota bene* (mark well)		supp., suppl.	supplement, supplementary
no., nos.	number (s)		trans.	translation, translator, translated by
non seq.	*non sequitur* (it does not follow)		viz.	*videlicet* (namely)
op. cit.	*opere citato* (in the work cited)		vol., vols.	volume (s)
p., pp.	page (s)		vs.	versus

B. NUMBERS

Deciding when to use figures (32) or to write out numbers (thirty-two) is not always easy, but in this section we provide a number of concrete suggestions. In general, figures are preferred in business and technical writing, especially for all numbers ten and above, and when numbers cannot be expressed briefly and simply (thus $179.82 rather than one hundred seventy-nine dollars and eighty-two cents). Use figures:

1. For numbers of 10 or more: **Three** birds, but **82** sheep, **19** dogs.

2. For dates, telephone, street, and room numbers, and zip codes: April **13**, **1911**, **118** Sycamore Lane, April **13**th, Wayne, Pennsylvania **19087**, **683-2000**.

3. For percentages, decimals, and money: **16** percent, **0.38** inch, **$0.13** or **13** cents, **$5** (not $5.00) per ton.

4. For hours followed by a.m. or p.m., but not by o'clock, noon, or midnight: **8:23** a.m., and **6** a.m. (not 6:00 a.m.), but **twelve** o'clock, **twelve** midnight.

5. For units of prose with frequent references to numbers: "At least **12** of the **35** students voted to wait **10** minutes for the teacher, **18** voted to leave, and **5** had already left."

6. For unit modifiers and ordinal numbers of 10th or more: **8**-hour day, **10**-pound shot, **19**th century, **13**th Congressional District, **118**th Street, **32**nd President, and **11**th precinct, but seventh day, first delivery, third strike.

(Note: If another number precedes one of these as part of a phrase, one, usually the smaller, is written out—e.g., three 10-man crews, 19 two-inch boards).

7. For temperature, longitude, latitude, measurements, proportions, and mathematical expressions: **18** by **12** feet, **600** horsepower, **20/30** vision, **2** to **4**, **1:150**, **7** days, divided by **9**, subtract **84**, **96**°F., **45**° **03'6"** E **83**° **19'6"** N.

Use words:

1. For single numbers less than 10: **three** reports, **eight** budgets, **five** departments.

2. For round numbers and approximations: about **fifty** employees, a **hundred** dollars, a **thousand** soldiers, the early **sixties**.

3. For fractions either used alone or followed by *of a* or *of an:* **one-half** acre, **three-fourths** of an inch (not 3/4 inch or 3/4 of an inch), **1/8** to **4/8** inches.

4. For numbers at the beginning of a sentence: "**Sixteen** men died in the fire."

5. For legal documents: **sixty-two thousand eight hundred and seventy-five,** or **two hundred and seventy-three thousand five hundred and thirty-three.**

Very large figures may be expressed by combining words and figures: therefore, $39,000,000,000 may be written as either **$39 billion** or **39 billion dollars.**

EXERCISES

ABBREVIATIONS AND NUMBERS

F.   In the following sentences correct any errors in the use of abbreviations and numbers.

1.   The co. report spelled out 3 ways in which profits could be increased.

2.   16 companies claim Dr. Fred Miller, PH.D., as their economic consultant.

3.   On July seventh at eight-thirteen a.M., they moved from nine Cedar Lane to thirteen Ransom Strt.

4.   The Xerox bill alone came to five thousand three hundred dollars.

5.   The meeting will begin promptly at 11:00 a.m.; the first discussion item is the $12,000,000 budget.

6.   Mr. Chas. Stimson, Esq., of Bailey-Barton Cor., called my attention to pg. fifty-one of their annual report.

7.   He needed a 3/5 inch drill for the hole.

8.   It was thirteen degrees Far. below zero in Montana one year.

9.   These homes were built in the eighteen-eighties.

10.   Most quarterbacks have twenty-twenty vision.

11.   The odds against a merger are thirteen to one.

12.   Around forty percent of our staff have medical insurance.

13.   The first, second, and twelfth floors are the best heated.

14.   He will be eighty years old on the fifteenth of July.

15.   It will take around 80 days to complete the job.

16.   He will need five twelve-hour days to make that much money.

17. He lives in apartment two-D on ninety-sixth Srt. in Raleigh, N.C.

18. Attendance at the regional training sessions varied from 75 at Dr. Thom's seminar to 59 at Mr. Barton's to seven at Mr. Menton's.

19. Many great inventors (q.v., Ford and Edison) were also shrewd businessmen.

20. See p. thirty three to forty for the stock quotations; International Bauxite is at twenty-seven, zinc at 0.82.

Chapter 14

STYLE POINTS

A few years back a national magazine published a sea story designed to imitate the writing style of Ernest Hemingway. There was the same absence of adjectives, the same collection of simple and compound sentences, the same declarative straightforwardness that we associate with Hemingway. All the elements were present, but the effect was not the same. You knew you were not reading Hemingway, but a clever imitation.

Style is important—an idea may be forceful or ineffective depending upon how well it is expressed. Would Abraham Lincoln's famous line still be famous had he said: "Eighty-seven years ago our ancestors revolted and established a democratic government . . ."? Think how much more powerful is "Fourscore and seven years ago our fathers brought forth upon this continent a new nation, conceived in liberty, and dedicated to the proposition that all men are created equal." Does "I arrived here, looked around, and then emerged victorious" have the same impact as "I came, I saw, I conquered"? We can't all be Lincolns, Hemingways or Caesars, or even all develop a distinctive style. In fact, we shouldn't be overly concerned about style in our business communications. What we need is to try to communicate our ideas as clearly as possible without confusing or boring our reader. We need to write letters and reports in a style that is both unified and coherent.

Unity in writing means being able to stick to the treatment of a specific subject, usually the one announced in a topic sentence or paragraph, without adding any unnecessary or irrelevant information. Individual paragraphs may deal with more than one important idea, but the ideas should all contribute to the primary subject; irrelevant material should be omitted. To test the unity of parts one must grasp the purpose of the whole. And while *Unity* deals with relevance, *Coherence* deals with relatedness. The ideas in the paragraph(s) should be connected clearly and logically.

Throughout this text we have discussed possible barriers to communication and how to overcome them. In Chapter 3 we also discussed ways to organize your material. We stressed the necessity of previewing your material from an organizational standpoint by asking yourself:

1. What is the conclusion I want my reader to reach?

2. What is the best plan to follow in arranging the information to lead my reader to the desired conclusion?

3. What techniques can I use to make sure that my reader is able to quickly and easily follow my informational plan to its conclusion?

Keep in mind the need for conciseness. This does not mean being abrupt or curt. It means that one should not confuse the reader by giving him more information than he needs. Do not quote official documents endlessly. Cite only the points relevant to the situation and make sure you translate technical material that your reader may not understand.

In this chapter we will discuss several stylistic devices you should also consciously employ to help your letters and reports achieve coherent organization. A list of the major points to be covered in some detail, though by no means exhaustive, follows. It consists of a few critical devices, which if mastered, can quickly improve your writing of letters and reports.

1. DEVELOPMENT BY CLASSIFICATION—Number the major points in your presentation: "The first thing necessary is to . . . ." "The second thing to be done is . . . ."

2. WORDINESS—Avoid long, complex sentences. The more complicated the material, the shorter your sentences should be. Make your sentences concise by eliminating wasted words and expressions.

3. SENTENCE VARIETY—Use a variety of sentence structures to avoid boring your reader.

4. TRANSITIONS—Use transitional words and phrases as directional signals to alert your reader that you have covered one point and are moving on to another. Transitions will also suggest logical relationships between points.

5. PARALLEL STRUCTURE—Repeat key grammatical structures in a sentence or paragraph to help your reader follow the development of your presentation.

DEVELOPMENT BY CLASSIFICATION

There are many ways to develop a topic sentence. These include amplifying specific details listed in the topic sentence, illustrating the topic sentence with an example or examples, defining a key point, using comparison and contrast, showing cause or effect, or using these devices in combination. One other method which we have found to be simple, orderly, and effective is development by classification.

Classification provides an instant form of organization, a convenient skeleton on which to hang your ideas. We have already discussed how and why people are intimidated by the written word. We have prescribed ways to organize your material, but perhaps we should offer additional thoughts on how actually to begin writing, how to overcome the initial trauma. Then we can show how classification fits in with our other suggestions.

Having carefully assessed your writing situation in light of tone, information, and organization, how then do you actually begin to write or dictate? You can clean off the top of your desk, place all relevant papers before you, sharpen all your pencils, clear your throat, even clean the smudges from your rubber erasers—but you still haven't started *writing*! We hope the following suggestions may be helpful:

1. Use an outline or a series of marginal notes as a first step in the writing process. (See Chapter 3 for further suggestions regarding outline preparation.)

2. If you are dictating, try a dry run based on your preliminary notes. Then revise, revise, revise following our principles of organization. If you are writing, try brainstorming, jotting down a variety of phrases, key words, anything that comes to mind. Be conversational and let your ideas flow. This will help you relax and will provide material for revision. Of course, individual temperaments are important here. Some of us write very quickly and then labor long in revision; others compose slowly, but produce a finished copy the first time through. The important thing is to *relax*.

3. Now examine what you have written. Draw out a statement of your central point in the communication, and use this thesis statement as a basis of classification.

Assume that you are writing a report on ways to recycle money accumulated by the Arab nations in their petroleum sales. You have done your research on past proposals and need now to pull your information together. A possible thesis statement might be: "Proposals for the recycling of petrodollars are as complex as they are varied." Having researched four proposals (i.e., those of the United States, OECD, IMF, and the Common Market), you now need to distinguish between them. You can classify these proposals under a numerical ordering principle and have an instant general organization. A possible six paragraph communication could have the skeletal or *box diagram* framework shown in Figure 14.1:

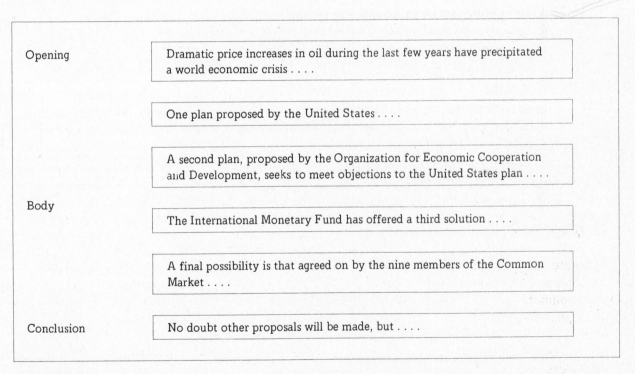

Figure 14.1.

Within this kind of general framework, you can then proceed to develop coherent paragraphs that explicate the elements of each plan. Finally, in a concluding paragraph, discuss the problems common to all four. The complete paper might look something like this:

> Dramatic price increases in oil during the last few years have precipitated a world economic crisis. A few Arab countries have amassed vast amounts of Western money in payments for their oil. Unless these funds are somehow channeled back into the economies of the oil-consuming nations we might witness a string of national bankruptcies. Proposals for such recycling of petrodollars are as complex as they are varied.

One plan proposed by the United States would create an international credit union of $25 billion borrowed from the industrialized nations. This money would be loaned out to needy nations and would be partially conditional on their measures to conserve energy. Proponents of this plan hope to produce cuts in world oil demand and a possible decrease in prices. They also hope to help insolvent nations avoid political turmoil.

A second plan, proposed by the Organization for Economic Cooperation and Development, seeks to meet objections to the United States plan. Some see the U.S.'s attempts to lower prices as futile since the oil countries would simply cut production if demand slackens. Also, The American plan does not allow for effective recycling of oil money. The OECD has proposed that a fund of $25 billion be established—but made up of loan guarantees, not cash. This way, stronger Western nations would insure loans to weaker members.

The International Monetary Fund has offered a third solution called the "Witteveen facility" after its managing director. The IMF loans out (at 7 percent interest) funds borrowed from the oil-producing nations. Two basic objections have arisen regarding this plan: 1) poor countries cannot afford the interest rate, and 2) the United States feels that the IMF credit supports the high level of oil prices.

A final possibility is that agreed on by the nine members of the Common Market. These European nations would produce a mutual assistance pact whereby bonds would be sold on the world market to support the credit problems of member nations. Should a borrower default, the other Market countries will cover the loan in proportion to their national wealth.

No doubt other proposals will be made, but they are meaningless unless the Organization of Petroleum Exporting Countries (OPEC) desires to have its money recycled. The Arabs may well resent being told where and how they should invest their money.

The subject of any letter or report that is amenable to a numerical breakdown can be developed by classification. You can arrange your points in what you consider to be the most effective order—either leading up to the most important point, or the reverse. You might even order the points by placing numbers in parentheses at the start of each relevant paragraph. Granting the somewhat mechanical nature of this organizing principle, we would still argue that:

1. It enables you to move into your topic quickly and efficiently. Your box diagram is an instant organizing principle.

2. It advances your ideas in a readily discernible form so that there is little likelihood of confusing your reader.

3. It can be easily combined with other methods of development to form more complicated structures.

Of course, no such organization is necessary in brief letters or memos, but it is invaluable in longer letters and reports.

A. Construct a block diagram similar to that in Figure 14.1 listing some initial sentences that might be used to develop the following general topics.

1. Create a hypothetical product (Bliss toothpaste, American Eagle Gin, My Scent Spray Cologne, etc.) and assume you are responsible for marketing it. Write a brief report outlining the kind of ad campaign you feel is needed.

2. As the sales supervisor for Marcom, a large computer firm, you are responsible for making recommendations both on how to improve sales operations and whom to promote. Outline two brief reports to the company president, one dealing with each of these responsibilities.

3. As a reputable stock broker with Wiggins, Tate & Momser you must keep abreast of market developments and periodically make specific recommendations to a few preferred customers. Structure a letter to your customers listing what you feel are possible growth stocks.

4. What are some of the ways in which your school can be run more efficiently? Select a particular area (comptrollers' office, academic administration, development, etc.) and then make specific recommendations on needed changes.

5. After four months of training with Belton Stores you feel fairly confident and familiar with all store operations. You notice especially that the Sporting Goods department is not producing much sales volume, probably because its selection of equipment is not complete. Write the store manager to propose some changes in the purchasing of equipment and the organization of the entire department.

WORDINESS

As English teachers we have been asked by many students, outside of class, to help them with their writing. Though impatient with composition classes, they had come to realize their importance. One particular student who came to us with problems was actually an older graduate. He worked at a local pharmaceutical plant as a chemist responsible for the production of penicillin. While in college, he told us, he never bothered too much with English; after all, he was going to work with test tubes and bunsen burners, not with words. Imagine his surprise, then, when his supervisor asked him to write a report on the plant's yearly production of penicillin. Imagine too his dismay when the boss rejected the very lengthy report he had labored over for many long nights. The boss, he told us, said the report was boring to read and far too long; he had better things to do with his time. Could we, the former student asked, help him simplify the report and thus help him regain the boss's favor? Well, we tried, and here are some general pointers we gave the student.

1. Remember that there is a distinction between speaking and writing. When we speak about being informal and conversational in your prose, we do not mean to relax completely and ramble on at will. Good writing demands that you place some restraints upon yourself. Never forget that your audience is not present, and that you cannot rely on facial gestures and voice intonations to communicate your ideas. Your writing must capture the reader's interest and hold it.

Here is a paragraph from a student's paper on an administrative case study:

> In spite of Worthington's very good ability to achieve successful results as an investor of the bank's money and as its chief official responsible for bank loans, and the good dividends which have been paid to our shareholders this year as a result of his labors, I feel compelled to ask for his being relieved as president of City Bank. My reason for this statement is that I feel that despite his past achievements his negative qualities are such that they are not in the best future interests of City Bank. There are two basic reasons why I feel he should be relieved. One is that he wants to make all the decisions and refuses to share authority with other administrators. This has resulted in a number of bright, able young employees leaving the bank to seek other positions where they will get more responsibility and thus have the experience and challenge of making important decisions. My second reason is that I feel by refusing to concentrate on new business he is not drawing in the additional savings that will be needed to help us compete with other banks in the future.

Does this paragraph meet Strunk and White's dictum that the "approach to style is by way of plainness, simplicity, orderliness, sincerity"?[1] We think not. It is a passage written off the top of the head, that is, without thought or genuine effort. The result is a boring, sometimes confusing paragraph. What follows is one possible revision:

> While Worthington's investment and loan policies generated excellent dividends this year, I believe that his resignation as president is in the best future interests of City Bank. I have two reasons for this proposal. One is Worthington's failure to distribute authority to junior administrators; the result has been a serious turnover in bright young employees who don't feel sufficiently challenged. Second, he is not attracting the new savings needed to make City Bank competitive in the future.

This passage, briefer and simpler, communicates the same ideas as the original.

2. Avoid the passive voice construction. Certainly this rule cannot be applied rigorously. There are times when it is permissible and necessary to use the passive voice. But remember that a verb in the

---

1. William Strunk, Jr. and E. B. White, *The Elements of Style,* 2nd. Ed. (New York: Macmillan, 1972), p. 62.

passive voice may weaken your message; it can suggest a desire for anonymity or an inability to accept responsibility. The passive voice construction also causes wordiness.

PASSIVE:	Errors **are caused** by careless typing.	(6 words)
ACTIVE:	Careless typing **causes** errors.	(4 words)
PASSIVE:	Shares of General Motors **were bought** by them.	(8 words)
ACTIVE:	They **bought** shares of General Motors.	(6 words)

3. Avoid rhetorical deadwood in the form of wordy or roundabout expressions. Often these occur as a kind of verbal throat clearing. We ruminate over our words instead of seeking the most concise equivalents.

WORDY:	In view of the fact that he missed three weeks of work, we fired him.
CONCISE:	Because he missed three weeks of work, we fired him.
WORDY:	Taking into consideration the fact that he is near retirement, we will not promote him.
CONCISE:	Since he is near retirement, we will not promote him.

4. Avoid tautologies (saying the same thing twice). We use some phrases without considering if each word is essential. **Free and clear,** and **null and void** are standard doublets in which one word is not really needed. If one word is implicit in the other, throw one of them out.

Vague intensifiers are also useless. We use them because of our insecurity. We are afraid that we may not be understood, so we underline our ideas with useless intensives, such as **absolutely essential, perfectly round, very simple.** These intensives may reassure the writer, but they are excess baggage to the reader.

WORDY:	He is a more or less exceptionally unique person.
CONCISE:	He is a unique person.
WORDY:	At this point in time we should be cautious.
CONCISE:	At this time we should be cautious.

5. Avoid using three or more words where one will do. Aristotle defined wordiness as "the accumulation of words that add nothing to the sense and cloud up what clarity there is." Congressman Maury Maverick of Texas called this impulse to confuse "gobbledygook." The Federal Government has been called the worst offender in the use of gobbledygook, as illustrated by the famous case of the plumber who wrote the Bureau of Standards in Washington to ask if hydrochloric acid was safe for cleaning drains. The Bureau answered: "The efficacy of hydrochloric acid is indisputable, but the chlorine residue is incompatible with metallic permanence." The plumber wrote back that he was glad the Bureau agreed with him. Washington replied with a note of alarm. "We cannot assume responsibility for the production of toxic and noxious residues from hydrochloric acid, and suggest you use an alternate procedure." And the plumber was again happy to learn that the Bureau agreed with him. Finally Washington exclaimed: "Don't use hydrochloric acid; it eats hell out of the pipes!"

Of course, this verbal disease, gobbledygook, is not confined to government communications. Why do ad-men call a razor a "portable shaving system"? Why does a school system talk about "terminal behavior objectives for continuous progression modules in early childhood education" instead of report cards? Why do people prefer "utilize" to use, "cognizant" to aware, "liquid refreshment" to drink, "optimal" to best, "ascertain" to learn, "initiate" to begin, "verification" to proof, "ocular fixation" to look, "modification" to change? Near relatives of gobbledygook are *jargon* (being unnecessarily technical) and *euphemism* (using unnecessarily formal synonyms to avoid embarrassing or painful words). Why does an insurance claims examiner speak with an ordinary insurance policy holder about "step-rated plans," "elimination period," and "exclusion date"? What moves a person to employ legal jargon such as "pursuant to" (according to), "with regard to" (regarding), "until such time as" (until)? Or why do we say "in the family way" instead of pregnant, "mortician" or "funeral director" instead of undertaker, "sanitary engineer" instead of plumber, or "culturally deprived environment" instead of slum?

All of these are the enemies of plain talk. Why do people use them? We suggested one reason in regard to the passive voice—the desire for anonymity, the refusal to take responsibility by hiding behind words. Many people substitute words for answers, terms for ideas, polysyllables for directness, impressive phrases for clarity. Also, there is a psychological appeal to using sophisticated terms and knowing that although your reader may be puzzled you have mastered the impressive maze of symbols. Needless to say, none of these impulses helps open the lines of communication.

Even though it is not directly related to wordiness, this seems the appropriate place to mention *slang* or substandard usage. As with jargon, only use slang when you are certain that your reader will understand you. For instance, you can be relatively certain that most readers will understand the "blahs" (mild depression), "hang-up" (emotional or psychological problem), or perhaps "uptight" (uneasy, anxious), but can you be certain about "honcho" (boss man), "yo-yo" (stupid person), or "coop" (a New York policeman's term for sleeping on duty)? Be safe and avoid slang.

6. Avoid clichés. Clichés are overworked expressions that can clutter the best of prose. They are often inherited sayings or phrases that were fresh when muttered by Adam in the garden, but have long since become very stale. Thus if asked to complete the simile "as quiet as a _____," most of us would unhesitatingly respond **mouse**. Why? Not because it is an apt comparison (although it is) or because we are being imaginative, but because we have heard the phrase before. Second-graders asked to complete the same simile, were not so Pavlovian or stereotyped in their responses as adults are. They came up with "as quiet as a **blink**" and "as quiet as an **elbow**" among others! Perhaps Thomas Babington Macaulay was right when he said that anyone who aspired to be a poet in an enlightened society "must first become a little child." Approach language, especially any similes or metaphors you might use, with a childlike wonder and freshness. Otherwise you will appear to be a lazy peddler of other's wares.

Below is a brief list of some common clichés. Supplement this list with those you may now rely on to fill up your own communication and avoid them all.

soft as a baby's bottom	good as gold
dead as a doornail	drop in the bucket
last but not least	slow but sure
by leaps and bounds	a shot in the arm
needle in a haystack	crying shame
it goes without saying	beyond the shadow of a doubt
truth is stranger than fiction	all's well that ends well
cold as ice	straight from the shoulder
to all intents and purposes	burning the midnight oil
finer things of life	the best things in life are free
better late than never	first and foremost
straight and narrow	more or less

7. Where needed for conciseness, reduce clauses to phrases and phrases to single words. Here are some examples:

a. Clauses reduced to infinitive phrases:

Carl decided that he would leave on the early train.

Carl decided to leave on the early train.

b. Clauses reduced to participial phrases:

When Biggins was left alone in the office last night, he made a number of long distance calls.

Left alone in the office last night, Biggins made a number of long distance calls.

c. Clauses reduced to gerund phrases:

If you work like him, you will finish by Monday.

Working like him, you will finish by Monday.

d. Clauses reduced to appositives:

Tom asked Mr. Howard, who is now serving as the assistant to the president, to pass along his request.

Tom asked Mr. Howard, the assistant to the president, to pass along his request.

e. Clauses reduced to prepositional phrases:

My uncle who is in the trade union predicts higher costs.

My uncle in the trade union predicts higher costs.

If you create new systems, the work will run more smoothly.

With new systems, the work will run more smoothly.

f. Clauses and phrases reduced to single words:

The Congressman who had been newly elected addressed his supporters.

The newly elected Congressman addressed his supporters.

He asked us in an angry way to leave his door.

He asked us angrily to leave his door.

The soldiers who were surrounded refused to surrender.

The surrounded soldiers refused to surrender.

EXERCISES

WORDINESS

B.   Give some simpler substitutes for the following:

1. accompanied by _____

2. accounted for by the fact that _____

3. along the lines of _____

4. am of the opinion _____

5. answered in the affirmative _____

6. answered in the negative _____

7. as on this date, as of this date _____

8. as to whether _____

9. at all times _____

10. at an early date _____

11. at this writing, at the present time _____

12. based on the fact that _____

13. concerning the matter of _____

14. due to the fact that _____

15. during the time that _____

16. for the purpose of _____

17. for the reason that _____

18. in a manner similar to _____

19. in addition to, in addition to the above _____

20. inasmuch as _____

21. in a satisfactory manner _____

22. in compliance with your request _____

23. in the absence of _____

24. in the event of, in the event that _____

25. in the meantime _____

26. in view of the fact that _____

27. is predicated on the assumption _____

28. in spite of the fact that _____

29. in the neighborhood of   _____

30. in this place   _____

31. is similar to   _____

32. make provision for   _____

33. one finds it necessary to   _____

34. previous to, prior to   _____

35. raise the question   _____

36. subsequent to   _____

37. taking into consideration the fact that   _____

38. the question as to whether   _____

39. there can be no doubt that   _____

40. through the use of   _____

41. we are in receipt of   _____

42. will you be good enough to   _____

43. with a minimum of delay   _____

44. with a view to   _____

45. with reference to, with regard to   _____

46. with the exception of   _____

47. with the result that   _____

C.   Edit the following combinations of words:

actual fact	self-acknowledged
alter or change	cease and desist
in the year 1967	first and foremost
green in color	necessary essential
modern styles of today	if and when
endorse on the back	very important essentials
close proximity	completely unanimous
intents and purposes	mix together
one example, for instance	revert back
photostatic copies	invisible to the eye
small in size	inaudible to the ear

one and the same	tasteless to the tongue
discuss in the lecture	living incarnation
part and parcel	before in the past
past history	one particular example
perfect square	circle around
descent down	ascend up
good and sufficient	component parts
further, as an additional point	rarely ever
exact same	nearly approximate
disappear from view	seesaw back and forth
square in shape	requirements needed for
gradually by degrees	the final conclusion
successively one after the other	each and every

D. Check available letters, reports, magazines, books or newspapers for:

   a. Five examples of passive voice constructions. Change them to active voice.

   b. Examples of gobbledygook, jargon, clichés, and euphemisms.

   c. Examples of roundabout expressions, tautologies, vague intensifiers.

E. Translate the following sentences into simpler, clearer English.

1. It will be the year 1980 that the steel foundations of the building will reach final completion.

2. He exhibited a proclivity for composing his correspondence using writing instruments of wood and graphite.

3. I would ask all employees to render assistance to each and every customer.

4. The home office recently made a survey of our company to make a determination of whether or not we were in agreement with their new provisions concerning rate of payment for hours worked by employees past the regular amount of hours required during each working day.

5. The nature of the company's product was such as to negate the feasibility of its being automated.

6. The construction project will be speeded up by the creation of new procedures.

7. John Marshall requested Tim Glenden, who is now serving as treasurer of the company, to send him a purchase order.

8. It is hoped that all employees of this company will give serious consideration to the recommendations.

9. To repeat again once more, there will be no smoking at all allowed in the halls.

10. The true birth of his degeneration begins with his blatant excess of the boundaries of moderation in pursuit of his academic ventures.

11. We hope the decision meets with the approval of the president.

12. He exhibited a proclivity for information which is cumulative and which covers any and all happenings.

13. My statement is predicated on the assumption that we have not yet made provision for the rejection of applications for employment.

14. There are about forty different flavors of ice cream to be found in the store called "Cake and Cream."

15. I would like to say that it is true that he exhibited a proclivity for hard work.

16. He delivered his report to the audience on the occasion of the final meeting.

17. A new computer which has been installed in our office in Seattle has resulted in an immeasurable improvement in the operations of said office.

18. He is cognizant that consummation of the agreement has been effected and that commencement of the work will soon be begun.

19. After perusing your letter I endeavored to ascertain whether the now existing regulations afford the opportunity for you to enter into negotiations with bargaining representatives from that country.

20. Needless to say, I am more or less on the button in affirming that the deal with Rochester Tool Company is as good as gold.

F. In a difficult trespass case, the state director of the Interior Department's Bureau of Land Management decided to give the trespasser a special-use permit. But he first asked for a legal opinion on the matter. Evaluate the memo he received, Figure 14.2, and revise it if necessary.

To: State Director

From: John Lawbook, Solicitor

Subject: Roland Occupancy Trespass

This responds to your memorandum dated February 21, 1964, requesting that we review and comment concerning the subject Roland trespass on certain lands under reclamation withdrawal.

We appreciate your apprising us of this matter and we certainly concur that appropriate action is in order to protect the interest of the United States.

We readily recognize the difficult problem presented by this situation, and if it can be otherwise satisfactorily resolved, we would prefer to avoid trespass action. If you determine it permissible to legalize the Roland occupancy and hay production by issuance of a special use permit, as suggested in your memorandum, we have no objection to that procedure.

Any such permit should be subject to cancellation when the lands are actively required for reclamation purposes and should provide for the right of the officers, agents, and employees of the United States at all times to have unrestricted access and ingress of all kinds, dig test pits and drill test holes, to survey for reclamation and irrigation works, and to perform any and all necessary soil and moisture conservation work.

If we can be of any further assistance in this matter, please advise. We would appreciate being informed of the disposition of this problem.[2]

Figure 14.2.

G. Pay careful attention to the language in the letter on the next page, Figure 14.3. See how much you can reduce the original without losing essential ideas.

2. From John O'Hayre, *Gobbledygook Has Gotta Go,* U.S. Department of the Interior, Bureau of Land Management.

Mr. Donald R. Wiggins
Chief
Office of Business Administration
U.S. Bureau of the Census
Washington, D.C. 20742

Dear Mr. Wiggins:

Authorized and empowered by the Public Works Act of 1967 and pursuant to its provisions, consideration is being given by the Urban Development Administration to the design and development of a prospectus at the present time for a construction project at Great Falls, Virginia for the purpose of full and complete review by the Bureau of the Budget and for the purpose of submitting said prospectus to the Committees on Public Works of the Congress.

Under and subject to said provisions, our planning contemplates the future construction of a multi-agency Federal building on an ecological site, located in the central business district; said site of such a nature as to be deemed accommodating to the sole and exclusive requirements of the U.S. Census and/or other federal activities in the aforementioned community. Eventual disposal of the extant Post Office and Courthouse building is contemplated when the construction of the before mentioned proposed new Federal building is finalized and completed.

In order to more easily facilitate the early and expeditious transmittal of the said prospectus, it is hereby requested that your current total space requirements be submitted on the format, UDA Form 342, which is attached herewith. Each and every change that you deem significant and that you can anticipate for and during the period of the next five years should also be furnished.

For the purpose of lending us assistance in connection with the discharge of our responsibilities in reference to the development of this project, it will be appreciated if this information can be submitted as expeditiously as possible and with a minimum of delay.

Sincerely yours,

Ronald W. Elliott
Director of Space Management[3]

Figure 14.3.

3. From *Writing Effective Letters,* Communications and Office Skills Training Institute, U.S. Civil Service Commission, pp. 4-26 through 4-27.

SENTENCE VARIETY

> **A.**   Scotch pine has become the country's leading Christmas tree. It meets a wife's
> demands. It shapes beautifully. Its size and smell are good. Its needles hang on
> and on. It is easy to grow. It is tolerant to a wide range of soil and moisture
> conditions. It survives planting shock well. It can be grown to Christmas tree
> size in about eight years. The fir requires ten to twenty years.

We'll start with a question. Is this an easy paragraph to read? Certainly not, and for good reasons.
The sentence structure is boringly repetitive with a series of brief subject-verb-object constructions.
The writer may have a number of individually interesting ideas, but he has not cared enough to
assemble them into an interesting paragraph. In fact, the writer has no respect at all for the reader's
sanity. Reading a series of such paragraphs would quickly put us to sleep.

Paragraph **A**, however, is our paraphrase of a paragraph from a published article on Christmas
trees; let's take a look at the original paragraph.

> **B.**   There is good reason why the Scotch pine has become the country's leading
> Christmas tree. First of all, it meets a wife's demands—it shapes beautifully, its
> size and smell are good, and its needles hang on and on. Second, it is easy to
> grow. It is tolerant to a wide range of soil and moisture conditions and survives
> planting shock well. And of particular interest to the grower is the fact that the
> Scotch pine can be grown to Christmas tree size in about eight years in contrast
> to the fir that requires ten to twenty years.[4]

This original paragraph, a much better version, is easier to read primarily because of the sentence
variety. The punctuation diagrams in Figures 14.4 and 14.5 illustrate the sentence mix of both of
the above paragraphs.

Figure 14.4. *Punctuation diagram of our paraphrase.*

4. From Evan B. Altderfer, "About Christmas Trees," *Business Review* of Federal Reserve Bank of
Philadelphia (December, 1971), p. 11.

Figure 14.5. *Punctuation diagram of Altderfer's original.*

Punctuation diagrams are a useful (though not infallible) way of indicating problems in sentence structure. Notice in **A** the total absence of any punctuation marks except the period. Also notice that most of the sentences are of a similar length. **B**, however, displays a more varied use of punctuation and sentence length. While **A** contains only simple sentences, **B**, although equally brief, uses a variety of sentence structures and stylistic strategies to create a more pleasing, interesting rhythm. Let's examine these in greater detail.

A. SENTENCE STRUCTURES

There are three basic sentence structures which can and should be used in combination to avoid the problems of a monotonous prose style. Although most of your sentences should be fairly brief (averaging fifteen to twenty words), you must take care to avoid choppiness. The ten sentences in **A** average seven words per sentence with a range of from three words to twelve. In **B** the five sentences (ranging from six to thirty-six words) average 19.6 words. More important, the sentences in **A** are all of a kind, while those in **B** show more variety.

1. Simple sentences consist of one independent (main) clause, no dependent clauses, and any number of phrases. Simple sentences are particularly effective as opening sentences and as breathing space between more complex constructions.

> Scotch pine has become the country's leading Christmas tree. . . . Second, it is easy to grow. **(B)**

2. Compound sentences join together two related independent clauses. Compound sentences help the writer avoid a string of simple sentences. Usually, these related ideas are joined either by a semicolon or a conjunction.

SIMPLE:	It is tolerant to a wide range of soil and moisture conditions. It survives planting shock well. **(A)**
COMPOUND:	It is tolerant to a wide range of soil and moisture conditions and [it] survives planting shock well. **(B)**

The "and" construction in compound sentences suggests a certain spontaneity of thought and generation of ideas, without indicating a relationship. Its overuse can make your prose too boringly talkative. The "but" and "or" conjunctions suggest a more thoughtful construction and a clearer subordination. An even more sophisticated linkage is achieved with the colon and semicolon.

3. Complex sentences are made up of one independent clause and one or more dependent (subordinate) clauses. These clauses express related ideas but are of unequal importance. Thus you must decide which elements you will subordinate. Your major idea will be stated in the independent clause, a related but less important idea in the dependent clause. Notice the following possible ways of combining simple sentences:

SIMPLE:	[The Scotch pine] can be grown to Christmas tree size in about eight years. The fir requires ten to twenty years. **(A)**
COMPOUND:	The Scotch pine can be grown to Christmas tree size in about eight years; the fir requires ten to twenty years. (The semicolon indicates that the two ideas are of equal importance.)
COMPLEX:	While the Scotch pine can be grown to Christmas tree size in about eight years, the fir requires ten to twenty years. (The sentence emphasizes the fir's aging.)
COMPLEX:	Although the fir requires ten to twenty years, the Scotch pine can be grown to Christmas tree size in about eight years. (This sentence emphasizes the pine's aging.)
COMPLEX:	The Scotch pine, unlike the fir which requires ten to twenty years, can be grown to Christmas tree size in about eight years. (The fir's aging is subordinated to that of the Scotch pine.)

B. WORD ORDER

Avoid a series of similar sentence beginnings. The most common problem here is the use of **I** or **We**. Example **A** especially overuses **It**. Pronoun connectors help produce coherent paragraphs; too many, however, become monotonous, as is true in **A**. **B** varies references to **Scotch pine** and to **it**, and does not begin a majority of sentences with either one.

Avoid using the same parts of speech at the beginning of every sentence. Every sentence in **A** has a subject-verb structure, while in **B** the word order is changed frequently to avoid a tiresome similarity. Notice, for instance, the author's use of numbers in **B** as a classification device. Also notice his variation on the third point where he uses the conjunction **and**.

C. PARALLEL STRUCTURE

Notice how four simple sentences from **A** are combined through parallel structure into one longer, easy to read sentence in **B**.

It meets a wife's demands. It shapes beautifully. Its size and smell are good. Its needles hang on and on. **(A)**
First of all, it meets a wife's demands—it shapes beautifully, its size and smell are good, and its needles hang on and on. **(B)**

Parallel structure will be discussed in more detail in a later section of this chapter.

D. LOOSE AND PERIODIC SENTENCES

In a *loose sentence* the main idea is stated at the beginning, and the rest of the sentence adds details. In a *periodic sentence* the main idea is stated at the end of the sentence. The first structure is forceful and direct; the latter is more suspenseful.

LOOSE:	Scotch pine has become the country's leading Christmas tree even though more consumers are purchasing artificial trees.
PERIODIC:	Although the fir requires ten to twenty years, the Scotch pine can be grown to Christmas tree size in about eight years.

E. TRANSITIONAL WORDS AND PHRASES

You know how using the words **first** and **second** lead readers from one point to another. A sentence like "Second, it is easy to grow." acts as a larger transition unit that moves us all the way from the first to the final part of a paragraph. The next section of this chapter is about Transitions, but before we move on we'll have some exercises concerning sentence variety.

EXERCISES

SENTENCE VARIETY

H. Consider the relationships between ideas in the following pairs of sentences. Join these sentences together, without using **and**, so that the relationships become clear. Subordinate ideas wherever necessary.

1. The senior accountant will address the meeting. Most of his staff will be attending.

2. He will compose the first draft of the report. The secretary will rewrite it.

3. We cannot prepare our tax returns. The final reports have not been sent out.

4. He agreed to collect the money. No one volunteered.

5. He likes to look over the receipts and read his mail in the morning. He also likes to do his dictation in the morning.

6. He received advance word of the impending merger. He bought twenty shares of Dynamic Corporation.

7. In order to make operations smoother the company hired an efficiency expert. The results have been inconclusive.

8. He asked the home office to send proper mailing lists and an updated budget statement. He also requested copies of the new brochure.

9. I cannot see him at the moment. Ask him to return tomorrow.

10. The deadline for budget requests is only a week away. He is confident that his statement will be ready.

11. Mike's job opportunities were limited. He became successful by working hard.

12. International Widget stock once cost $32 a share. It is now selling for $83 a share.

13. The published manual contained 382 pages. The earlier version of the manual has 506 pages.

14. You will be absent from work for a week. Please notify the supervisor.

15. The accountants examined the firm's records. They discovered several substantial errors.

I. Rewrite the following groups of simple sentences, combining them according to the directions given:

> Margaret Keller was hampered by early injuries.
>
> She worked hard.
>
> She became vice-president of Talcot Industries.

1. Stress the last sentence; de-emphasize the first and second ones.

2. Make the ideas in all three sentences equal.

3. Stress the last two ideas; de-emphasize the first.

> Bob Forster is our senior accountant.
> He graduated from Webster College.
> He has worked for Benton and Forbes for thirteen years.

4. Stress the first sentence; de-emphasize the last two.

5. Stress the third; de-emphasize the first two.

6. Stress the second; de-emphasize the first and third sentences.

> Ipinol is our latest product.
> It cures pain from arthritis.
> It can only be ordered by a doctor's prescription.

7. Stress the third sentence; de-emphasize the first two.

8. Make the first and third sentences equal; de-emphasize the second one.

9. Stress the second sentence; de-emphasize the first and third.

J. Rewrite the following paragraph to provide for greater sentence variety.

> Kevin McCarthy has been asked to supervise registration at our regional meeting. He has certain procedures to follow. He should first make certain that there is a table. There should be at least two chairs available for a registration desk. He should borrow or rent a typewriter to fill out name tags properly. He should use this typewriter to type up a list of those attending the meeting. He should do this after the registration period is completed. He should ask each person attending to complete a 4x6 index card. This should be done at the registration desk. He should have them place on the card the person's name and address. They should indicate their position in the company and what they hope to learn at the conference. He should make available to the person similar cards. These must be filled out after the meeting. The person gives on this card their general reaction, whether they found the conference valuable or not. He should arrange for a large blackboard or cork board to be placed near the registration desk. He should direct people to use this board as a message center. He should submit results of the conference back to the home office.

TRANSITIONS

The bulk of your business writing will have a deductive structure; you will begin with a general statement and then support it in a clearly organized, logical manner. You will seek *coherence* in your thoughts; you'll try to make them hang together. Two effective ways of achieving coherence are *transitions* (or connectors) and *parallel structure*. We'll deal here with the first of these first.

The cohesive bonds that allow sentences to hang together in logical paragraphs are transitions. These are the words and phrases that link ideas together. They provide directional signals to your reader enabling him to follow your argument. Without such guides he is in danger of both boredom and confusion. Let's examine some important linking devices that you can apply in your writing. Read the following paragraph on the heroin industry.

> The demand for heroin differs from other commodities primarily because possession is illegal. Because of a need for secrecy a seller cannot advertise his wares. *Thus*, it is expensive for a would-be consumer to obtain information about availability price, quality of the product, and sales locations. These characteristics are shared by other commodities such as marijuana, abortion, and prostitution when made illegal. In the case of heroin, quality is so unreliable and varies so greatly that death can often result from its use. *As a result*, many new heroin users rely on friends to introduce them to heroin and to verify its quality. *Thus*, the spread of heroin addiction is much like a contagious disease, spread by person-to-person contact.[5]

The use of common linking expressions helps produce coherent paragraphs. Notice the italicized words in the paragraph above. These are common linking expressions which promote the logic and order of the paragraph. **As a result,** for instance, shows how one statement is the result of the preceding one. Thus this phrase links both statements together. This is also the case with the word **thus.**

A. IMPORTANT TRANSITIONS AND THEIR NORMAL USE

Transitions amplify or carry forward an idea from one sentence to the next:

furthermore	first, second, etc.	in other words
also	in particular	finally
in addition	for example	too
that is	similarly	besides
moreover	namely	indeed
last	especially	then
in the same way	likewise	
in fact	next	

Transitional words show how one statement results from another:

thus	for this reason	after all
as a consequence	hence	then
therefore	so	as a result

You can use transitions to indicate time or place:

meanwhile	at the same time	below
soon	formerly	here

5. From Stephen L. Mehay, "The Control and Use of Heroin: An Economic Perspective," *Business Review* of the Federal Reserve Bank of Philadelphia (December, 1973), p. 17.

later	immediately	next to
earlier	up to this point	behind
afterward	beyond	in front of
until now	above	

Transitions compare or contrast ideas:

likewise	on the other hand	but
similarly	yet	still
in the same way	and yet	though
however	on the contrary	nevertheless
by contrast	otherwise	although

Transitional words show emphasis:

in fact	admittedly	yes
truly	of course	no
certainly	indeed	

To summarize or conclude your thoughts, use a transitional phrase:

to sum up	in sum	in brief
in conclusion	as stated above	altogether
finally	most important	

B. THE BUILT-IN CONNECTOR

Built-in connectors link ideas and help achieve coherence within paragraphs. The basic connectors are: 1) repeated words and phrases, and 2) substitute words or phrases, which can be either demonstrative adjectives or pronouns that refer to antecedents in previous sentences. All these devices are used in the following paragraph:

> *Other damaging rips in the social fabric* [1] also can be directly traced to heroin, even though no solid quantitative estimates of the size of the tears are available. Most links in the heroin distribution chain from importer to street retailer are characterized by some degree of monopoly and high *profit* [2] rates. *These* [3] monopoly *profits* might be used to "purchase" the cooperation of law enforcement and other criminal justice officials. When *it* [4] is discovered, this debasement of law enforcement services can seriously weaken citizens' confidence in public officials. *In addition,* [5] organized crime is involved at least in the upper links of the distribution chain. The *profits* that organized crime derives from the narcotics trade help maintain its large-scale criminal enterprise and provide funds to finance its activities in other fields, legal as well as illegal. In many cities, the narcotics trade, police corruption, and organized crime are closely related problems.[6]

This paragraph deals with addict-caused crime. It is part of a discussion linking the impact of the heroin trade's high profits to police corruption. This clearly written, coherent paragraph is aided by the author's use of transitions and connectors (we have italicized and numbered these for purposes of the following discussion).

1. The transition from the previous paragraph is accomplished by the phrase "Other damaging rips in the social fabric . . . ." **Other** is a good indicator that the effects of the heroin traffic will be discussed further and enlarged upon.

---

6. Mehay, "The Control and Use of Heroin," p. 16. Italics indicate our emphasis.

2. **Profit** is a key repeated word. It is clearly linked to the corruption of public officials, and its repeated use threads this element throughout the paragraph.

3. The demonstrative adjective **these** modifies **profit** in one case. Either **profits** or **these** could be left out of the sentence and the weight of meaning would remain, but the predicate adjective, in this case, also reinforces the main idea being built up throughout this paragraph, namely that **profits** link the illegal heroin trade with law enforcement.

4. The pronoun **it** also refers back to the link between heroin profits and the corruption of justice officials, and also provides a way to unify this already established fact with a new idea—that public confidence in the law is weakened.

5. The transitional phrase **in addition** ties yet another organization into the struggle for heroin profits, organized crime. **In addition** amplifies all the linkages discussed previously in the paragraph and stresses their combination.

EXERCISES

K. We have jumbled the sentences of three paragraphs and numbered them. Read over each paragraph and then decide how the sentences should be correctly ordered. Place your answers (by number) in the appropriate categories at the end of the selections.[7]

1st paragraph:

1. The unusually long distribution chain and the lack of vertical integration help to minimize the number of transactions each dealer must make.

2. Much of this opium is converted into heroin in secret laboratories in France and Lebanon.

3. Heroin is derived from the opium poppy which is grown mainly in Turkey and Southeast Asia.

4. The fewer transactions each dealer must make the less visible he is to the authorities and the less vulnerable to arrest.

5. Between the producer and the final consumer are often as many as six distribution stages— importer, kilo connection, connection weight dealers, street dealers, and "jugglers."

6. Few, if any, dealers operate at more than one of these distribution stages: that is, there is virtually no vertical integration in the industry.

7. The peculiar organization of the industry serves to minimize sellers' risk.

2nd paragraph:

1. At the top levels—importers and kilo connections—very few firms serve each geographical market area.

2. Both of these factors contribute to the high profit rate earned by distributors at the top.

3. The heroin distribution chain resembles a pyramid with a few large firms at the top and many small firms at the bottom.

4. Also, the grip of organized crime tends to be tightest at these levels.

3rd paragraph:

1. Economists would say that the "opportunity cost"—the value of occupations they forego—to them of being in this line of business is very low.

2. Also, there are few barriers (for example, capital requirements or technological) to block the entry of new competitors.

7. Mehay, "The Control and Use of Heroin," p. 16.

3. At the base of the pyramid, suppliers, especially street dealers and jugglers, are more numerous.

4. So the combination of greater competition and lower opportunity cost tend to depress profit levels for heroin retailers compared to higher-level distributors.

5. Heroin retailers are often addicts themselves; they can do few other things as well as they can traffic in heroin.

Topic Sentence: Paragraph 1 _____

                             Paragraph 2 _____

                             Paragraph 3 _____

Developmentary   Paragraph 1 _____
Sentences
(arranged in   Paragraph 2 _____
coherent sequence):
                             Paragraph 3 _____

Concluding Sentence: Paragraph 1 _____

                             Paragraph 2 _____

                             Paragraph 3 _____

L. Make use of transitions and connectors in developing paragraphs around the following topic sentences.

1. Accounting can be a very exciting profession.

2. An increasing percentage of products are being made outside the United States.

3. Corporations have an important impact on the growth patterns of some communities.

4. Increased oil costs have produced shock waves throughout our economic system.

5. Television advertisements are often more creative than the shows they help sponsor.

6. Federal Government agencies touch our lives in many ways.

7. I have mixed feelings about the growth of unions in this country.

8. The graduating senior must often choose between working for an older, established firm or a younger, developing one.

9. Business can be an effective partner with city governments in rehabilitating downtown areas.

10. Banks have used many marketing devices to lure potential customers.

M. Obtain a copy of a firm's annual report or a copy of a prominent business magazine (*Business Week, Barron's, Forbes, Fortune, Harvard Business Review, etc.*). Select what you feel is a representative paragraph in terms of an author's use of transitions and connectors. Copy a paragraph or two, circle and number all major transitions and connectors, explain how each of these are used, and submit the report to your instructor.

N. Rewrite the following short report on the choice of a new plant location. Use appropriate transitions and connectors.

> I have analyzed the situation regarding which location to choose for our new plant. The Selma, Atlanta, and Charleston locations have advantages and disadvantages. Charleston is the most advantageous area. It has many benefits to offer. The city will donate fifteen acres of land (worth $45,000) with all utilities. We would need to pay for the cost of the building. The building will require seven acres for itself. The extra land will be used for parking and other needs. The remaining eight acres may be used for future expansion or may be sold in the future. The location is near a highway and a railroad line. There are no state taxes. The local real estate taxes are low. The savings each year would be high. Charleston is close to our home office. Travel and telephone expenses would decrease. Wages are lower in this area. I feel Charleston is the best site.

PARALLEL STRUCTURE

Parallel structure, called by Sheridan Baker the "masonry of syntax,"[8] involves using similar grammatical constructions to express ideas that are closely related. Like the use of transitions, parallelism is an aid to coherence, but in addition to providing an ordering principle within a sentence or paragraph, parallel structures please us psychologically. They satisfy our need for order and symmetry by compressing and organizing related thoughts.

Examine the following sentences:

> James Brooks is our senior accountant. He has had many jobs. He once worked with the Belman Corporation, a California firm, and with Argyll Limited in Minnesota. He worked with the Oklahoma National Trust. He also worked with the Kansas Railroad Corporation.

Since these sentences contain related ideas, parallel structure can help compress and organize them to eliminate the monotonous rhythm of brief, simple sentences strung together. Let's try rewriting these sentences to join the ideas together:

> James Brooks, our senior accountant, once worked with the Belman Corporation in California, with Argyll Limited in Minnesota, with Oklahoma National Trust, and he also worked for the Kansas Railroad Corporation.

As you can see, something is still wrong. The final part of the sentence mars both the organization and rhythm of the whole. Instead of conforming to a parallel structure, with four prepositional phrases following the introduction, we have combined three prepositional phrases with a main clause. The reader's expectations, both grammatical and psychological, are not fulfilled, for the parallelism is faulty. The sentence should read:

> James Brooks, our senior accountant, once worked with the Belman Corporation in California, with Argyll Limited in Minnesota, with Oklahoma National Trust, and with the Kansas Railroad Corporation.

This is better. The ideas, now nicely structured, fall smoothly into place. Readjusting the structure of your sentences to make items parallel is a sure way of improving the readability and appeal of your prose style.

Here are some other examples of parallel structures:

> He is not only intelligent, but also charitable. (Parallelism of correlatives followed by adjectives.)
>
> I came, I saw, I conquered. (Three verbs.)
>
> Three qualities essential to a good secretary are efficiency, humor, and discretion. (Three nouns.)
>
> He is either an opportunist or an idealist. (Correlatives with nouns.)
>
> The man was Xeroxing the manuscript, and Beth was typing the final pages. (Two simple sentences.)
>
> Let every nation know, whether it wishes us well or ill, that we shall pay any price, bear any burden, meet any hardship, support any friend, oppose any foe to assure the survival and the success of liberty.[9] (Verb phrases.)

8. Sheridan Baker, *The Practical Stylist,* 3rd Ed. (New York: Crowell, 1973), p. 43.

9. From John F. Kennedy's "Inaugural Address," Washington, D.C., January 20, 1961.

EXERCISES

PARALLEL STRUCTURE

O.   Rewrite the following sentences to correct any faulty parallel structure.

1.   It will be necessary to purchase a new machine or try repairing it ourselves.

2.   Not only the building site costs but also the cost of utilities would be eliminated.

3.   One advantage of the Chicago plant is that travel and telephone expenses are smaller. Wages are also lower in this area.

4.   He is either an able stock analyst or a man whose analyses of stocks are lucky ones.

5.   The accountant is an honest man, but sometimes he can be careless.

6.   The Komar Aircraft Corporation offered him stock options, a good salary increase, and he would get a six-week vacation.

7.   Your letter to our company shows your interest in the improvement of and in caring for our national parks.

8.   We hope in the next seven months to establish three new franchises in the Washington area, review and evaluate our operations with all area managers; also, we hope to generate more capital through the sale of real estate.

9.   Not only has he been promoted, but also a salary increase was given him.

10.   He decided that writing the letter was better than to dictate it.

11.   Our foreign operation needs a director skilled in international law and who knows the French language.

12.   According to the personnel director, he has neither the ability nor is he personable enough to fill the position.

13.   We prefer early morning conferences not only because everyone is present but also more time for discussion.

14.   The brochure circulated by the business machine company was colorful, informative, and held our interest.

15.   The responsibilities of branch managers depend upon job experience, whether they are located in particular geographical areas, market conditions, and the fact that the company president likes some more than others.

P.   Write or locate five different examples of parallel structure. Provide examples of different types of construction.

Q. Rewrite the following paragraph using the principles studied in this section.

You can, if you wish, choose an individual to act as chairman of the symposium. Approach him as soon as possible. Discuss with him the structure of the meeting. Solicit his suggestions on guest speakers and meeting location. Also, solicit his advice on possible sponsors of the symposium. The chairman is very important to the success or failure of the meeting. Be careful in selecting this individual. The chairman will assist with planning the symposium's content and will make suggestions for speakers. He will also help decide on the meeting site and date. His availability is an important consideration. He should not be too busy to assist with the meeting. He should be willing to assist with the details. He should help get the co-sponsorship of the organization for whom he works. He should have enough knowledge of his field to choose prominent speakers. He should be able to put together a quality program to attract the interest and support of his colleagues. He should have enough leadership ability to run the program. Be certain the chairman knows what is expected. He should not commit himself if he can't do the work. Choose someone you can work with and with whom you will probably establish a lasting relationship.

Chapter 15

WORD PROBLEMS

SPELLING

> **I** before **e**
> Except after **c**,
> Or when sounded as **a**
> As in **neighbor** or **weigh**.

This old jingle gives us a ready solution to the spelling of troublesome words such as **receive, vein, weight, receipt, ceiling**, and so on; therefore it is convenient and useful. Yet, like many rules, it cannot be applied with universal rigor. Otherwise you end up misspelling exceptions like **seize, either, leisure**, etc.

Grammar texts provide a variety of spelling rules to help you avoid the teacher's red pencil or the brand of illiteracy. They include the dropping-of-the-silent-**e** rule and the retention-of-the-silent-**e** rule ("When a word ends in a silent **e** preceded by **c** or **g**, retain the **e** when adding **able** or **ous**."), the **y**-to-**i** rule, and others. But while granting their usefulness, we feel that memorizing too many rules (and numerous exceptions to the rules) loads an unnecessary burden on students, one similar today to learning the function of a slide rule before learning to use a pocket calculator. We have opted instead to provide two handy lists of frequently used words that are often misspelled, or confused, as well as the following hints:

1. Always keep a reputable, hard-bound dictionary on hand. The hard-bound editions are more complete and more durable.

2. Your eyes should give you the first indication of something wrong with the assemblage of letters in a word. When in doubt, first consult the list of Words Frequently Misspelled (pp. 268-271); if the word is not there, then go to your dictionary.

3. You might ask yourself, "But how can I find a troublesome word if I can't spell it?" Well, you certainly will have some sense of the word, especially the possible first letter. For instance, take the word **cancel**. You know what it means, but suppose you are uncertain if it begins with **k** or **c**, and whether it has one **l** or two. A simple process of elimination and page shuffling will give you the answer.

4. Also, you should keep a personal list of the words *you* usually have trouble spelling. Consult this list frequently and try to formulate your own memory devices. For instance, remember that **stationery** is spelled with **er** like **paper**, that **February** is **br** cold, that **desert** has one **s**, as in *sand*.

WORDS FREQUENTLY MISSPELLED

abbreviate	apparent	chosen
absence	appearance	clothes
absolutely	appetite	column
accede	appreciate	coming
accelerate	approaching	commission
accessible	appropriate	committee
accessory	approximately	comparative
accidentally	arctic	competition
accommodate	argument	completely
accompanied	arrangement	concede
accumulate	article	conceit
accustom	ascend	conceive
accurate	athlete	condemn
achievement	athletic	conquer
acknowledge	audience	conscience
acquaintance	awkward	conscientious
acquainted	barbarous	conscious
acquire	barely	consider
across	becoming	continually
address	before	control
adolescence	beginning	controlled
adolescent	believed	controller
advantage	benefited (benefitted)	convenience
affectionately	breathe (verb)	coolly
aggravate	brilliant	copies
all right (alright)	bulletin	cordially
altogether	buried	corner
always	business	counselor
amateur	calendar	courteous
among	canceled (cancelled)	criticism
amount	candidate	criticize
analogous	carrying	curiosity
analysis	category	dealt
anonymous	cemetery	debatable
apologize	changeable	decided

decision

defense

definite

definitely

definition

dependent

describe

description

desirable

despair

desperate

destroy

develop

different

dining

disappeared

disappointed

disastrous

discipline

diseases

dispensable

dissatisfied

dissension

dissimilar

dissipation

divided

division

doesn't

due

eerie (eery)

eighth

efficiency

efficient

eligible

eliminated

embarrass

embarrassed

emphasize

enclosed

environment

equipment

equipped

especially

esthetic (aesthetic)

exaggerated

exceed

excellent

exhausted

exhilaration

existence

exorbitant

expense

experience

explain

explanation

extremely

familiar

fascinate

fascinating

February

finally

focused

foreign

foreman

formally

formerly

forty

fourth

friend

fulfilled

fundamental

gardener

generally

genius

government

grammar

grievance

grievous

guarantee

guard

handkerchief

handle

harass

height

hindrance

hundred

hurriedly

hypocrisy

iced tea

imagination

immediately

incidentally

independent

indispensable

inevitable

intelligence

interesting

interfered

interpretation

interpreted

interrupted

irresistible

itself

knowledge

label

laboratory

laid

led

leisure

library

lightning

livelihood

loneliness

losing

machinery

maintenance

management

manufacturer

mathematics

meant

medicine

miniature

minute

mischievous

misspelled

mobile

movable

mysterious

naturally

necessary

nevertheless

nickel

niece

ninety

ninth

noisily

noticeable

nowadays

obstacle
occasion
occasionally
occurred
occurrence
omission
omitted
operated
opinion
optimistic
opportunity
original
outrageous
paid
pamphlet
parallel
paralysis
paralyzed
parliament
particularly
partner
pastime
payable
peaceable
perceive
perform
performance
perhaps
permanent
permissible
perseverance
persistent
persuade
phase
phenomenon
phony
physically
piece
pleasant
portrayed
possess
possession
practically
precede
precedent
preceding

preference
preferred
prejudice
prepare
preparation
privilege
procedure
proceed
professional
professor
programmed
prominent
propeller (propellor)
psychology
pursue
quantity
queried
query
quiet
quite
quitting
realize
really
receipt
receivable
received
recipe
recognize
recommend
referred
regretfully
relieve
religious
remembrance
repetition
resistance
resource
restaurant
rhyme
rhythm
ridiculous
roommate
sacrifice
sandwich
satisfactorily
scarcely

scene
schedule
secretary
seize
sense
separate
separately
sergeant
severely
shining
siege
similar
sincerely
sophomore
specimen
strength
strenuously
stretched
studying
succeed
successful
superintendent
supersede
suppress
surely
surprise
synonym
temperament
temperature
thorough
through
together
tomorrow
totaled (totalled)
toward
tragedy
transferred
transferring
treasurer
tremendous
tries
truly
Tuesday
twelfth
undoubtedly
unnecessarily

unnecessary

until

usually

vacuum

valuable

varieties

various

vegetable

vengeance

vice versa

view

vigorous

village

villain

weather

Wednesday

weigh

weird

whether

whole

wholly

whose

women

worrying

wreck

writing

written

Xerox

zealous

COMMONLY CONFUSED WORDS

accede (verb): to agree to
exceed (verb): to surpass

> The advertising agency **acceded** to our wishes and deleted the misleading slogan.
>
> The agent **exceeded** his quota of new insurance policies.

accept (verb): to receive, agree to
except (preposition): excluded

> The stockholders **accepted** their generous merger offer.
>
> **Except** for Bill, all the branch managers were promoted.

advice (noun): recommendation or information
advise (verb): to give advice

> My broker's **advice** about gold prices proved to be true.
>
> He **advised** me to sell immediately.

affect (verb): to influence
effect (noun): the result
effect (verb): to cause or produce

> The damp weather **affected** my asthma.
>
> One **effect** of the loss will be a cut in salary.
>
> His attempt to **effect** changes lost him his job.

alley (noun): a narrow street
ally (noun): an associate or comrade

> The body was found in the **alley**.
>
> Albania is considered a firm **ally** of Communist China.

allude (verb): to refer
elude (verb): to avoid or escape

> He **alluded** to a recent discussion he had with his secretary.
>
> The lucky rabbit somehow managed to **elude** the traps.

all ready (adjective): everything is prepared
already (adverb): previously, prior to

> The accountants are **all ready** to examine the books.
>
> The accountants **already** examined the books.

all together (adverb): everyone acts in unison
altogether (adverb): wholly or completely

> "Come **all together**, please," the guide said.
>
> Board members were not **altogether** pleased with his performance.

altar (noun): table of worship
alter (verb): to change or modify

> The priest placed the chalice on the **altar**.
>
> He refused to **alter** his bad business practices.

angel (noun): a spiritual being
angle (noun): geometric figure; point of view

> **Angels** are higher on the chain of being than men.

> My **angle** of vision was distorted by the post.

breath (noun): air drawn into or expelled from the lungs
breathe (verb): to draw air in and expel it from the lungs

> His **breath** indicated that he had been drinking.

> He made the mistake of **breathing** into the policeman's face.

capital (adjective): serious or important
capitol (noun): meeting place of a state legislature
Capitol (noun): building in which the U.S. Congress meets

> He was found guilty of a **capital** crime.

> Our **capitol** is a lovely old building.

> The **Capitol** is an important piece of American architecture.

cite (verb): to summon or to refer to
site (noun): location

> The judge **cited** two precedents for the antitrust action.

> The **site** of our regional headquarters is still being debated.

complement (noun): that which completes or makes perfect
compliment (noun): expression of respect or flattery

> Her dry wit perfectly **complements** his robust laughter.

> The boss **complimented** us on the job enrichment program.

council (noun): important or official group
counsel (noun): advice or advisor
counsel (verb): advise or consult

> The **council** of economic advisors meets today in the Holiday Inn.

> **Counsel** for the defense decided against an appeal.

> He enjoys **counseling** the kids at camp.

descent (noun): decline or move downward
decent (adjective): that which is proper, moral, or in good taste
dissent (verb): to differ

> Our **descent** from the mountain was easier than the ascent.

> He wore a **decent** suit to the conference.

> He **dissented** on the third article of the bill.

desert (noun): sandy, barren land
dessert (noun): a course served at the close of a meal

> The Sahara is the largest **desert** in the world.

> For **dessert** we had ice cream and cake.

dual (adjective): two or double
duel (noun): combat between two individuals

Frank had a **dual** set of pistols.

The **duel** left Hamilton fatally wounded.

elicit (verb): to draw forth, evoke
illicit (adjective): illegal

Our competition tried to **elicit** information on our new model.

He attacked gambling and other **illicit** activities in his campaign speech.

emigrant (noun): one who leaves his country
immigrant (noun): one who settles in another country

Emigrants from Poland found their way to Israel.

American **immigrants** quickly became familiar with Ellis Island.

eminent (adjective): conspicuous, prominent
imminent (adjective): ready to happen, impending

Madame Curie was an **eminent** French scientist.

My sore shoulder tells me a storm is **imminent**.

explicit (adjective): clear, obvious
implicit (adjective): implied, potential

The boss's order was very **explicit**.

A threat to cancel funds was **implicit** in his proposal.

imply (verb): to hint or suggest
infer (verb): to guess or draw a conclusion

He **implied** that bonuses would be distributed.

We **inferred** from his actions that he was upset.

its (possessive pronoun): belonging to it
it's (contraction): it is

The dog was looking for **its** bone.

It's nice to see a cat lick its kitten.

later (adverb): at a future time
latter (adjective): more recent; relating to the end

Let's deal with this contract **later**.

Spread your seed in the **latter** part of the summer.

lay (transitive verb—requires an object): to put or set down (principal parts: **lay, laid, laid**)
lie (intransitive verb—does not require an object): to rest or recline (principal parts: **lie, lay, lain**)

Please **lay** that report on my desk.

I **laid** the records there yesterday.

I found my dog **lying** on the new oriental rug.

He just **lies** there and sleeps.

He **lay** there all night.

I wish I could have **lain** there.

liable (adjective): responsible for
libel (noun): written or oral attack

libel (verb): to attack or slander

> The court found her **liable** for the damage done by her pet elephant.

> Barry Goldwater once sued *Fact* magazine for **libel**.

> The court found that he had been **libeled**.

loose (adjective): not fastened securely
lose (verb): fail to hold onto

> The nut worked **loose** during the long ride.

> Did you **lose** your key at the party?

missal (noun): a mass book
missile (noun): a projectile self propelled or thrown

> The church we attend keeps changing its **missals**.

> Kennedy debated Nixon in 1960 on the "**missile** gap."

passed (verb): past participle of pass (move or proceed)
past (adjective): taken place before the present

> The teacher **passed** him to the ninth grade.

> During the **past** year our sales doubled.

personal (adjective): private or individual
personnel (noun): group of employees

> She felt her yearly income was a **personal** matter.

> Mr. Thomas handles all **personnel** problems.

principal (adjective): most important or chief
principle (noun): law, doctrine, or code of conduct

> He was the **principal** labor mediator in Washington.

> Some businessmen have no **principles** at all.

raise (transitive verb): to awaken or lift up (principal parts: **raise, raised, raised**)
rise (intransitive verb): ascent, emergence, or increase (principal parts: **rise, rose, risen**)

> Please **raise** the window.

> He **raised** the flag yesterday.

> I **rise** promptly at eight every morning.

> She **rose** from her seat and addressed the audience.

> That stock has **risen** ten points since Monday.

set (transitive verb): to place or put (principal parts: **set, set, set**)
sit (intransitive verb): ascent, emergence, or increase (principal parts: **sit, sat, sat**)

> **Set** those flowers on this table.

> She had **set** the table hours ago.

> **Sit** here where you can see the game.

> My boss **sat** there for hours staring at the graphs.

stationary (adjective): fixed, immobile
stationery (noun): writing paper

> The soldiers remained **stationary** during the parade.

The company **stationery** is blue with red type.

than (conjunction): used for comparisons
then (adverb): indicates time

He is a better manager of people **than** I.

Why wait until **then**?

their (possessive pronoun): belonging to them
there (adverb): indicates position or place
they're (contraction): they are

The secretaries lost **their** jobs to a computer.

There is no better wax than this one.

I'm sure **they're** going to have a good time in Ocean City.

to (preposition): direction toward
too (adverb): also, besides

Throw the switch **to** the left.

He **too** wanted the job.

use (verb): to accustom or utilize
used (adjective): accustomed to or second hand

Use these forms for the application.

He was **used** to being the alternate.

A **used** Volkswagen is a good buy.

whose (possessive pronoun): relating or belonging to whom
who's (contraction) who is

Whose report was best written?

Who's going to dinner after work?

your (possessive pronoun): relating or belonging to you
you're (contraction): you are

Your paycheck was left in your desk.

You're going to be promoted if you work hard.

EXERCISES

Cross out any misused words and write in the correct one.

1. The girls were already to go to the beach.

2. My angel of vision was blocked by the trees near the office.

3. Visits to the country allow me to get a breathe of fresh air.

4. Please set in the last row of the auditorium.

5. We are use to better food than this.

6. You're attitude needs improvement if you want the job.

7. I am libel to go crazy with the constant noise.

8. Did he infer that you would be named regional supervisor?

9. During our trip to Egypt we slept overnight in the dessert.

10. Every dissent American should learn the value of descent.

11. My secretary gave me good council about the client.

12. Her fine cooking illicited many complements.

13. He was deeply effected by the death of his wife.

14. The corrupt merchant failed to allude the police.

15. Perhaps we should send him a missile to read.

16. The cat had lain it's collar on the kitchen table.

17. In passed times stationary could be purchased cheaply.

18. Grave principals of conduct were involved in the case.

19. They're is no better time then the present for the rising of the flag.

20. Who's basket was laying on the bench?

USAGE

Levels of usage are difficult to define, for they tend to shift and change. What was once considered colloquial sometimes comes to be accepted in most standard speech and writing; the use of contractions is but one example. Also, degrees exist within categories that may make some borderline usage more acceptable than others. **Shape** used as a synonym for **condition** is a colloquial usage but is sometimes found in business writing. But **real** used as an adverb is a colloquialism seldom found in standard speech and writing.

Both of the above examples from the following Glossary of Usage necessarily reflect current taste (which may change) and the authors' prejudices. Questions of usage often deal not with what is wrong, but with what is appropriate. **Reckon** may be used as a spoken substitute for **suppose** in certain areas of the country, but it should not be used in standard speech or writing. You should attempt to be informal and even conversational in your business communication, but you should never become carelessly casual or familiar; these defects are as annoying as pomposity.

You must ultimately decide if the situation warrants your using one level of language or another. We'll attempt to guide you in your choices and make you aware of the possibilities. Some words we designate "colloquial" are not glaring errors. We simply feel that if you hope to be company president or division manager you should use the most standard level of language. There are three major designations for levels of usage that we will use:

1. Standard—acceptable for serious speech and writing.

2. Colloquial—acceptable in informal speech but not in the best writing.

3. Nonstandard—unacceptable in speech and writing.

One final reminder: when in doubt, rewrite the sentence!

GLOSSARY OF USAGE

a, an. Use **a** before words beginning with consonants (**a** dog, **a** boat) or a "yew" sound (**a** usual tour, **a** university). Use **an** before words beginning with vowels (**an** octopus, **an** unusual contract) and *unpronounced* h's (**an** honor, but **a** hill).

above, below. These are acceptable terms for written material that precedes or follows a particular passage, as in "the case cited above" or "the graphs below." However, it is often preferable to use "the preceding" or "the following" which is less stuffy but no less accurate. Avoid the legalistic "in view of the above" or "the above cited reasons," and wherever possible, use "therefore," or "for these reasons," etc.

acknowledge receipt of. Simply say "Thank you for" or "we received."

ad. A shortened form of **advertisement** that is acceptable in informal correspondence. This applies as well to the entire range of clipped forms, such as **auto** (automobile), **lab** (laboratory), **phone** (telephone).

adequate enough. Redundant.

advise. A cold substitute for "tell" or "inform."

again. Do not use after words with **re**-prefix when these words mean *again* or *back*.

> He regained **(again)** the position lost yesterday.

ain't. A nonstandard contraction of "am not," "is not," "are not," "have not," or "has not."

> He **is not** (not **ain't**) a good manager.

alright, all right. The second usage is preferred:

> In his opinion it was **all right** to leave early.

all the farther, all the longer, etc. It is preferable to use "as far as," or "as long as."

> This was **as far as** (not **all the farther**) he could go in his bid.

allude, refer. The first applies to an indirect reference, while the second is very direct:

> During his speech he **alluded** to recent articles criticizing wage and price controls; when questioned about this he **referred** us to Compton's article in the April issue of *Fortune* magazine.

alumnus, alumna. An **alumnus** is a male graduate (plural **alumni**), an **alumna** (plural **alumnae**) is a female graduate. **Alumni** is used when referring collectively to male and female graduates. Use "graduates" if your reader might object to the male plural.

among, between. **Among** is used with three or more persons or things:

> The work was divided **among** the branch managers.

> **Between** usually refers to two persons or things, but may be used when the relationship is both several and individual:

> The conflict **between** the two men lasted for a year.

> The lawyer saw no conflict **between** the parent company and its three subsidiaries [between, that is, the parent company and each individual subsidiary].

amount, number. **Amount** refers to a large, indivisible quantity, **number** to countable units.

> They recovered a large **amount** of aluminum from the trash dump.

> There were a **number** of people in the elevator.

analyzation.   An incorrect substitute for "analysis."

and etc.   Redundant since **etc.** is an abbreviation for "and so forth."

ante-, anti-.   **Ante-** used as a prefix means "before," as in **ante**diluvian or **ante**date; **Anti-** means "against," as in **anti**-Semite or **anti**slavery.

as.   Do not substitute for "that:"

> He didn't see **that** (not **as**) it was coming.

> Introduce dependent clauses with "since" or "because" rather than **as**.

> **Since** (not **as**) we were in the state, I called him.

> Do not overuse the preposition **as**:

> Kissinger was named (**as**) Secretary of State.

as, like.   See **like, as, as if**.

at.   Redundant when used with "where:"

> Where is my coat (**at**)?

> Where is he (**at**) when we need him?

attached hereto, attached herewith, enclosed please find. Be direct and say simply "Here is."

awfully, terribly.   These are acceptable only in speech as synonyms of "very."

> STANDARD: He is **very** good at tennis.

> COLLOQUIAL: He is **awfully** good at tennis.

> Note: It is wise to limit the use of all intensifiers. "He is good at tennis" is more forceful than "He is very good at tennis."

awhile, a while.   **Awhile** is an adverb, **while** a noun.

> That happened **awhile** ago.

> I will be with you in **a while**.

badly.   An adverb often confused with the adjective "bad:"

> I feel **bad** (not **badly**).

> It is colloquial usage to substitute **badly** for "very much," as in: "He needed a drink **badly**."

barely, hardly, scarcely.   These adverbs, which mean "not quite," should not be used with negatives. The result is a double negative.

> He is (**not**) **hardly** around anymore.

> He **scarcely** (**never**) visited his mother.

because of.   See **due to**.

beg.   Don't "**beg** to advise" or "**beg** to acknowledge receipt of." Whatever it is, it's not worth begging for.

being as how, being that.   Nonstandard for "because" or "since."

> STANDARD: **Since** he was in the building, she decided to wait.

> NONSTANDARD: **Being that** he was in the building, she decided to wait.

below.   See **above.**

beside, besides.   **Beside** is a preposition meaning "by or at the side of"; **besides** is generally used as an adverb to mean "in addition to."

> He took his place **beside** her on the train.

> **Besides** John, we have Tim and Bill ready to travel.

be sure and.   See **try and.**

between.   See **among.**

between you and I.   Never a correct substitute for "between you and me"; **me** is object of the preposition **between.**

but that, but what.   Colloquial substitutes for "that."

> STANDARD: There is no doubt **that** the school faces a deficit.

> COLLOQUIAL: There is no doubt **but that** the school faces a deficit.

can, may.   In formal usage, **can** means "to be able":

> **Can** I lift the chair?

May asks or indicates permission:

> **May** I have the last piece of cake?

Colloquial usage is flexible, but these basic distinctions should be kept in mind.

cannot, can not.   Use **cannot** unless you wish to stress the **not.**

center around, center about.   Some argue that these idioms are illogical since centers would never revolve around anything.

> STANDARD: The discussion **centered on** (or **upon**) the patent application.

> COLLOQUIAL: The discussion **centered around** the patent application.

come and.   Colloquial for "come to," as in:

> **Come to** (not **and**) see me if possible.

consensus of opinion.   Redundant since **consensus** means "general agreement."

contact.   Acceptable as a general term meaning "communicate with," yet it is best to make your wishes more specific, as in: "call," "write," "meet," "interview," etc.

continual, continuous.   **Continual** means recurring at brief intervals, while **continuous** means uninterrupted.

> We were awakened by **continual** visitors to the office.

> The **continuous** roar of the waterfall discouraged speech.

contractions.   Abbreviated forms of words, such as **he's** for **he is** or **you're** for **you are.** Contractions are acceptable in business usage.

data.   Although the plural form of **datum, data** is frequently treated as a collective noun with a singular verb, as in:

> This **data** is useful.

> If problems arise substitute "information."

definite, definitely.   Avoid using these words as useless intensifiers, as in:

> He is (**definitely**) an excellent plumber.

different from, different than.   *Different from* is generally preferred, though **different than** can be preferable when introducing clauses.

> Her typewriter was **different from** mine.

> His position on this issue was **different than** I expected.

doesn't.   Not to be confused with the plural contraction "don't."

> She **doesn't** (not **don't**) like working on the bottom floor.

due to.   Supporters of formal usage accept **due to** after the verb **to be,** but object to it at the beginning of a sentence when introducing an adverbial phrase; they prefer "because of" or "owing to."

> STANDARD: His report was late **because of** an error in the computer program.

> COLLOQUIAL: His report was late **due to** an error in the computer program.

> GENERALLY
> ACCEPTABLE: The accident was **due to** (or **caused by**) his tiredness.

each and every.   Redundant—use either one but not both.

enclosed please find. See **attached hereto.**

endeavor.   Pompous for "try."

equally as good.   Eliminate the unnecessary **as.**

expect.   Colloquial when used to mean "suppose."

> STANDARD: I **suppose** I will be seeing him soon.

> COLLOQUIAL: I **expect** I'll be seeing him soon.

fact, of the fact that.   Often **of the fact** can be deleted.

> WORDY: He was unaware **of the fact that** she had hired him.

> BETTER: He was unaware **that** she had hired him.

farther, further.   In formal usage **farther** refers to distance and **further** to degree or quantity. In informal usage the words are used interchangeably. The superlative forms are **farthest** and **furthest.**

> STANDARD: The office is eight miles **farther.**

> COLLOQUIAL: The office is eight miles **further.**

faze.   Colloquial for "bother."

fellow.   Colloquial for "person."

fewer, less.   **Fewer** refers to number, **less** to quantity or degree.

> There is **less** turnover since we began the enrichment program.

> **Fewer** workers are leaving the company.

figure.   Colloquial for "think," "believe," or "suppose."

> STANDARD: I **believe** I will leave early tomorrow.

> COLLOQUIAL: I **figure** I will leave early tomorrow.

fine.   Used colloquially as an adjective of praise and as an adverb meaning "well," as in, "the machine works just **fine**." Avoid this usage.

first-rate.   Colloquial if used as an adjective or adverb meaning "excellent" or "good."

> STANDARD: He is **excellent** at dictating organized letters.
> COLLOQUIAL: He is **first-rate** at dictating organized letters.

flunk.   Colloquial for "fail."

former, latter.   **Former** refers to the first-named of two, **latter** to the second-named of two.

> We saw John Timmons and Stanley White today; the **former** [John] is at Yale University while the **latter** [Stanley] is at Brown.

further.   See **farther.**

good and.   Colloquial in such expressions as "good and angry," "good and ready," etc.

good, well.   **Good** is an adjective, **well** is an adverb.

> STANDARD: He runs the conference **well**.
> NONSTANDARD: He runs the conference **good**.

had of, had ought.   Both forms are nonstandard. Use **had** or **ought**.

> I wish I **had** (not **had of**) purchased the stock earlier.
> They **ought** (not **had ought**) to go for a vacation.

half a.   This is acceptable, but should not be preceded with a redundant **a**:

> There is **half** (not **a half**) a pie left in the refrigerator.

hardly.   See **barely.**

herein set down.   This is legal jargon for "listed here."

himself.   See **myself.**

I have before me your letter. Avoid this pompous expression.

in lieu of.   This is legal jargon for "instead of."

in regards to, with regards to.   The correct forms are singular, "in regard to" and "with regard to."

in my opinion.   Wordy and unnecessary. Substitute "I think," "I feel," or "I believe."

inside of, outside of.   When used as prepositional phrases, drop the **of**:

> The dog was found **inside** (not **inside of**) the house.

interpose no objections.   Avoid this legal jargon. Use "I approve" or "I agree with."

in the affirmative, in the negative.   Pompous for "yes" and "no."

in the neighborhood of.   Wordy—use "about."

invite (noun).   Nonstandard for "invitation."

irregardless.   A nonstandard substitute for "regardless."

> **Regardless** (not **irregardless**) of her feelings, I am leaving on Monday.

is when, is where.   Avoid using these to introduce noun clauses defining terms.

> STANDARD: A merger **occurs when** two companies join together.

COLLOQUIAL: A merger **is when** two companies join together.

kind of, sort of.   Colloquial for "somewhat" or "rather."

STANDARD: They were **rather** tired after the trip.

COLLOQUIAL: They were **sort of** tired after the trip.

latter.   See **former.**

learn.   See **teach.**

led.   **Led** is the past tense and past participle of the verb "to lead" (conduct). It should not be confused with the noun "lead" (metal), which is spelled and pronounced differently.

The guide **led** us to where the piece of **lead** had fallen.

lend, loan.   See **loan.**

less.   See **fewer.**

let's.   This is a contraction for **let us** and should *not* be followed by **us.**

STANDARD: **Let's** go to the beach.

NONSTANDARD: **Let's us** go to the beach.

like, as, as if.   **Like** is a preposition, **as** and **as if** are conjunctions. Language purists insist on these distinctions, but it is common to find **like** used as a conjunction to introduce clauses.

STANDARD: Winston tastes good **as** a cigarette should.

COLLOQUIAL: Winston tastes good **like** a cigarette should.

literally.   **Literally** means "in a strict sense without exaggeration." Thus "he **literally** hit the ceiling when he heard the news" makes no sense unless he really did hit it. If he did not, the word **literally** becomes a meaningless intensifier.

loan, lend.   These words are now both used as verbs, as in:

Loan (or **lend**) me a dollar.

Loan is the only noun.

lots, lots of.   These are colloquialisms for "much" and "many."

STANDARD: There are **many** vice-presidents at the central office.

COLLOQUIAL: There are **lots of** vice-presidents at the central office.

mad.   Colloquial for "angry."

many, much.   **Many** refers to quantity, **much** to amount. Their comparative and superlative forms are **many, more, most; much, more, most.**

The Salvation Army got **much** more money from the **many** shoppers in the mall.

may.   See **can.**

may of.   Nonstandard for "may have."

media.   Like **data, media** is sometimes used with a singular verb, even though it is plural (singular is **medium**). Be safe and use only the plural verb.

most.   Colloquial for "almost."

STANDARD: **Almost** all the secretaries bring their own lunch.

COLLOQUIAL: **Most** all the secretaries bring their own lunch.

Ms.   An acceptable abbreviation for salutations when you are uncertain of a woman's marital status. However, use **Miss** or **Mrs.** if your correspondent specifically indicates this.

much.   See **many**.

muchly.   An incorrect substitute for "much."

myself, yourself, himself.   Only in nonstandard usage does the intensive pronoun replace personal pronouns. They may be used, however, for emphasis.

> STANDARD: Bob and **I** worked on the Beltzer contract.
>
> NONSTANDARD: Bob and **myself** worked on the Beltzer contract.
>
> ACCEPTABLE: Bob **himself** drew up the agreement.

nice.   Overused to express pleasure or approval. Seek greater precision in your choice of words.

nothing.   Should not follow a negative.

> Jack can't do **anything** (not **nothing**).

nowhere near.   Colloquial for "not nearly."

nowheres.   Use "nowhere."

number.   See **amount**.

off of.   Eliminate the **of**:

> She chased them **off** (not **off of**) her desk.

O.K., OK, okay.   All three versions are acceptable colloquialisms, but the first is more widely used.

on account of.   "Because of" is preferable.

ought.   See **had of**.

ourself.   Incorrect form of "ourselves."

outside of.   See **inside of**.

owing to the fact that.   Wordy—use "because" or "since."

> WORDY: **Owing to the fact that** he was continually drunk, he was not promoted.
>
> BETTER: **Because** he was continually drunk, he was not promoted.

party.   **Party** refers to a group and should not be used in place of "individual," "person," "man," etc.

> The operator said that the **person** (not **party**) would call back.

permit me to state.   Avoid this pompous expression.

plenty.   Nonstandard when used as an adverb meaning "very" or "fully."

> STANDARD: Her backhand is **very** good.
>
> NONSTANDARD: Her backhand is **plenty** good.

prepositions.   Take care to avoid such superfluous prepositions as "blame **on**," "where **at**," "cover **over**," or "fill **up**." Also, be sure to use correct prepositions in idiomatic phrases:

addicted **to**	agree **to** (a thing)
adhere **to**	agreeable **to**
agree **with** (someone)	angry **at** (a thing)

angry **with** (someone)
argue **for** (a point)
argue **with** (someone)
argue **about** (a question)
arrive **in** (a city)
capable **of**
compare **to** (shows similarity)
compare **with** (shows similarity and difference)
concur **in** (an opinion)
concur **with** (someone)
devoid **of**
differ **with** (disagree with a person)
differ **over** (a question)
different **from**
dissent **from**

hint **at**
impatient **with** (a person)
impatient **at** (conduct)
independent **of**
invest **in** (business)
invest **with** (authority)
join **in** (activity)
join **to** (one thing to another)
join **with** (people)
part **from** (leave)
part **with** (release, give up)
profit **by**
prohibit **from**
sensitive **to**

pretty.   Colloquial when used as an adverb meaning "somewhat" or "moderately."

> STANDARD: Her chances of being promoted are **moderately** good.
>
> COLLOQUIAL: Her chances of being promoted are **pretty** good.

pursuant to.   This is legal jargon for "according to."

question as to whether, question of whether.   Shorten to "whether."

real, really.   **Real** is an adjective, **really** an adverb. **Real** may be used colloquially as an adverb, but should be avoided.

> STANDARD: They had **real** plants growing in their kitchen.
>
> STANDARD: I **really** would like to see him president.
>
> COLLOQUIAL: This is **real** good ice cream.

reckon.   Colloquial for "think" or "suppose."

refer.   See **allude.**

regardless.   See **irregardless.**

same, said.   Except in formal legal documents, don't use **same** as a pronoun or **said** as an adjective.

set forth.   When possible, use "explain" or "describe."

shall, will.   The wide acceptance of **will** to express the future is almost making **shall** obsolete.

shape.   Colloquial for "condition."

should of.   Nonstandard for "should have."

so.   **So** is colloquial when used as an intensifier to mean "very."

> STANDARD: He was **very** helpful on the project.
>
> COLLOQUIAL: He was **so** helpful on the project.

sort of.   See **kind of.**

stall for time.   Redundant for "stall."

such.   Colloquial when used as an intensifier.

> STANDARD: He is a **nice** person.
>
> COLLOQUIAL: He is **such** a nice person.

sure.   Colloquial for "certainly" or "really."

> STANDARD: He **really** likes to criticize.
>
> COLLOQUIAL: He **sure** likes to criticize.

take the liberty, take the opportunity.   These are wordy, meaningless phrases.

teach, learn.   **Teach** means "to impart knowledge," **learn** means "to gain knowledge:"

> He **taught** me tennis during the summer; I **learned** a great deal.

terribly.   See **awfully.**

than, then.   **Than** is a conjunction that implies a comparison, while **then** is an adverb indicating time.

> **Then** he said; "Tim is taller **than** I."

that there, this here, them there.   Nonstandard forms.

> STANDARD: Give me **that** directory.
>
> NONSTANDARD: Give me **that there** directory.

there is, there are.   Be careful that these do not become habitual fillers at the beginning of a sentence. Overuse can lead to wordiness and vagueness.

theirselves.   An incorrect substitute for "themselves."

them.   Should never be used as an adjective.

> STANDARD: I enjoy **those** records.
>
> NONSTANDARD: I enjoy **them** records.

thusly.   The **ly** is not necessary.

trust.   This is a stilted substitute for "I hope."

try and, be sure and.   Colloquial for "try to" or "be sure to."

> STANDARD: Be **sure to** lock the office.
>
> COLLOQUIAL: Be **sure and** lock the office.

together.   Redundant if its meaning is inherent in another word.

> To complete the puzzle, connect the two pieces **(together)**.

type.   Colloquial for "type of."

> STANDARD: This is the **type of** job I prefer.
>
> COLLOQUIAL: This is the **type** job I prefer.

use, utilize; use, utilization.   **Utilize** and **utilization** are pompous substitutes for **use** (verb) and **use** (noun).

we are not in the position to.   Substitute "we cannot."

where.   Colloquial as a substitute for "that."

> STANDARD: I see **that** prices are rising again.
>
> COLLOQUIAL: I see **where** prices are rising again.

where . . . at.   See **at.**

will.   See **shall.**

with regard to.   See **in regards to.**

would like for.   Often a colloquial, wordy substitute for "want."

> STANDARD: The boss **wants** me to go to Dallas.
>
> COLLOQUIAL: The boss **would like for** me to go to Dallas.

would of.   Nonstandard for "would have."

yours of recent date.   This is an outdated reference to an incoming letter. Rather than "I have **yours of recent date**" say "Thank you for your recent letter."

yourself. See **myself.**

Appendices: SAMPLE COMMUNICATIONS AND CASE STUDIES

Appendix A

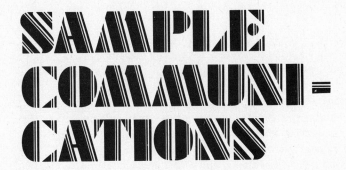

In the Appendices we have provided additional case studies and sample letters that will enable you to determine whether you learned the earlier lessons. We wrote some of the letters ourselves, but most come from actual correspondence sent to or from government and private industry. So these exercises are practical in the best sense of the word; they contain the kinds of letters and situations that you will encounter in your own job.

In Appendix A you will merely need to critically evaluate letters and responses sent to customers or clients. This may be done in discussion or in writing. In Appendix B you will be asked to compose original responses. In both cases, keep in mind all the points on style, grammar, and usage made previously in this text, especially Part I with its discussion of the Communications Triangle—*Tone, Information, Organization.*

FROZEN DINNER PROBLEM

A. INCOMING LETTER

March 3, 197__

President
Gutessen Frozen Dinners, Inc.
618 Hessell Boulevard
Los Angeles, California 90024

Dear Sir:

As a long-time fan of your Gutessen frozen dinners, I felt it my duty to report a loosening of previously high standards in their manufacture. I refer to a recent experience with respect to a "Loin of Pork" (with orange muffin) dinner. I followed directions in heating the dinner, having taken it from my freezer. The muffin, however, did not prosper as pictured on the front of the package (see enclosed sample). Apparently during the manufacture the major portion of the muffin shifted over into the pork and gravy producing when heated a not very delectable combination and a badly burnt residue of what should have been a full muffin. This marks the second time I have had such an experience with a Gutessen frozen dinner, and would appreciate your looking into the matter.

Thank you for your assistance.

Sincerely,

Claude L. Renfro
376 Bodin Way
Baton Rouge, Louisiana 70803

Figure A. 1.

B.   RESPONSE

GUTESSEN FROZEN DINNERS, INC.
618 Hessell Boulevard
Los Angeles, California 90024

March 15, 197___

Mr. Claude L. Renfro
376 Bodin Way
Baton Rouge, Louisiana 70803

Dear Mr. Renfro:

We regret that our product did not meet your expectations, but can assure you that the problem
is not in its manufacture. We carefully control the quality of our products up to the time when
they leave the factory. Sometimes during their handling in the various stores, they are allowed to
thaw and are then refrozen. This sometimes causes problems when customers prepare them.

Since the responsibility is not ours, we suggest you check with your local stores for a possible
refund of money. Thank you.

Sincerely,

Peter T. Soames
Vice-President
Consumer Complaints

Figure A.2.

C. RESPONSE

GUTESSEN FROZEN DINNERS, INC.
618 Hessell Boulevard
Los Angeles, California 90024

March 15, 197__

Mr. Claude L. Renfro
376 Bodin Way
Baton Rouge, Louisiana 70803

Dear Mr. Renfro:

Thank you for contacting us. We regret that anything has occurred which might cause you to question the care used by us in the preparation of our Gutessen frozen prepared dinners.

To insure that our packing and processing techniques are properly followed, supervisors employed by the company as well as supervisors of the United States Department of Agriculture are always present in the processing area. All products are carefully compounded according to established recipes and are supervised very carefully in the preparation.

Immediately after preparation, while the food to be frozen is under such supervised care, it is routed into the freezing tunnels where temperatures of from 20 to 40 degrees below zero are maintained. It takes but a few minutes under these sharp freezing conditions for the food to be solidly frozen. Then the frozen foods are packaged in the kind of containers that keep contamination away from them. Of course, the products had been covered with aluminum foil before ever reaching the freezing tunnels so that contamination in the freezing tunnels would be impossible. Following the packaging they are still maintained in refrigerated areaways with temperatures considerably below zero.

All the frozen products are dispatched to different distribution centers and placed in specially designed freezer trucks that maintain temperatures below zero so that they will arrive in a frozen state.

In spite of all of our care, however, something very unusual must have happened to cause your disappointment. Unfortunately, it is possible for frozen foods to be mishandled after leaving our control so that they are allowed to thaw and then are refrozen. Based on your description we believe this is what had happened to the product you purchased.

Even though this condition was beyond our control, we sincerely regret your disappointment and trust that you will never again be similarly displeased.

Very truly yours,

Peter T. Soames
Vice-President
Consumer Complaints

Figure A.3.

INSURANCE CLAIM

A. INCOMING LETTER

January 4, 197__

Alpha Insurance Company
137 Elton Drive
Baltimore, Maryland 21229

Dear Sir:

All you people care about is collecting payment, but when it comes for a person to collect there is an excuse to get out of paying. July 24 I went to State Hospital and then sent you all bills immediately, and immediately I get a letter from your claims dept—no payment—and other excuses. I wrote to cancel my policy immediately and now I see your ads every day in the local paper. In my opinion, your insurance stinks and you people are rotten.

Mrs. G. Stone
199 Willow Road
Baltimore, Maryland 21229

Figure A.4.

B. RESPONSE

ALPHA INSURANCE COMPANY
137 Elton Drive
Baltimore, Maryland 21229
January 10, 197__

Mrs. G. Stone
199 Willow Road
Baltimore, Maryland 21229

Dear Mrs. Stone:

Your recent letter has been referred to my attention.

The above captioned policy provides benefits in the amount of $500.00 per month for hospital confinements due to accidental bodily injury. Hospital confinement is the primary basis on which claims are paid. According to the information submitted with your claim of July 24, 197__, you were not confined to the hospital. We therefore could not approve payment of benefits.

Your policy has been cancelled as you requested.

Sincerely,

Elton R. Haggerty
Claim Services Representative

Figure A.5.

ASTHMA MEDICINE

A.   INCOMING LETTER

February 23, 197__

President
Levit Laboratories, Inc.
Cherry Hill, New Jersey 08034

Dear Sir:

Since childhood I have been bothered with asthma and only recently, with my doctor's recommendation of Almadine, have I gotten any relief. Your medicine is excellent, but expensive. I refer to the recent price increase. A few months ago, I paid $2.25 for a pint of Almadine, now I was recently charged $4.55 for the exact same amount. Why this outlandish increase? Why too is it necessary for this drug to be purchased by prescription? Wouldn't its sale under its generic rather than its brand name reduce the cost?

Unless my letter is satisfactorily answered, I intend to pursue this matter with my Senator through his committee on Food and Drug Laws.

Sincerely,

George P. Young
369 Main Street
Solon, Ohio 44139

Figure A.6.

B.   RESPONSE

LEVIT LABORATORIES, INC.
Cherry Hill, New Jersey 08034
March 1, 197__

Mr. George P. Young
369 Main Street
Solon, Ohio 44139

Dear Mr. Young:

I want to thank you for your letter of February 23, 197__, concerning your recent purchase of Almadine.

In February, 197__, we did increase our price for Almadine by approximately $0.42 per pint which would in no way explain the increase of $2.30 that you experienced.

We are always concerned when we hear of the high prices charged by pharmacies for our products. Several states are proposing bills to require pharmacies to post their base prices; see attached article from the New York Times on this matter.

Whenever you are charged a price that seems excessive, you should ask the proprietor to see his base price list to determine what his markup on the product has been. If the markup seems excessive, you should suggest to him that you will refer the matter to the control board.

As Levit Laboratories is a Tier 2 company under Phase III of the Federal Economic Stabilization Act, we are not required to prenotify the Price Commission regarding price increases. However, our management has tried to maintain the lowest price possible without sacrificing the quality of our products and we are satisfied that the increases we have made are in accordance with the federal regulation.

As to your question regarding Almadine being a prescription drug, this is required to eliminate the dangers of misuse in terms of overdosage or use by patients with some other complicated disease which can only be determined by a qualified physician.

If the above explanation is not satisfactory and if you require additional information, please feel free to contact me. We also wish to take this opportunity to thank you for your support of Levitt products and I hope that Almadine has relieved your asthmatic condition.

Cordially yours,

Hilton T. Barner
President

Figure A.7.

ANNOUNCEMENT OF EXAMINATION[1]

Arrangements have been made for the administration of a special examination designed to appraise supervisory skills and test qualifications and knowledge regarding supervision. It has been determined that this examination will be offered in the afternoon, Friday, September 29 in the first floor training area. The test consists of more than one part and will take a few hours.

Employees who recently entered Government service and those who have never entered such competition prior to this time are eligible to compete.

Employees in grades ranging a grade above the GS-2 level through one or two grades below the so-called executive level who have not previously participated in this type of examination before and are desirous of doing so at this juncture should contact those persons in their own respective offices to whom they are directly responsible. The appropriate portion of this communication should be signed and returned by employees wishing to compete to the employee in charge of these matters who operates in the division having as its major function the responsibility for handling personnel affairs.

John Nash
Director of Personnel

- -

NAME _____ GRADE _____

POSITION TITLE _____ BUREAU _____

I wish to take the examination to be given September 29.

Figure A.8.

1. From *Writing Effective Letters,* U.S. Civil Service Commission, p. 2-23.

MOWER REPAIR

A.   INCOMING LETTER

42 Maple Terrace
Houston, Texas 77036
August 23, 197__

Mr. Michael Caldman
President
Barnfeld & Smith
624 Leggett Drive
Tulsa, Oklahoma 73111

Dear Mr. Caldman:

I have not yet received from your Houston appliance repair center the lawn mower sent for repair on June 23, sixty two (62) days ago. The delay has cost me both money (around $25 so far) for lawn cuttings and additional aggravation over the fact that Barnfeld & Smith never bothered to inform me about the delay (it became necessary for me to contact your customer service department).

Such carelessness and inefficiency extend beyond this particular department, for I have been equally frustrated, along with many other customers, with your automotive repair center at Houston. In what I consider a typical experience, I had to wait over nine hours on December 13 for the simple installation of a brake hose, all the time never being informed why this wait was necessary.

I certainly can understand that in an enterprise as large and complex as yours, problems will arise. What I can't understand or forgive is the basic neglect of good customer relations and what would seem to me common sense business practices (such as a basic rotation system or service board in your automotive center to indicate when a car is being serviced, or a simple call from your customer service department when there is a delay in appliance repair).

The personnel of your company are courteous and helpful, but they could use better direction and sounder management.

Sincerely,

Harlan T. Redburn

Figure A.9.

B. RESPONSE

BARNFELD & SMITH
624 Leggett Drive
Tulsa, Oklahoma 73111

August 29, 197__

Mr. Harlan T. Redburn
42 Maple Terrace
Houston, Texas 77036

Dear Mr. Redburn:

Thank you for your recent letter. We always want to know when customers are not receiving good service.

You are correct in asserting that we kept your lawn mower an unpardonably long time. This was necessary, however, because of a delay in receiving proper parts from the factory. We wanted to be certain of returning the machine to you in the best possible condition though we sincerely apologize for the delay.

Concerning your other suggestions, I have directed the manager at your Houston branch of Barnfeld & Smith to look into this matter.

Thank you again, Mr. Redburn, for taking the time and effort to write me. Please contact me again should further problems occur.

Sincerely,

Michael Caldman
President

Figure A.10.

LOST COMMISSARY CARD[2]

A.   INCOMING LETTER

Department of the Army
The Pentagon
Washington, D.C.

To whom it may concern:

My husband, Martin Keller, served in the Army and was proud to be helping his country.
Now I, his widow, am in need of my identification card because I don't make much money and
I need to keep on getting things from the commissary where things don't cost as much. The fellow
there says I need to get the card renewed so please renew the card right away.
Thank you in advance for my card.

Yours truly,

Mrs. Sarah Keller

Figure A.11.

B.   GOVERNMENT MEMO FOR THE RECORD

Basis for Action:

Pvt. Martin Keller served from 7 June 1918 until discharge 26 August 1919; died 15 May 1961.
Since Pvt. Keller was neither on active duty nor retired at time of death, identification card should
not have been issued to widow.

*   *   *

Uniformed Services Identification and Privilege Cards authorize medical care in uniformed services
facilities; and commissary, post exchange, and theater privileges. Widows of military personnel are
eligible for cards

(1)   if their husbands died while on active duty or while in a retired status
and

(2)   if they have not remarried.

Cards issued by mistake are to be returned to your office, ATTN: AGAO-CC, for destruction.

Figure A.12.

2. From *Writing Effective Letters,* U.S. Civil Service Commission, pp. 5B-7 through 5B-9.

C.   RESPONSE

Dear Mrs. Keller:

This is in reply to your letter of 10 October 1967, requesting the renewal of your identification card.

Only unremarried widows of military personnel who died while on active duty or in a retired status are eligible to be issued Uniformed Services Identification and Privilege Cards authorizing medical care in uniformed services facilities, commissary, post exchange and theater privileges. Since your late husband was discharged and subsequently died, you are not eligible for an identification card.

In view of the above, the identification cards previously issued you were in error. It is requested that the card referred to in your letter be returned to this office, ATTN: AGAO-CC, for destruction in accordance with pertinent regulations.

Sincerely yours,

Major General, USA

Figure A.13.

INSURANCE CANCELLATION

A.   INCOMING LETTER

113 Falton Road
Concord, New Hampshire 03301
June 10, 197__

TVAT Insurance
Bell Terrace
Portland, Maine 04103

Sir:

I'm sending your check back to you. I wish you'd check your files again. You say my insurance is cancelled. I have paid all my payments. I don't understand how you can say this. If I didn't need insurance I wouldn't of been paying you all this time.

In October of 72 I sent you two checks for payment of my insurance and for W. E. Cochian. The nos' were 4407 & 4408. One was for $6.96 and one for $4.35. Please tell me why you say I've been cancelled.

Thank you,

Dorothy Master

Figure A.14.

B. RESPONSE

TVAT Insurance
Bell Terrace
Portland, Maine 04103

June 20, 197__

Mrs. Dorothy Master
113 Falton Road
Concord, New Hampshire 03301

Dear Mrs. Master:

We are again returning the Refund Draft for $6.95.

Our records show that the due date on your policy had been September 7, 197__. We have no record of receiving a payment for the September due date or of another payment in October. Please forward photocopies of both sides of the cancelled checks of any payments made in September or October.

Our records further show that we have no policy in our alphabetical files for W. F. Cochian. Please send us the policy numbers.

Enclosed is a specially coded envelope to my attention for your convenience in replying.

Sincerely,

Adeline Williams
Policy Owners' Service.

Figure A.15.

CONFEDERATION OF LOCAL GOVERNMENTS

TO: The Local Government Group of California Institute of Cities

FROM: Toby Hartwell—Executive Director CIC

SUBJECT: Loose Federation of Local Government Association Members of CIC

It is recommended that consideration be given to initiating steps at an early date to bring the Local Government Association members of CIC together in some sort of a federation for purposes of:

1. Representing the aggregate local-government interest more effectively and visibly within the CIC organizational framework;

2. Facilitating the interface between the local government segment of CIC and the State and Federal segments;

3. Providing fully researched and well reasoned local positions on various issues and policy questions to the State and Federal segments;

4. Providing the local segment with the maximum possible strength and unity in negotiating issues with the State and Federal segments, and in influencing State and Federal policies; as well as in responding to issues raised by the State and Federal levels;

5. Creating the most favorable possible conditions in inter-local and inter-association relationships such as to encourage State and Federal seed or matching money assistance for creating and sustaining on-going association capacities adequate to put the local segment on a more equal partnership footing with the State and Federal governments on research of policies and issues and on advocacy of positions.

It is therefore further recommended that the local government associations create for these purposes a non-profit corporation constituted of and governed by the associations which can, among other things, serve as a local vehicle for:

1. Pooling existing association resources, including certain staff resources, for research on and advocacy of shared local objectives; and

2. Applying for technical and financial assistance from State and Federal agencies, foundations, and other sources.

The strength and adequacy of local initiatives become of prime importance in the context of Federal decentralization, general revenue sharing, and the principles now asserted in the Housing and Community Development Act of 1974.

Indeed, the shape and efficacy of the whole emerging system of inter-governmental relationships induced by these national trends are contingent largely on the exercise of the leadership role now cast into the hands of the local general purpose governments.

Figure A.16.

Page 2

The benefits to local governments of the CIC itself as a new and unique channel of negotiation with and communication to and from the State and Federal governments will either become real or will fade away as lost opportunities to the extent that they are captured by aggressive and unified local action.

The general and special revenue sharing acts accord <u>prime policy-making prerogatives</u> and responsibilities to every unit of local general-purpose government, and encourage the development of individual local capabilities for discharging these responsibilities.

It follows that somewhat parallel prerogatives and responsibilities devolve on the State Associations which represent the aggregate interests of these constituent local government units vis a vis the State and Federal governments; and parallel capacities on the part of the Associations to perform together must be developed to enable the associations to serve and support their individual members most effectively in these new dimensions of local responsibility.

The foregoing recommendation addresses itself to this need.

Figure A.16. *(continued)*

COMPANY RECORDS

A.   INCOMING LETTER

5813 Brook Road
St. Louis, Missouri 63131
June 5, 197__

Car-Life Insurance Company
82 Smith Place
Cedar Rapids, Iowa 52406

Gentlemen:

I think it is about time that we get one thing perfectly clear. Mrs. Jean Roberts is deceased. We no longer want you to send to us those bills for premiums. How can you collect on a person who is dead!

We have given you all the information we can give; now it is your turn to start doing something about the last claim. If this is not done, action will be taken.

C. R. Roberts

P.S. What kind of a company are you that you don't even have policy numbers on your clients? I want an immediate response from you people.

Figure A.17.

B. RESPONSE

CAR-LIFE INSURANCE COMPANY
82 Smith Place
Cedar Rapids, Iowa 52406

June 20, 197__

Mr. C. R. Roberts
5813 Brook Road
St. Louis, Missouri 63131

Dear Mr. Roberts:

Your recent letter has been referred to me for my attention.

We are sorry you received a premium notice in Mrs. Roberts' name after you notified us of her demise. This was a technical error due to our automatic billing system and we would like to apologize for it.

You should not, in the future, receive any further notices in Mrs. Roberts' name. If you do, however, please notify us so that we can determine if there is an error in our billing system.

Thank you for your patience in the matter.

Sincerely,

Atalanta N. Calidon
Policy Owners' Service

Figure A.18.

POLICY PROBLEM

A. INCOMING LETTER

81 Sharon Drive
Danville, Illinois 61832
February 1, 197_

Cromer Insurance
901 Fels Road
Decatur, Illinois 65222

Dear Sir:

I want you to verify your records, as to this Hospital Indemity Rider—I have received two of these—since I accepted and added the extra benefit to my policy.

The Rider attached to my policy is dated 09/28/7_. I want you to verify to me—that I am covered from that date—so there will be no mistake on my part, or yours. Why have I received two notices, if I'm already covered??? I have my cancelled check showing payment of $17.53 on 09/17/7_.

> 11.83   original policy
> 5.70   Hosp. Rider
> 17.53

I do not want to find out, that through some error, I'm not covered—when I have paid for benefit! Awaiting reply.

Bonnie Turner

Figure A.19.

B. RESPONSE

CROMER INSURANCE
901 Fels Road
Decatur, Illinois 65222

February 18, 197__

Ms. Bonnie Turner
81 Sharon Drive
Danville, Illinois 61832

Dear Ms. Turner:

I received your recent correspondence regarding the above policy.

Our records indicate that you accepted a rider on September 28, 197__. The same rider is again being offered with an effective date of December 28, 197__.

If you wish to accept this rider offer, please send up a payment of $8.15. You may be insured up to $1,000.00 per month on this policy.

I trust this information has been helpful. If you have any further questions, please do not hesitate to contact me.

Sincerely,

Hilda T. Watson
Policyowners' Service

Figure A.20.

Appendix B

CASE STUDIES AND EXERCISES

1. Use semiblock form in writing an order letter from David Quinn, 781 Euclid Road, Radford, Virginia 24141 to Carnac Galleries, 813 Sunset Lane, Long Beach, California 90804. Mr. Quinn wishes to purchase the following items listed in Carnac Galleries' rare map catalogue #83:

> 72. *Nova Virginiae.* Centered on Chesapeake Bay, with west at the top. Based upon John Smith's famous map of Virginia, 1612. This particular one is the fourth derivation of the Smith map. $150

> 118. *Virginia and Maryland.* The Tidewater region of both states. Delaware is not yet present; primitive counties labeled throughout. Lower one third of map reinforced, with two unobtrusive tears, repaired. $60

> 235. *Phaenomena.* Seven separate representatives of the solar system demonstrating different theories as to its nature (Plato, Ptolemy, etc.). With attractive vignettes, text and a handsome chart showing various aspects of the movement of the Earth around the sun. $100

Even though this is Mr. Quinn's first order, he would like these maps sent on credit.

2. Use a block style in responding to Mr. Quinn's letter in the previous exercise. You are Carson P. Rhodes, the owner of Carnac Galleries. Indicate that you would be happy to set up an account after receiving proper credit references, but that the present order must be sent out C.O.D.

3. An advertising agency—Shields, McDermott & Pyles—handles the account of Groper's Dog Food, 312 Kennel Building, Lexington, Kentucky 40506. To pump up sagging sales, Alison Pyles comes up with the following scheme: Groper's will run a contest to name its new line of dry dog food pellets. Contestants may submit only one name and must attach a label from a can of Groper's Dog Food with each entry. First prize is $10,000. The contest is a success

with over 100,000 entries. The winning name is "Gropettes." The agency now plans to send a sales letter to all entrants encouraging them to purchase Groper's products. Draft such a letter.

4. As special assistant to Mayor Tomlinson of Canton, Iowa, it is your responsibility to deal with correspondence from constituents. You receive the letter shown in Figure B.1.

1801 Barton Terrace
Canton, Iowa 69302
August 18, 197__

Mayor Carl P. Tomlinson
Court House
Canton, Iowa

Dear Mayor Tomlinson:

Debris-covered lots are both a public eyesore and a hazard to residents of the community, especially small children. In an effort to help you promote Canton as a safe, clean city, we have compiled the following list of debris-covered lots and sincerely request that these situations be corrected:

813 Cardale Drive   1863 Lois Lane
Oak Terrace and Barton Road   139 Felcher Street
983 Hubert Lane   Conway and Tilsen Streets
Manning and 24th Streets   4901 Hollins Road

Thank you for your attention to this matter.

Sincerely,

Thomas V. Higgins
Scoutmaster
Scout Troop #18

Figure B.1.

You first check with the Bureau of Public Works. They confirm that these conditions exist but that other pressing matters, notably drain damage caused by a recent flood, prevent their attending to this problem at the present time. Presumably it can be scheduled for one month from today. Write Scout Troop #18 confirming this report. You might also suggest that should the scouts wish to become involved in the clean-up, the city would welcome their assistance.

5. Create a hypothetical company and write to its president suggesting ways to improve the company's major product or service. Structure your suggestions either in memo or brief report form. For instance, you might write K. L. Armstrong, President of Crescent Moon Paper Products,

regarding the firm's line of toilet tissue. Possible suggestions: 1) the tissue doesn't tear evenly because of improper perforation; 2) the diameter of the cardboard core inside the roll is too large, causing excessive run-off and waste when someone pulls hard on the roll; 3) colors other than white should be used; 4) scents might be used, such as heather, morning dew, spring bouquet, etc. Show how your ideas will improve the profitability and marketability of a particular item. Where necessary, include illustrations or charts to reinforce your points.

6. Dr. Frederick K. Morrow, a member of the Anesthesia Associates of New London, 613 Harder Road, New London, Connecticut 06320, performs a saddle-block during the delivery of Mrs. Alma P. Fertitta's baby. The charge is $75, of which her insurance covers $20. Mrs. Fertitta, who lives at 690 Clarence Drive, New London, Connecticut 06320, does not pay the bill immediately but instead writes Dr. Morrow requesting an explanation for the high charge, especially since the physician doing the delivery only charged $40. Write Dr. Morrow's response. You might suggest that the high cost of malpractice insurance forces you to charge so much.

7. Assume in the previous example that Mrs. Fertitta receives Dr. Morrow's response but still does not pay the bill. Dr. Morrow sends several reminders, but these are ignored. Write Mrs. Fertitta a fourth reminder in which Dr. Morrow indirectly threatens legal action and appeals to her sense of fair play. After all, he saved her from a great deal of pain during a difficult delivery, and she may require his services in the future.

8. Most major corporations publish annual reports in which they discuss the year's achievements, present financial statements, list Trustees or Board Members, chart growth patterns, project future plans, note major investments, etc. Locate one such report published during the last five years. Briefly summarize the company's report. Then indicate whether or not you feel the company is worth investing in.

9. Crawford Savings & Loan Association, 318 Bedford Building, New Orleans, Louisiana 70119, opened its Shreveport branch one year ago. Armand K. Coffin deposited $50 at that time in a new account and received a free chopping block; he has made no further deposits. Patricia Waddell, Crawford's head of Marketing, must compose a letter to attract old customers. She decides to celebrate the first anniversary of the Shreveport office by offering free balloons and frisbees to all children of depositors and a chance to win a $500 saving account by filling in an entry form at the bank. Write Ms. Waddell's letter, beginning it with "We miss you" Go on to announce the anniversary celebration and mention the services available at Crawford— travellers checks, mortgage loans, money orders, retirement accounts, etc. Should you point out that Mr. Coffin previously received a gift from the bank?

10. Using the following outline of information, write a memo to be posted on all police bulletin boards:

    A.   Test for Promotion to Police Lieutenant

    B.   Three Parts
        1)   knowledge of criminal law
        2)   supervisory ability
        3)   knowledge of police operations

    C.   When—Tuesday, April 18 at 4:00 P.M.

    D.   Where—City Hall, Room 832

    E.   Eligible—all patrolmen with at least four years experience

F.   Action Needed
    1)   receive approval and solicit recommendation from immediate supervisor
    2)   return attached application form to Chief Bartram Taylor, Personnel Division, City Hall, Room 832 by Friday, April 14.

11. As President of First-Line Foods, Inc. you receive the letter shown in Figure B.2.

---

38 Locust Lane
Falls Church, Virginia 22042
May 27, 197__

President
First-Line Foods, Inc.
Stamford, Connecticut 06105

Dear Sir:

I have long purchased and respected your various products. However, after recently preparing a pitcher of your concentrated grape juice, I became sick at seeing a deposit of some material clinging to the inside of the empty can (sample enclosed). This discovery certainly makes suspect any claims your company might make regarding cleanliness and careful inspection.

I would appreciate your attention to this matter.

Sincerely,

Emily P. Duckett

Figure B.2.

Assume that an analysis of the material submitted by the customer indicates that it is a sealant. Send the customer a free supply of products with this explanation. Be careful in your wording. This gift should not be construed by the customer as a bribe to avoid legal problems and bad publicity, but rather a thank you by the company for the customer's indicating a defect in the production process.

12. Assume that you are running for township supervisor. You are 38, an accountant with the State Utility Commission, a Democrat. You are married and the father of three children. There are three definable voting blocks within your township:

Precinct 1:   mostly wealthy, conservative landowners interested in horses and the Republican Party.
Precinct 2:   a blue-collar area composed of workers in the local canneries.
Precinct 3:   a section of older homes inhabited mostly by young professionals and academics— a more liberal group.

Compose a different letter for each precinct. Try to sell yourself as a candidate.

13. Belmar Publishing Company receives the letter in Figure B.3 from an angry customer.

---

8 Cornwall Avenue
Durham, North Carolina 27514
October 31, 197__

Office of the President
Belmar Publishing Company
1402 Regent Place
St. Davids, Pennsylvania 19087

Dear Sir:

On August 4 of this year, I ordered two books from your company (Psychopathia Sexualis and
The Collected Drawings of Aubrey Beardsley), for which I sent you a check for $6.15 (Check #861,
North Carolina National Bank). You then mailed me a package containing the copy of Psychopathia
and two books which I did not order. At my own expense, I returned these two books to you and
requested my Beardsley book plus the mailing charges incurred in rectifying your mistake (approximately 60¢). You ignored my request.

This letter marks my third and final attempt to get satisfaction or even a response of some sort
from your firm. Unless I hear from you in one week regarding this matter, I intend to send a copy
of this letter to the Better Business Bureau.

Sincerely,

Charles L. Trent

Figure B.3.

Imagine two situations in responding to this customer: 1) you discover the customer is correct
and decide either to refund his money or to send him the books; 2) you must admit that you
have no records of the purchases (a possible reason for not responding earlier?) and would like
the customer to send a photostatic copy of the check.

14. At five o'clock one afternoon as he leaves the office, your boss hands you a hastily scribbled
memo (which we've typed for you). "Please type this and sign it," he says, "and mail it today."
Correct your boss's errors and send out the letter.

MEMORANDUM TO: Chief Inspection Officer

FROM: R.C.

Reference is made to your letter of July 2 in which you inquired about my investigation of the Office of Printing and Publications, Public Service Agency.

In reply, I wish to advice that in May of this year BIA asked me to go to Santa Maria to make a weeks inspection of the O.P.P. They are the only office in our chain of facilities which is not showing a profit. The total office operation, as well as the personal and the procedures were to be thoroughly investigated.

Mr. Kyle the office director is one of those men who shows an interest in his job. He only began the work last December, however and has hardly had time to affect changes. He is trying desparately to solve the many serious problems that confronts him. His Board of Directors hold various views as to remedial steps to be taken. Maintaining the chief trouble lies in inadequate personnel training, this view is held by the Chairman of the Board. It must have been him who recommended a series of time and motion studies. The machine operators which have been trained in the past year have never been given production standards. Everyone works at their own pace. Showing signs of wear and tear and in need of periodic oiling and immediate repairs, the machine shop workers moral has hit rock bottom.[1]

Figure B.4.

1. From *Perk Up Your Grammar: Workshop in Better English,* United States Civil Service Commission (Washington, D.C.: U.S. Government Printing Office, 1971), p. 160.

15. Evaluate the correspondence shown in Figure B.5.

---

                                                      430 Oake Avenue
                                                      Lowell, Massachusetts 01905
                                                      January 3, 197__

President
Belco Oil Corporation
Madison Avenue
New York, New York 10016

Dear Sir:

The attached check for $23.72 is submitted despite the fact that my own records indicate that I already sent you a check in November (Provo National Bank #345) for what you state is a past due balance of $16.25. I do so in order not to damage my credit rating in any way.

Please inform me should my earlier check appear. Thank you for your assistance.

                                                      Sincerely,

                                                      Thomas B. Means

---

Figure B.5.

In response to the above letter, Mr. Means receives a form response letter from Belco on which one of several boxes was checked. Next to the box was the following statement: "Thank you for your payment. The balance of your account is now: $0.00." Mr. Means then wrote the reply in Figure B.6.

430 Oake Avenue
Lowell, Massachusetts 01905
January 25, 197__

President
Belco Oil Corporation
Madison Avenue
New York, New York 10016

Dear Sir:

What I assuredly do not need is a form letter telling me that you received my check for $23.72 (#404, Provo National Bank) and that my balance is $0.00. What I do need is a response to my earlier letter indicating that I was sending you the check for $23.72 despite the fact that your December statement erred in showing a past due balance of $16.25. As I indicated in my letter of January 3, I sent you this payment in November (the check, which I have taken the time and effort to Xerox, is 345, Provo National Bank, apparently deposited by you on December 20).

I would appreciate your attention to this matter.

Sincerely,

Thomas B. Means

Figure B.6.

Write the president's of Belco Oil Corporation's response to Mr. Means' second letter.

16. Write a memo to your boss (John K. Marston, President of Board and Box) summarizing clearly and briefly Title 15 U.S. Code, section 1473(b), Figure B.7.[2]

2. Title 15 U.S. Code, section 1473(b), pp. 496-97.

§ 1473. Conventional packages, marketing—Noncomplying packages for elderly or handicapped persons; labeling statements

(a) For the purpose of making any household substance which is subject to a standard established under section 1472 of this title readily available to elderly or handicapped persons unable to use such substance when packaged in compliance with such standard, the manufacturer or packer, as the case may be, may package any household substance, subject to such a standard, in packaging of a single size which does not comply with such standard if—

(1) the manufacturer (or packer) also supplies such substance in packages which comply with such standard; and

(2) the packages of such substance which do not meet such standard bear conspicuous labeling stating: "This package for households without young children"; except that the Secretary may by regulation prescribe a substitute statement to the same effect for packaging too small to accommodate such labeling.

Noncomplying packages for substances dispensed pursuant to orders of medical practitioners

(b) In the case of a household substance which is subject to such a standard and which is dispensed pursuant to an order of a physician, dentist, or other licensed medical practitioner authorized to prescribe, such substance may be dispensed in noncomplying packages only when directed in such order or when requested by the purchaser.

Exclusive use of special packaging; necessary circumstances

(c) In the case of a household substance subject to such a standard which is packaged under subsection (a) of this section in a noncomplying package, if the Secretary determines that such substance is not also being supplied by a manufacturer (or packer) in popular size packages which comply with such standard, he may, after giving the manufacturer (or packer) an opportunity to comply with the purposes of this Act, by order require such substance to be packaged by such manufacturer (or packer) exclusively in special packaging complying with such standard if he finds, after opportunity for hearing, that such exclusive use of special packaging is necessary to accomplish the purposes of this Act.

Pub.L. 91-601, § 4, Dec. 30, 1970, 84 Stat. 1671.

Figure B.7.

17. Create sales letters for the following situations. Pay particular attention to your first paragraph:

    a.   Sell a camera to an amateur photographer.

    b.   Sell a camera to a professional photographer.

c.   Sell fire insurance to a home owner.

d.   Sell fire insurance to the owner of a jewelry store.

e.   Sell fire insurance to the owner of a canning factory.

f.   Sell a typewriter to the purchasing officer of a large corporation.

g.   Sell a typewriter to a housewife who makes extra money typing term papers.

h.   Sell a watch to a carpenter.

i.   Sell a watch to an accountant.

j.   Sell a burglar alarm system.

k.   Sell a computer dating service.

l.   Sell a subscription to the following magazines: *Good Housekeeping, Field and Stream, TV Guide, Reader's Digest, Ebony, Business Week.*

18.   As T. Walter Harrington, Senior Vice President of Marketing for Regency Insurance Company, write four possible sales letters to be sent to new parents. Attempt to sell them a) life insurance on the baby, b) additional life insurance on themselves, c) home mortgage insurance, d) disability insurance.

19.   Write an evaluation of the following form letter, Figure B.8, as an example of "a" in the previous exercise:[3]

Schedules, schedules!

The new baby is home and doesn't know what "schedule" means. Sleeping and eating come at the oddest times.

But before long you'll all be sleeping through the night. Then there'll be the first smile, the first step, the first word—all this and more on a schedule of baby's own.

Right now is when you should give serious thought to another kind of schedule—Regency's insurance rates for children. These rates are low, because your child is young.

You should take advantage of these rates to start the baby out with a sound future. When your youngster grows up, a strong financial asset will be waiting.

I'll call shortly to tell you about the insurance plans we offer for your child.

Figure B.8.

3. Courtesy Metropolitan Life Insurance Company, New York.

20. Locate one of the following business administration articles and write a clear summary of it:

    a. Robert S. Sobeck, "A Manager's Primer on Forecasting," *Harvard Business Review* (May-June, 1973).

    b. R. N. Ford, "Job Enrichment Lessons from AT & T," *Harvard Business Review* (January-February, 1973).

    c. Robert Tannenbaum and Warren H. Schmidt, "How to Choose a Leadership Pattern," *Harvard Business Review* (May-June, 1973).

    d. Gilbert Burck, "The Hazards of 'Corporate Responsibility,' " *Fortune* (June, 1973).

    If these articles are unavailable, choose any substantial article from the last five years of *Harvard Business Review, Business Week, Forbes, Fortune,* or *The Journal of Management Studies.*

21. Kay Sando has for ten years been credit manager of Randall's 5 & 10 at its central office on Barcladen Boulevard, South Orange, New Jersey 07079. In addition to its retail trade, Randall's supplies several fabric outlets with wholesale goods. One such customer–Paul Schall, Creative Mill Outlet, 82 Ramrod Road, Rutherford, New Jersey 07070–has been a customer for eight years. He has always been a little tardy in his payments, but recently, because of a slump in business, has fallen three months behind on his March 1 bill of $453.87 for yarn and drapes. Mrs. Sando writes Schall four letters before indicating that she will be forced to resort to legal action. Assume a time gap of one month between each letter and compose these letters.

22. Create a hypothetical resumé and application letter suited to each of the following job advertisements:

    a. ACCOUNTS PAYABLE. Suburban company has an opening in the accounting dept. Excellent opportunity for dependable person exp. in accounts payable function & communicating with vendors. Typing skills a definite plus. Salary commensurate with exp. Write Armiter Employment Agency, Crowder Building, Commerce, Texas 75428.

    b. TECHNICAL WRITER NEEDED for a major organization offering an attractive salary as well as a rewarding career. We're looking for a person skilled in written communication, preferably with an engineering background. You're needed to prepare technical reports that meet federal, state, and company standards, as well as legal requirements. You'll also review contract proposals for conformity to specifications and recommend changes. The ability to work together with technical and nontechnical personnel is necessary. Send resumé and salary history to P. O. Box 613, Philadelphia, Pennsylvania 19107.

    (Note: Assume you are Ralph Perkins, Hormel Road, Allentown, Pa. 18104. You just graduated from college and are job hunting. You majored in English, but the only technical part of your background was a summer job with Regis Mining Company where you were a clerk. You write well and are industrious.)

    c. SALES TRAINEE with large copy equipment company. We seek articulate graduate to train for local terr. Must be promotable. Sal to $12K + bonus + car. Send application and supporting documents to Photorite, Inc., 630 Arno Road, Glenwood, Illinois 60452.

    d. SALES INTERVIEW. Challenging, creative, noncompetitive, sophisticated inside sales. Must be completely poised, positive, aggressive and highly intelligent. Previous sales experience helpful but not required. Do not write unless you can sell yourself and expect an excellent income. No travel or solicitation. Box 318 Honolulu, Hawaii 96816.

    (Note: You once worked in drug store part-time; you also sold encyclopedias for two summers. You feel you meet the criteria demanded.)

23. Write office memos dealing with the following subjects:

    a.   From Bartram P. Comer, Vice-President of Acme Tool Company, to Sales Personnel regarding use of company automobiles.

    b.   From Helen Carmichael, Plant Supervisor of Egan Steel Company, to all employees regarding energy conservation, especially the use of electricity in both the plants and the offices.

    c.   From Carter T. Sitwell, President of Amana Foods, to all Vice-Presidents, soliciting suggestions on ways to improve company morale.

    d.   From James R. Farrow, Vice-President of Finance, Amana Foods, containing three specific recommendations to "c" above.

24. Thomas M. Johnson, Director of Personnel for Cardiff Clothes sends the following memo, Figure B.9, to all division heads:

                                                   February 1, 197__

TO: All Division Heads

FROM: Thomas M. Johnson, Director of Personnel

On July 1, 197__a letter was sent from Personnel to all Division Heads informing them that the Administrative and Hourly Personnel of the company were covered under the Federal Fair Labor Standards Act (Wage-Hour Law) and that under this law the company must keep a complete record of each employee's present rate of pay and exact <u>hours</u> worked.

To avoid the use of time cards we asked that all absences for whatever reason (illness, vacation, personal, jury duty, etc.) be reported to the Personnel Office so that the records are accurate at all times.

Enclosed is a copy of the absence record of each employee in your division and the dates absent as reported to this office. Please check this record against your division record, make any corrections or additions, and return it to the Personnel Office as soon as possible so that we may complete our 197__ report.

Figure B.9.

Constance Hood, Director of the Sewing Division, is responsible for eight employees. Write a memo from her responding to Mr. Johnson's request. List any corrections in Personnel's absence record and bring the record up to date through December 31, 197__ .

Page numbers in italics are examples

1.) Make Request — Attract Attention.
     Direct or wait awhile

2.) State reson for Request

3.) Provide the reader with the info. so he can understand
   details (only needed ones)

4.) Omit details. that are not needed.

5.) If asking questions
     Alot # them. or Each in a paragraph

6.) If it costs the reader   send him a self addressed envelop
     or say you'll pay for it yourself.

7.) watch for the I's at the beginning.

8.) Don't Apology for writing & be polite. Be positive!

9.) Colon not comma

10) Use dates

11) Close Courteously, express appreciation

12) Make it easy to reply (if asking favor)